D1595451

Literary Criticism in Perspective

Editorial Board

Literary Criticism in Perspective

James Hardin (*South Carolina*), General Editor

Stephen D. Dowden (*Brandeis University*), German Literature

Benjamin Franklin V (*South Carolina*), American and
English Literature

***

About *Literary Criticism in Perspective*

Books in the series *Literary Criticism in Perspective* trace literary scholarship
and criticism on major and neglected writers alike, or on a single major work,
a group of writers, a literary school or movement. In so doing the authors—authorities on the topic in question who are also well-versed in the
principles and history of literary criticism—address a readership consisting
of scholars, students of literature at the graduate and undergraduate level,
and the general reader. One of the primary purposes of the series is to illu-
minate the nature of literary criticism itself, to gauge the influence of social
and historic currents on aesthetic judgments once thought objective and
normative.

The Ironic Dissident

Wedekind in 1917, the year before his death

PT 2647 .E26 Z727 1997
Lewis, Ward B.
The ironic dissident

Ward B. Lewis

The Ironic Dissident

Frank Wedekind
in the View of His Critics

CAMDEN HOUSE

RITTER LIBRARY
BALDWIN WALLACE COLLEGE
WITHDRAWN

Copyright © 1997
Camden House, Inc.

Published by Camden House, Inc.
Drawer 2025
Columbia, SC 29202 USA

Printed on acid-free paper.
Binding materials are chosen for strength
and durability.

All rights reserved, including the right of reproduction inany form.
All rights to this publication will be vigorously defended.

Printed in the United States of America
First Edition

ISBN: 1–57113–023–3

Library of Congress Cataloging-in Publication Division

Lewis, Ward B.
The ironic dissident: Frank Wedekind in the view of his critics /
Ward B. Lewis.
     p.   cm. – (Literary criticism in perspective)
Includes bibliographical references and index.
ISBN 1–57113–023–3 (alk. paper)
    1. Wedekind, Frank, 1864–1918—Criticism and interpretation.
I. Title. II. Series.
PT2647.E26Z727   1996
832' .--dc20   96–30113
                                               CIP

Acknowledgments

I would like to thank those who contributed to this undertaking in numerous ways: the Stadtbibliothek München as the source of the photographs of Wedekind, the courteous and efficient staff of Interlibrary Loan at the University of Georgia, Robert Stamper for his editorial assistance, and James Hardin for his advice and patience.

W. B. L.
October 1996

To Erika

Contents

Preface

Although in 1960 Claude Hill writes of Wedekind as "forgotten" (92), some three decades later the works of this author have experienced a healthy reawakening of interest. In 1987 the "Editions- und Forschungsstelle Frank Wedekind" was established in Darmstadt under the direction of Hartmut Vinçon, from which the series *Pharus* issued two years later. An historical-critical edition of *Die Büchse der Pandora* appeared in 1990 edited by Vinçon, and valuable manuscripts such as the first version of *Der Marquis von Keith* followed thereafter.

Further activity in 1990 included a new edition of Wedekind's works by Erhard Weidl as well as *Benjamin Franklin Wedekind. Biographie einer Jugend* by Rolf Kieser, a significant biography of the dramatist's early years providing new material beyond that contained in the early, seminal work of Artur Kutscher.

Kieser together with Reinhold Grimm edited the *Frank Wedekind Yearbook 1991*. In the introduction to the *Yearbook,* Grimm refers to the current renaissance in Wedekind scholarship, the contributions to which number about a fifth in English language research and especially American German studies (x).

The corpus of Wedekind's literary production embraces about thirty dramas and pantomimes accompanied by his commentaries on them, seventeen prose tales, twenty-one essays, and almost one hundred and fifty satirical poems. Some of these first appeared in the *Gesammelte Werke* in six volumes from the press of Georg Müller beginning in 1912 with the sixth volume appearing in 1914 on the occasion of Wedekind's fiftieth birthday. A seventh volume containing the late dramas and divers pieces appeared in 1920 edited by Artur Kutscher. Together with Joachim Friedenthal, Kutscher edited the two volumes including the final papers (*Nachlaß*) that were published in 1919 and 1921 thus completing the edition of nine volumes.

Other editions followed: a five-volume set by Fritz Strich (1924) as well as a two-volume edition of the letters the same year, editions in two volumes by Hansgeorg Maier (1960, 1964), three volumes by Manfred Hahn (1969), and the two volumes by Erhard Weidl (1990) mentioned above. All editions to date omit some of the early and late work, and a critical edition is yet to be compiled.

The treatment accorded the Nachlaß by Kutscher and Friedenthal in the eighth and ninth volumes published by Müller fails to constitute a complete presentation of Wedekind's literary effects. Omissions and variants are not indicated; dates are often missing or inaccurate as may be the orthography. Kutscher in his three-volume biography treats the literary effects chronologically, and what remains of the manuscripts is to be found in the canton library in Aarau, Switzerland and the Stadtbibliothek München.

Pursuant to the desire to illustrate how critics have responded to Frank Wedekind, understood and misunderstood him, and consistent with the objectives of the series *Literary Criticism in Perspective*, scholarship from Wedekind's own time until the present day is considered in a chronological order emphasizing the manner in which tastes and fashions change. Each chapter is preceded by a brief synopsis of the works beneath the heading.

References to primary works by their German titles are followed by a translation and the year of publication of the work in parentheses. The English rendering of the title is neither an indication that Wedekind's work has been translated nor a reference to whatever title a translation may have assumed. About half of the sixteen dramas considered in these pages appear in English as do two of his short prose pieces. With reference to the latter, the English term *novella* and its plural *novelle* have been employed rather than the German counterparts.

In order to streamline the text, the titles of critical works are omitted; a citation is limited to the surname of the critic, date of his or her work, and the pages concerned. The first name of a critic may be employed on occasion to suggest gender as a factor in his or her attitude, especially in the context of feminist criticism.

At the turn of the century *Lebensphilosophie*, or vitalism, was the fashion. Life, or *das Leben*, was conceived as a principle or concept and was influenced by the idea of the affirmative will to power as expressed by Friedrich Nietzsche. The vital force constitutes a power beyond comprehension, a paradox, and in the eyes of Wedekind was grounded in sexuality. *Lebensphilosophie* has attracted scholarship only relatively recently and is first treated by Rothe (1968) and thereafter by Rasch (1969) and Kalcher (1980). When the critics refer to "Life" in this abstract sense, the noun will be capitalized.

When reference is made by Roman numeral to a single volume among three or more, as in the case of Kutscher and Hahn, the volume number when it remains the same is provided only once in any paragraph. The critical works are arranged chronologically in the Bibliography. Alphabetical cross-reference is provided by the index, which also includes bibliographic entries enabling one to locate a critic by name or date. Unpublished dissertations have not been included.

All of Wedekind's comments on his own dramas are from "Was ich mir dabei dachte" (What I Was Thinking about at the Time), remarks composed about 1911 and not published until 1921 in the final volume of the Collected Works.

For the following works short titles have been adopted:

> *Der Erdgeist, Die Büchse der Pandora* = *Lulu*
> *Der Marquis von Keith* = *Keith*
> *König Nicolo oder So ist das Leben* = *Nicolo*
> *Karl Hetmann, der Zwerg-Riese (Hidalla)* = *Hidalla*
> *Simson oder Scham und Eifersucht* = *Simson*
> *Mine-Haha oder Über die körperliche Erziehung der jungen Mädchen*
> = *Mine-Haha*

1: Introduction
Frank Wedekind and the Modernist Turn

At the turn of the century Frank Wedekind made himself heard by provoking the establishment in his attacks upon bourgeois conventions and the authority of church and government. He celebrated sensuality, the joys and perils of the flesh, satirized the institutions of marriage and family, and attacked repressive moral standards. An outspoken pacifist, antimilitarist, and nonconformist, his private life was considered as scandalous as his works. Associated closely with the brothers Heinrich and Thomas Mann and serving as a model for the youthful Bertolt Brecht, Wedekind prepared the way for the expressionists and proved formative in the development of the theater of the absurd.

Benjamin Franklin Wedekind was born on 24 July 1864 to German parents returning from the United States where they had met and married. Two decades earlier the father, Friedrich Wilhelm Wedekind, had joined the ranks of the Forty-eighters, those liberals who left Germany after the failure of the Revolution of 1848. Still motivated by political sentiments accounting for his opposition to Bismarck, the father removed the family to the canton of Aargau, Switzerland, in 1872. There Frank Wedekind was educated in the Gymnasium, where he was regarded by his colleagues as "The American," a status he attempted to preserve in later years in order to establish his foreign nationality before Prussian authorities. Attainment of the *Abitur* concluding his secondary school studies in 1884 left the young Wedekind free to undertake university study in Munich, a city in which he was drawn to literature, theater, and ballet as well as the company of artists and writers, whose interest he shared as a contributor to newspapers and journals.

A break with his strong-willed father was precipitated by Wedekind's lack of enthusiasm regarding legal studies. The episode became a literary event when depicted by Gerhart Hauptmann in his drama *Das Friedensfest* (The Coming of Peace: A Family Catastrophe, 1890), thereby initiating a lifelong feud between the two writers. While now no longer prevented from pursuing his own interests, Wedekind was at the same time deprived of financial support and assumed a position in advertising with Maggi, a food concern, where he remained for about half a year.

Upon the death of his father in 1888 Wedekind inherited sufficient means to settle first in Berlin, then in Munich, where he became acquainted with the bohemian life of Schwabing, a district providing the models for those marginal social types on the fringes of bourgeois culture which would emerge thereafter in his works.

Problems with the censors evoked by *Frühlings Erwachen* (The Awakening of Spring, 1891) were exacerbated by *Erdgeist* (Earth-Spirit, 1895), but Max Reinhardt's production of the former in 1906 confirmed Wedekind's position. A cycle of his works was produced three years later.

In 1906 he married the actress Tilly Newes, who had starred in his dramas, and they had two daughters, Pamela and Kadidja. On 9 March 1918, in his fifty-fourth year, Wedekind died, lamented widely by writers and bohemians alike.

Wedekind appeared on stage in a number of roles from his own works, demonstrating a characteristically grotesque and exaggerated manner which became his trademark. In the cabaret, as well, he assumed the role of entertainer. Associated with his perception of himself in this capacity was a love affair he harbored throughout his life with the circus. He was fascinated by clowns, fools, dwarfs, acrobats, bareback riders, and aerialists.

The imagery of the circus is crucial to Wedekind's work. The trick rider Fritz Schwigerling is hired to teach gymnastics and runs off with Katharina to prepare her for a life under the big top. The animal trainer introduces Lulu as a serpent and wild, beautiful animal; a dancer, she will be trained as an acrobat by the carnival strong man Rodrigo Quast. She is accompanied throughout the tragedy by her portrait as Pierrot, the popular clown. The Marquis von Keith is quite conscious of his balancing act as a financial tightrope walker. The king appears as jester at his own court in the person of Nicolo. The literary artist is associated with the vagrant and popular player. Hetmann, the minigiant, is a prophet recognized by the circus director Cotrelly as a clown.

Lulu is brought before the audience in the prologue by an animal trainer with whip in hand. The object is familiar in the context of the circus, of course, where it represents that mastery which elicits submission from the beast. This instrument assumes heightened meaning in Wedekind's works and is associated with female sexual arousal. Background is suggested by well-known lines attributed to Friedrich Nietzsche: "Du gehst zu Frauen? Vergiß die Peitsche nicht!" (You are going to women? Do not forget the whip!).

The primacy of the circus performer is established in Wedekind's essay "Zirkusgedanken" (Thoughts about the Circus, 1887). The governing principle of the circus ring is perceived as elasticity, "die plastisch-allegorische Darstellung einer Lebensweisheit" (the clearly allegorical representation of a truth of life; IX, 297). Modern life requires for survival that elasticity demonstrated by the trick rider and his colleagues. Two kinds of circus performers—the trapeze artist and the tightrope walker—represent two different types of human beings: the "abstract-sublime idealist" and the "realistic-practical idealist." Suspended in a stable equilibrium supported at a point above the middle of the trapeze, that artist takes his suspension for granted. He embodies independence of movement and the pursuit of abstract, lofty ideals high above humanity. This artist typifies a class to which prophets, political rebels, poets and philosophers belong. The tightrope walker, on the other hand, illustrates realistic, practical idealism since the performer works with a labile equilibrium that demands a continuous struggle to preserve balance. Such people are useful and persevere on the small path before their eyes. To this group belong workers, officials, and Faust and Goethe (IX,301–5).

Wedekind's publisher Albert Langen founded the satirical magazine *Simplicissimus* in 1896. This publication was committed to new and controversial literary works and included among its contributors Thomas and Heinrich Mann as well as Wedekind, whose paths all crossed here. In sketches and text the magazine satirized the stuffy Wilhelmine regime and provided a congenial intellectual atmosphere for the writers. *Simplicissimus* criticized the authoritarian school system and promoted reform and sexual education in the spirit of *Frühlings Erwachen*. The first chapters of Heinrich Mann's novel *Der Untertan* (The Patrioteer, 1918), the most resounding satire of the time, appeared here, comprising an indictment in a direct line of descent from *Frühlings Erwachen* of the patriarchal, authoritarian, male-dominated familial and social structure.

Simplicissimus was continuously scrutinized by the censors. A central episode during the time of Wedekind's association with the magazine has come to be known as the Langen affair and was to be reworked in his dramas. Wedekind's satirical poems "Meerfahrt" (Ocean Voyage) and "Im Heiligen Land" (In the Holy Land), dealing with the visit of Kaiser Wilhelm II to Palestine, were published in 1898 and caused outraged authorities to raid the editorial offices and confiscate the offensive material, including Wedekind's verse manuscript. A scandal broke. Facing the threat of arrest, Wedekind fled to Zurich and then Paris, finally returning to Germany to face trial for *Majestätsbeleidigung*, or lèse-majesté. He served a sentence of imprisonment lasting almost six months, for which he held Langen responsible since Wedekind interpreted the entire affair as a scheme to gain publicity and increase circulation of the magazine. Wedekind's farce *Oaha* (1908) treats the personalities and events associated with *Simplicissimus* in an attempt to make them appear ridiculous. The playwright sought revenge upon Langen in the dramatic figures of Rudolf Launhart in *Hidalla* (1904) and Georg Sterner in *Oaha*, characters that present unflattering portraits of the publisher. The trial and the subject of lèse-majesté are also treated in *König Nicolo* (King Nicolo, 1902). The theme of unrecognized greatness is readily applied by Wedekind to himself, especially when associated with features of the Langen affair. A corollary to this theme is the wretched curse of ridicule ("Fluch der Lächerlichkeit").

Another acquaintance of the dramatist likewise assumed a place in his writing and influenced the picaresque novel of a colleague. Wedekind's friend was Willy Grétor, whom Lion Feuchtwanger (1952) describes as a painter, writer, businessman, and swindler: "This Grétor was the most brilliant forger of pictures of his time, no doubt many a picture by him hangs in many a gallery. He knew no scruples, acknowledged no restraints" (9). The inspiration for *Simplicissimus* may have been conveyed to Langen by Grétor; the latter had sold Langen some forged paintings but later allegedly remarked that the suggestion that Langen found the magazine amounted to full compensation for the swindle. Wedekind dedicated *Erdgeist* to Grétor, and he serves as the inspiration for the confidence man known as the Marquis von Keith in the work by that name.

Thomas Mann accepted a position with *Simplicissimus* from Korfiz Holm, who was trying to hold the magazine together after Langen and Wedekind fled the country. Mann was quite taken by Wedekind's drama *Der Marquis von Keith* (The Marquis of Keith, 1901), which he had seen performed in Munich with its author in the central role. Mann felt that one of the scenes spoke to him personally. He even claimed it figuratively as one of his own. The drama inspired Mann's own version of the tale of a confidence man and artistic performer, who fools both himself and society by hiding behind a succession of masks, enabling him to lead lives both public and private as he employs various names and identities. *Die Bekenntnisse des Hochstaplers Felix Krull* (The Confessions of Felix Krull, Confidence Man) occupied Mann intermittently for a good part of his life; the writing first appeared as a single chapter in 1922, was expanded for publication in 1937, and was largely rewritten for reappearance in 1954. The work borrows heavily upon the conception of art as spectacle and is set at the operetta, the circus where the aerialist Andromache performs, and the bullfight arena.

At Wedekind's funeral in the Waldfriedhof cemetery in Munich on 13 March 1918, both Thomas and Heinrich Mann attended, and the latter delivered the funeral oration. He remembers Wedekind with great respect in his memoirs *Sieben Jahre* (Seven Years), written in 1923. There lines recall Wedekind's association with *Simplicissimus*, the betrayal by Langen, his performances on the stage, and the first success of *Frühlings Erwachen*. Mann describes Wedekind as a dramatist who recognized bourgeois existence for what it was—ruthless struggle, shameless exploitation, and naked bestiality.

Wedekind's critical analysis at the turn of the century anticipated the death of an age concluded by the First World War, but his admonition that society reexamine its foundations fell on deaf ears. The pacifist Wedekind is included in Heinrich Mann's *Der Kopf* (The Head, 1925), a massive novel which attempts to show in microcosm the part that the German intelligentsia had played in the catastrophe of the Great War.

Wedekind's work became popularized. Lulu was reduced from her mythic proportions and disassociated from subconscious fears of unfettered sexual freedom when she emerged as a vamp or femme fatal on stage and screen during the twenties and thirties. She appeared as a seductress played by the Danish star Asta Nielsen in Leopold Jessner's film *Erdgeist* (1923); the American actress Louise Brooks played the role in the film *Die Büchse der Pandora* (Pandora's Box) directed by Georg Wilhelm Pabst in 1929.

That criticism of the school system central to *Frühlings Erwachen* flowed directly into Heinrich Mann's *Professor Unrat* (Small Town Tyrant, 1905), which depicts a hypocritical, repressive society where a tyrannical pedant dominates the classroom. This work was directed as the film *Der blaue Engel* (The Blue Angel) by Josef von Sternberg in 1930. Here Marlene Dietrich transforms Rosa Fröhlich of the prose to the celluloid Lola Lola, and Lulu reappears in caricature as a bawdy cabaret singer.

Songs by Wedekind from the literary cabaret *Elf Scharfrichter* (Eleven Executioners) were just one of the many influences the dramatist exerted on his young literary disciple Bertolt Brecht. Artur Kutscher, Wedekind's friend and biographer, taught a seminar on drama at the university in Munich during 1918, and at the celebration marking the conclusion of the course he introduced the students to Wedekind, who accompanied himself on the lute to some of his songs. Bertolt Brecht took part in the seminar, and the twenty-year-old idolized the older man and reflected him in the central figure of his first drama, *Baal* (1918), written for Kutscher's course. Brecht imitated Wedekind's risqué ballads intended to shock the respectable bourgeoisie. In an obituary for Wedekind composed six weeks after this memorable evening, Brecht recalls the songs Wedekind sang and the vitality of his personality. More profound was the influence Brecht found in Wedekind's drama; Wedekind's work manifested those concepts of anti-Aristotelian theater, open form, and alienation which were further developed in Brecht's theater, thereby influencing the drama of the entire twentieth century.

The ranks of the expressionists that followed Wedekind were greatly influenced by his themes. *Frühlings Erwachen* initiated the motif of youthful rebellion against the older generation. This revolt against authority together with sexual emancipation and the rejection of traditional values were embraced, as was the idea of the writer as the prophet of social change. His language left its mark on the work of Georg Kaiser and that of Wedekind's son-in-law Carl Sternheim.

The technique of Wedekind's drama made itself felt in the theater of the absurd, especially as represented in the works of Max Frisch and Friedrich Dürrenmatt. Here we find language that is curt, terse, and epigrammatic employed in unresponsive, unindividualized speech exchanged by one-dimensional figures. Bourgeois hypocrisy and decadence are unmasked in grotesque, cynical satire. Inherited from Wedekind is the mixture of caricature and farce in works representing distorted social values. Examples of such farce are Frisch's *Die große Wut des Philipp Hotz* (The Great Wrath of Philipp Hotz, 1958) and Dürrenmatt's *Die Physiker* (The Physicists, 1962). Wedekind is similarly a model for satire, especially where Dürrenmatt employs epigrams as in *Ein Engel kommt nach Babylon* (An Angel Comes to Babylon, 1953).

The critics have been quick to point out thematic parallels in the works of these authors. Criticism of the school system originating with *Frühlings Erwachen* is reflected in Frisch's *Nun singen sie wieder* (Now They Sing Again, 1946). The insane asylum to which Scholz retires in *Keith* reappears in *Die Physiker;* Dürrenmatt's Anastasia in *Die Ehe des Herrn Mississippi* (The Marriage of Mr. Mississippi, 1950) amounts to a Super Lulu, who anticipates Claire Zachanassian in his *Besuch der alten Dame* (The Visit, 1956).

Wedekind's grotesquely Herculean circus world of the showman and trick rider Fritz Schwigerling and the extortionist and muscle man Rodrigo Quast, who can balance prancing ponies on his sternum, is reflected in central dramatic figures who operate outside the system of bourgeois morality. A gymnast performs as executioner in Dürrenmatt's *Besuch der alten Dame,* and in Frisch's *Biedermann und die Brandstifter* (The Fire Raisers, 1958) the two arsonists are Schmitz, the wrestler, and

Eisenring, the former waiter.

In 1952 Tilly Wedekind, the author's widow, raised the charge before the Schutzverband Deutscher Schriftsteller (Protective Association of German Authors) that Dürrenmatt had plagiarized from her husband's work. She accused him of borrowing from *Erdgeist*, *Hidalla*, and *Franziska* (1912); she charged especially that the theme of his play *Die Ehe des Herrn Mississippi* had been taken from *Schloß Wetterstein* (Castle Wetterstein, 1912), where the widow Leonore marries Rüdiger, the man who murdered her former husband.

Dürrenmatt admits in his essay "Confessions of a Plagiarizer" to having been influenced by Wedekind's language and borrowing from him. Denying his indebtedness to those dramas Tilly Wedekind identified, however, Dürrenmatt concedes having appropriated for *Die Ehe des Herrn Mississippi* a dramatic idea behind Wedekind's *Marquis von Keith*. Here the two central figures embody an ideology and appear in a spotlight as in the ring of a circus. Dürrenmatt borrowed the dialectic represented by characters; the configuration Keith-Scholz is recast in the persons of Anastasia-Mississippi. As in Wedekind's drama, this play poses the struggle of opposing powers represented by people against the background of a decadent world in decline.

2: *Frühlings Erwachen* (1891)
The Awakening of Spring
and the Tragedy of Youth

Frau Bergmann prudishly avoids the questions of her fourteen-year-old daughter Wendla regarding the origin of babies. Young boys who feel the stirrings of puberty are captives within the school system; Melchior Gabor, self-assured and successful, attempts to help Moritz Stiefel with his studies and writes a pamphlet to explain their sexual fantasies.

When Wendla meets Melchior in the forest, she begs him to beat her as her friend Martha is beaten by her parents. On their next encounter they have sexual intercourse in a hayloft.

Failing to avail himself of that hope for happiness held out by Ilse, a child of sensual pleasure, Moritz kills himself since he will not be advanced with his class. Melchior is dismissed from the school when his pamphlet is discovered, and a letter to Wendla unites his parents in the decision to send him to a correctional institute. He breaks out and upon the headstone in a graveyard reads the epitaph for Wendla Bergmann, who has died from an abortion.

Over the graves comes Moritz, with his head under his arm, enjoining Melchior to accompany him in the realm of the dead; but the Masked Gentleman interferes and leads Melchior with his questioning skepticism forward into the world of the living.

The primary question in the critical literature concerns the nature of the drama *Frühlings Erwachen* (The Awakening of Spring, 1891). What is it all about? Is it an allegory in which a character such as the Masked Gentleman has a meaning of its own? Is Wedekind in this way trying to explain or illustrate something? Or is it a problem play ("Tendenzstück"), a work with a message, written for the purpose of advancing a particular view? And with regard to the content, is the author providing a representation of puberty, advancing social criticism, seeking pedagogical enlightenment, or some combination thereof?

In a letter written in 1891 to an anonymous critic, Wedekind revealed his intention to depict poetically the phenomenon of puberty in order to facilitate more humane and rational views among parents and educators (Hahn III, 452). This lyrical and pedagogical light held little appeal for Wedekind's earliest critic, Pissin (1905), and for many subsequent critics. Pissin interprets the drama as allegory, and the final scene with the Masked Gentleman as grotesquely allegorical at that. Here it is suggested that the solution to Melchior's problems lies in his daring to devote himself to the enjoyment of life and to a penetrating study of the world (14–15). The lyrical qualities of the work are recognized, however, by another early voice in a remarkably sensitive reading, which would remain influential, albeit unacknowledged, a half century later. Lou Andreas-Salomé (1907), a woman significant in the lives of Friedrich Nietzsche, Rainer Maria Rilke, and Sigmund Freud, distinguishes herself as a critic in the pages of the journal *Die Zukunft*. Here treating the work as neither problematic nor allegorical, she emphasizes its poetry and psychology as it represents the awakening urge of the sexes for each other (97). The fantastic aspects of the final scene correspond both to the way children see and to the figments of youthful imagination (98–99).

Andreas-Salomé is the first to observe that the Masked Gentleman and the author are one (99), a perception that lives through the history of criticism of the work and is accepted as a verity during the years when Wedekind increasingly played the actual role upon stage.

Subsequent critics read for social content. Writing in exile in Vienna in 1908, Leon Trotsky is taken aback by the representation of a mindless school and a nasty family, manifesting the author's "social cynicism." The message of the drama is interpreted as sensual aestheticism; the sexual drive breaks the chains of the family and rises above social barriers to become an uninterrupted series of aesthetic experiences. Admiring Wedekind's attack on patriarchy, Trotsky is inclined to tolerate that bourgeois aestheticism represented by the Masked Gentleman (381–82). Appearing as a problem play also in the eyes of Goldmann (1908), *Frühlings Erwachen* constitutes a plea for sex education and a positive contribution of Wedekind in this regard (121). The theme of the play is a child's awakening to perversity (118); and Wendla is so perverse, the critic observes, that she would have followed Melchior into the hayloft even if her mother had told her the truth about pregnancy since that is in the nature of Wedekind's female characters (122–23). The message remains paramount a year later when Kapp (1909) interprets the drama without allegory as an indictment of human negligence (112). The Masked Gentleman is the devil in a top hat, considering the advantages of life and death (117); and the critic's sole reservation lies in Wedekind's alliance with youth in ruthless opposition to parents and teachers (118).

In remarks on the drama written around 1911, Wedekind notes that prior to the production by Max Reinhardt at the Deutsches Theater, Berlin, in 1906, *Frühlings Erwachen* was viewed as pure pornography; thereafter, it was seen as the driest pedantry (IX, 1924). And indeed in 1912 Elsner interprets it as a plea for sexual education in the school, an institution highly unsuitable therefor (15). The critic, however, has scant sympathy for the children; they are nasty little creatures obsessed with sex (23). Wendla feigns ignorance and innocence and lets herself be seduced in order to teach her mother the lesson that parents should not leave their children uninformed regarding such matters (19–20).

That the play is both tendentious and allegorical is suggested by Friedenthal (1914), who interprets the Masked Gentleman as *das Leben* leading Melchior from the cemetery of youth out into the distance and the years ahead (52). At the same time the critic maintains that although too great an emphasis has been placed on the work as an indictment of parents and the school system, nevertheless the drama is exactly that (54). Assuming, without acknowledgment, the perception of Andreas-Salomé (1907) that the work constitutes the poetry of puberty (98–99), Friedenthal invokes the spontaneous, elemental lyrical quality of youth (54); sensitive impressions are exquisite and rare; the work radiates the breath of adolescence (57).

Although Friedenthal generally adopts prevalent attitudes towards the work, he does contribute one insight which is influential in the history of criticism. This is in his emphasis upon the dramatic representation of the out-of-doors: flowers and trees, a sun-drenched garden, a meadow, and a vineyard. Conveying a spontaneous feeling for nature originating in the biography of the author, the drama represents Wedekind's strongest expression of an exciting and rich youth that reaches back to the small town of Lenzburg in Switzerland. Friedenthal confirms the autobiographical connections further by noting that during adolescence the author attended the Gymnasium in neighboring Aarau, where two acquaintances committed suicide (90).

The tendentious nature of the play is faced straightaway by subsequent critics. Blei (1914), for example, rejects the suggestion of tendency, asserting that the work stands for itself and that any authorial intent of treating an educational problem is secondary (148–49). Echoing the sentiments of Friedenthal that the adolescents in this work are illuminated by the warmth of youthful vitality in a way not to be equaled in subsequent work by Wedekind, Fechter (1920, 41), too, denies that the drama is tendentious; he argues that it amounts to the author's lament for the death of his belief in the beauty of love and life (43). The dramatist treats the theme of puberty as it awakens to Life without adult guidance; dark, compulsive aspects cause entrapment and horror since the bourgeois world treats the problem as nonexistent or immoral; nature, sexuality, and Life are left to the young to struggle with in torment (35).

The autobiographical identity noted by Andreas-Salomé (1907, 99) between the dramatist and the Masked Gentleman is furthered by Fechter. Employing a Faustian allusion, he observes that Wedekind projects upon the stage ideas from the two souls which dwell within his breast (40). Whereas the Masked Gentleman provides to Melchior affirmation of life in this world for all of its error and horror, he may also be the devil (41), speculation which opens the door for the emergence of Mephistopheles in postwar criticism. The drama does not move by the development of conflicts and their resolution but by the impulses and moods which the work conveys, Fechter notes, anticipating subsequent critics (42–43).

Nature understood by Friedenthal (1914) as the outdoors is now interpreted by Diebold (1921) in a poetic sense as a metaphor for that voice which sings with intoxication from desirous blood (44). The drama is not limited to society and education; Wedekind is an anarchist attacking civilization, which is ashamed of nature (44–45). Elaborating upon the concept of nature in a manner similar to Diebold, Elster (1922) describes the full sweetness of spring's awakening in a warm atmosphere quivering with yearning. He is, however, less lyrical in his expression of Wedekind's intended lesson, namely, that parents and educators should provide children guidance during puberty (28).

Wedekind's foremost spokesman was Artur Kutscher (1922), who observes that the dramatist avoided any inartistic or negative message. Unable to argue that Wedekind was not trying to present a problem, Kutscher asserts that he advocated regard for nature and love of life. Avoiding allegory, Kutscher submits, nevertheless, that the Masked Gentleman represents the concept of Life as well as continued living, attitudes of both Melchior and Wedekind, and that the dedication of the work to the Masked Gentleman stands for the thanks of the boy he saved (I, 248).

A great hiatus appeared in Wedekind criticism throughout the thirties and middle forties until the postwar years. From the literary estate of Friedrich Gundolf in 1948 emerged criticism which attempted to preserve continuity with more sophisticated earlier interpretation and at the same time avoid simple categorization of the drama. Conceding that the work is satirical and has a message, the critic moves away from considering it in terms of theme and content as a conflict between youth and the older generation. Gundolf focuses upon the scenes, which are for the most part unstructured in their relation to one another. He further develops an idea of Fechter (1920) who noted that the drama consists not of conflict and the resolution thereof, but of mood and atmosphere (42–43). The scenes, according to Gundolf, constitute a collection of poetic portrayals of inner conflicts, emotions, character, and space, all of which emanate from the moment as it is illuminated (209).

The view that the work is both allegorical and problematic, argued by Friedenthal, is supported by Dosenheimer (1949), who exercises her prerogative to have it both ways. Although the drama is too good to be simply advancing an argument, she observes (190), it does deal with a problem: that of the human being in society. In Wedekind's work, life means sexuality, and in his dramas he wishes to give predominance to urges of the flesh; but society negates these, and therefore he attempts to revolutionize society (191).

Considerable ingenuity is demonstrated when critics skirt the issue. Faesi (1956) and Natan (1963) do this by defining the theme of the work in such an abstract manner that it is appropriate for practically any drama portraying youth. *Frühlings Erwachen*, according to Faesi, deals with the problem of the growing person fitting him- or herself into life (245). Granted the drama consists of variations on one and the same subject, namely the appearances of puberty among a group of adolescents and the reactions of their parents thereto (244); but the author does not advocate sexual enlightenment. Wedekind simply lets nature unfold before one's eyes and speak for itself (245). With more subtlety than exercised by Faesi, Natan achieves the same effect, observing that the play conveys "the troubled spirit of young people" (104). The critic makes an autobiographical connection with the assertion that the moral presented in the final scene constitutes an element of Wedekind's philosophy, namely "only he who is willing to jump over open graves will find life interesting and rewarding" (105).

Reading the play as an allegory, Michelsen (1965) interprets it so conservatively that it poses no serious social criticism or threat to the status quo. The work constitutes the depiction of characters and their distress, and the message suggests that there is no other solution for those complications associated with the growing awareness of sexuality than unrestrained enjoyment of the senses or death (52). The drama has, however, suffered from the ravages of time, and consistent with Faesi (246) and Hill (1960, 84), Michelsen adds his opinion to the postwar consensus that the problem is dated and the play has lost its impact of shock (54).

In 1968 the literary criticism felt a jolt. The influence of the interpretation of Friedrich Rothe in that year is intimidating; it casts into doubt much of the literary criticism which preceded it and into shadow all that would follow. In the light of vitalism, or *Lebensphilosophie*, Rothe considers the Masked Gentleman an allegorical representation of Life, a dominating power before which the nature of social reality is immaterial (18). Further, the clothing of the Masked Gentleman—high hat and frock coat—establish his identity with bourgeois society. This identification of society with Life sharply reduces the social critical aspects of the work (10). The scene is a confrontation of vitalism and social criticism, and vitalism triumphs.

A year later in a journal article, Rothe (1969) recants with an overtly political interpretation, a revision to which the scholars pay scant attention. Emphasizing the major plot development of the drama rather than the conclusion, Rothe now adopts the ideas of Spalter (1967, 118, 116) regarding the bourgeois mentality and exercise of power. *Frühlings Erwachen* is not a message play concerning sexual enlightenment (Rothe 1969, 30); the sexual question is secondary (32). The work is an illustration of the system of bourgeois repression in the institutions of family, school, church, and reformatory (31). Order must be enforced so that it may be reproduced in succeeding generations to preserve the bourgeoisie (32). Whereas a year before the children were metaphors of nature (1968, 8), now they reproduce bourgeois moral views and patterns of behavior (1969, 37). The Masked Gentleman appears as "a reflex of imperialist ideology," providing unfounded hope to be realized in the great, distant world (39); but he is ambivalent since reminiscent of Mephistopheles in the pact scene with Faust (40).

Attempting to come to grips with Rothe's earlier interpretation of 1968 whereby social criticism is radically diminished by the dominance of a figure representing both vitalism and bourgeois society, Rasch (1969) argues that vital exuberance and social criticism are one. Because emancipated sexuality is opposed by society it cannot be realized (416). Therefore individual recognition of sexual urges constitutes social criticism, which is necessary to natural existence and moral order (415).

Wedekind is seen as anarchistic because he attacks civilization which is ashamed of nature, according to Diebold (1921, 44–45). And from what was then the German Democratic Republic emanates a similar interpretation characterizing the author as anarchistic and therefore wrong; Kaufmann, in 1969, equates nature and individuality and assumes that Wedekind's concept of vitalism was antisocial. The critic sees human nature in the drama defended not against a particular society but against every society, against the sociability of the human being. The individual, in the dramatist's eyes, exists free of society, egocentric and sensual, naive and unrestrained. And Kaufmann, remaining true to the concepts of Marxism, concludes that the idea of an individual who is not socially determined is nonsense, a false abstraction (69).

Another voice from the German Democratic Republic in the same year assumes a perfect equation between the moral of the work and Wedekind's own personal views. It is the voice of Hahn (1969), who analyzes the final scene of *Frühlings Erwachen* and expresses a solution amounting to the pursuit of Life in spite of everything (I, 16). Wedekind does not try to change bourgeois, capitalist society but makes his own way in it. The playwright is ambivalent; he is a destroyer of bourgeois ideology who in destroying constructs the bourgeois ideology of egoistic survival (20–21).

An aura of optimism is perceived by both Gittleman (1969) and Shaw (1970), the former understanding the work as an allegory of good and evil by which the dramatist advocates a new standard of education for adults and adolescents (51–52). Unlike Hahn (I, 20), Gittleman interprets the words of the Masked Gentleman as a suggestion that man can change his world (52). Shaw emphasizes that the theme is not primarily sex but puberty, a time when aberrations of sexuality are natural (57).

The vein that emanates from Spalter (1967, 116–18) becomes strongly political, that is anticapitalist, with Rothe in 1969; this continues with Hahn the same year and is sustained by Irmer (1970), who also writes from the German Democratic Republic. Irmer is heavily indebted to Rothe, to whom he pays no due, for his exposé of the authoritarian nature of capitalism as it is manifested in educators and the method of instruction. A premise of capitalist society assumes teachers and parents beat lessons into the youth physically; these lessons consist of submission to authority, subordination, obedience, and a feeling of duty. The children are beaten in order that they learn to turn about and do the same to the next generation. Related questions of instruction and education are ignored (109). The Masked Gentleman, who in the view of Rothe (1969, 39) appeared as an image of capitalism extending indefinite hopes to be realized on distant shores, now assumes greater proportions and is a full-blown capitalist promising access to the wealth of the world (Irmer, 196). Irmer sustains Rothe's parallel to Mephisto and the devil's pact.

Fleeting attention paid the Masked Gentleman by White (1973) tends to undercut Rothe's influential 1968 interpretation of this figure. For two reasons White argues that the Masked Gentleman is not to be understood as a representative of bourgeois society as Rothe suggests: an identity exists between this figure and Ilse, a character to be discussed below; and the top hat and tails which the Masked Gentleman wears are not prescribed in the stage directions (118). Indeed, this attire is merely what Wedekind wore when playing the role, a fact made widely familiar by a photograph of him in the part. White submits that the figure offers a reconciliation of the generations since the figure shows there are things worth living for beyond the morality of the school system and a patriarchal society; the Masked Gentleman represents "a *saner* adult world" (118).

Best (1975) deftly appropriates the gist of Rothe's article from 1969 and Irmer's ideas of 1970, removing them from their anticapitalist context. Bourgeois life is perceived as a vicious circle as one generation applies to the next those standards which had been enforced upon it. The development of adolescents is stunted, and they are emotionally crippled in the process, just as their parents before them (64–65). Life, for that reason, has nothing desirable to offer Melchior, and the role of the Masked Gentleman is anything but positive (64–65).

Wedekind's intentions are clearly didactic and socially critical in the eyes of Kuhn (1981), the central theme of the work being the discrepancy between actual and pretended motivation in the adult world. The scenes depicting both children and adults provoke criticism of the latter; when they judge the children, the process becomes reversed, and the behavior of the adults reveals itself in a negative light (79). The Masked Gentleman is an allegory of Life as well as a mouthpiece for Wedekind; when he promises to make the world accessible to Melchior, he is inviting the public to active participation in social criticism (77–79).

Pickerodt (1984) stands in awe before the complexity of the drama. After the example of Gundolf, Pickerodt perceives a diffuse montage of lyrical atmospheric segments as well as literary parody, naturalistic family drama, and social satire (22).

The history of the literary criticism is oversimplified by the generalization of Chick (1984) when he states that the drama is traditionally seen as "a message piece" advocating vitalism. But he argues that it is also anti-vitalist since sex is not represented as beautiful and pure but as "an unavoidably painful, maddening, perverse, sometimes lethal force" (26). And Gonçalves da Silva (1985), too, interprets the work as a problem play representing the tragedy of puberty and the need for pedagogical enlightenment; her view, however, is colored by fatalistic pessimism since she perceives "a society bent on destroying its tender links with nature in an irrevocable pursuit of a doomed civilization" (3).

The feminists Boa (1987) and Diethe (1988) take different stands with regard to the drama, that of Boa being more in conformance with the history of the criticism. She describes the play as an analysis of a sexually oppressive culture accompanied by a representation of the sexual fantasies engendered by that milieu (26). Children experiment with attitudes and roles, but adults adhere in a rigidly hypocritical or self-deluded way to their roles (35); these modes of behavior are harmful and include sexual pleasure, the exercise of power, and extension of one's ego to children (37–38). Diethe, on the other hand, finds that the play amounts to an unequivocal statement in behalf of a young woman's right to sex education. Wedekind in this regard goes beyond that which he took in later works, especially *Mine-Haha*, where education is confined to physical fitness and music (79).

In the final scene the Masked Gentleman ceremoniously delivers a dictum: "I understand morality to be the real product of two imaginary factors. The imaginary factors are obligation and desire. The product is called morality, and its reality cannot be denied!" ("Unter Moral verstehe ich das reelle Produkt zweier imaginärer Größen. Die imaginären Größen sind Sollen und Wollen. Das Produkt heißt Moral und läßt sich in seiner Realität nicht leugnen!" II, 172–73) Friedenthal (1914) recognizes the message for what it is, Wedekind's little joke, the mathematical differential of life (56). Diebold (1921, 47) construes the Masked Gentleman's words as advocation of the golden mean realized by the product of "Sollen" (obligation, morality) and "Wollen" (flesh, desire), and the subject is ignored for a half century thereafter. Indeed, Dosenheimer (1949) observes that no moral is appended to the conclusion of this work as Wedekind does so often (190).

But then, enter the Anglo-American Germanists, who with terrible seriousness attempt to construe a moral statement. Shaw (1970) argues that since tragedy in *Frühlings Erwachen* is the consequence of the given moral system, the Masked Gentleman redefines this. This character substitutes a natural morality for that grounded in social institutions by offering the boys a formula (61), which is regarded "as a kind of existential magic spell" (51). The new morality consists not of "an inherited system of pieties" but a measure applied to the particular circumstances; it is not absolute, but a dynamic product of relative and arbitrary values. That the factors are imaginary mean they are as one conceives them or that they do not exist and are only apparent (60–61).

Shaw's conception of a natural morality, as opposed to a social one, is refined a bit by Bullivant (1973) with his idea of a personal moral code far removed from the facade of social respectability (44). The critic, however, makes a sudden reversal. One may recall the turnabout in the interpretation of the Masked Gentleman when Rothe (1968, 10) finally characterizes him as a bourgeois figure identifiable with repressive society. Bullivant executes such a maneuver when he suggests that the personal moral code is contradicted by the term *obligation* (Sollen) since such duty must be external and social (45).

White (1973) assumes an intermediate position with the argument that the Masked Gentleman advances a bourgeois morality, which reveals itself as false and empty since it is the product of imaginary quantities and unreal concepts (116). The Masked Gentleman thereby plays a conciliatory role between the generations (118).

Distinguishing his position from that of Shaw (61), who posited relative and arbitrary values, and taking issue with the view of Bullivant (45) that an external ethic must necessarily be of bourgeois derivation, Burns (1975) argues that absolute values are represented by Sollen and Wollen, and the proposed synthesis of them is unreal since they cannot be united in a social context. This lack of union is the reflection of a work where values conflict as a consequence of the interaction between the individual and society in a dialectical relationship (155).

In a refreshing fashion, Best (1975, 80) characterizes the words of the Masked Gentleman as "impressive sounding nonsense." With no due respect to Best, Hibberd (1979) adopts his attitude that the proposition consists of dubious abstractions (634) and agrees with White (116) that the term *imaginary* is to be understood as unreal since the words constitute dismissal of an erroneous bourgeois moral code. Hibberd argues further that no new morality is offered to replace the old (647). The dictum of the Masked Gentleman constitutes Wedekind's use of comic irony to create distance and objectivity in his audience. Borrowing heavily from

Spalter (1967) without recognition, Hibberd contends that what in the context of Brecht would be described as an "alienation effect" startles the viewer, causing him to disengage the emotions and observe critically. Melchior's behavior then reveals itself as an affirmation of life which is a matter of faith, an instinctual response beyond rational comprehension (645).

Borrowing the argument of Burns (155) about the dialectical relationship of the individual and society, Jelavich (1983) observes that individual inclinations and social expectations interact in a dynamic way to produce morality. The polarization of these concepts—Melchior's egoism and the retribution of society—lead to tragedy (139).

In the spirit of Best (80) and Hibberd (645), Stewart (1985–86) characterizes the words of the Masked Gentleman as too abstract to tell one what he offers Melchior (62). The critic assumes the position of Dosenheimer (1949, 190) that no moral is set forth, but he does assert that the Masked Gentleman functions as a "moral arbiter" (61–62).

Boa (1987) considers the term *imaginary* as it is understood by Shaw (1970, 60), White (116) and Hibberd (647).The term may refer to the fact that there are no objective moral truths in the external world or that imperatives engendered by the imagination or internalized social conventions are delusory if thought to be objective. Further, the interaction of Sollen and Wollen (both subjective) has real consequences which amount to "desire disguised as the moral imperative"; we will, or determine by an act of choice, in accordance with our desires and call it morality (Boa, 37).

Frühlings Erwachen bears the subtitle "Eine Kindertragödie" (A Tragedy of Children), but critics fret over the absence of elemental concepts of the genre; these writers concern themselves with humor, the central dramatic figure, the development of plot, and dramatic structure. And words of the author foster confusion.

In a letter written to Fritz Basil in 1907, Wedekind divulges his intention to emphasize humor in some passages, especially those reflecting on Wendla and in the scenes with her mother. He contends that it the work is interpreted as harmlessly amusing, it is more moving; however, when the passionate and tragic qualities of it are stressed, the effect may be offensive (Hahn 1969 III, 580).

The work is tragedy with Melchior in the central role as hero, according to Goldmann (1908, 114); the remaining figures, however, are caricatures, which are so crude and tasteless that they demonstrate the author's lack of humor (120). Kapp (1909) interprets not Melchior stage center as the tragic hero but the children as multiple heroes (113); the coherence of the traditional dramatic development is here superseded by an episodic arrangement consisting of many small genre pictures (111). The very same aspect of structure elicits from Hofmiller (1910) the objection that the work is fatally flawed: formlessness renders the work incapable of being performed and suitable only for reading (92); the work is not a drama consisting of acts but a collection of dreams and nightmares tinged with feverish anxiety (100). Friedenthal (1914) expresses dissatisfaction with the structural arrangement of scenes (57), and Fechter (1920) describes it simply as loose (42), but Elster (1922) is more positive and notes a series of concentrated visions that evokes suspense (21).

The concept of tragedy receives a Freudian interpretation from Faesi (1956), who sees fate in the operation of the libido as a blind, elemental force (245). But Völker (1965) cautions that Wedekind's use of the term *tragedy* in his subtitle is misleading and recalls the author's letter to Fritz Basil; Völker argues that the work must be played to emphasize its fantastic, bizarre humor or otherwise the language becomes stilted and ridiculous (27).

That each of the children constitutes a central tragic figure is the view of Kapp (1909, 113) and Dosenheimer (1949, 189), which is borrowed and refined by Rothe (1968) in his contention that the children collectively play the role usually assigned a central character as hero in tragedy; they represent the vital force of elemental sexuality and innocence beyond the boundaries of morality. Childhood becomes the scope of the drama (8), and what Wedekind refers to as his humor is that parody with which he establishes distance from his child heroes (20).

Tragicomedy with skeptical humor is identified by Böckmann (1969, 86), and what Rothe described as parody is recognized by Hahn (1969) as the dramatist's objective aloofness and superiority (I, 17). All of the children, including Melchior, experience tragedy since their innocent, childish, natural state of being human is disregarded, deformed, and destroyed by social norms; adolescent survivors will forget the questions they have been posed by Life (10–11).

That the work cannot be played as unqualified tragedy since the text would be awkward and ridiculous is the position of Völker (27), acknowledged and adopted by Gittleman (1969, 27); on the contrary, any production must emphasize the strangely grotesque humor. Gittleman characterizes the work most accurately when, leaving Völker behind, he makes the offhand observation, "Deeply tragic scenes mingle with moments of hilarious farce" (52). Without referring to Natan (1963), Gittleman borrows his opinion that the dramatic figures are so one-sided that the customary relationship of protagonist and antagonist is lacking as are motivation and conflict (46).

With regard to the structure of the work in the absence of a coherent plot development, Gittleman appropriates directly from Feuchtwanger (1952) not only the idea but the very term *antithesis*. Feuchtwanger employs this term with reference to the juxtaposition, for example, of scenes of "poetic delicacy" with those of "savage irony" (18), and Gittleman notes antithesis manifested in the "beautiful, lyrical sensitivity" of the adolescents as juxtaposed to the "wholly grotesque stupidity" of the adults (46).

Shaw (1970) identifies the work as tragedy, not in "the technical generic sense," but because changes normally taking place at puberty do not occur, enabling adolescents to enter the adult community rather than remaining isolated from it (59).

Irmer (1970, 111–12) is less decisive, describing *Frühlings Erwachen* as a tragedy in theme and content. Allying himself with Rothe (1968) and Hahn (1969 I) without acknowledging them, Irmer identifies Wedekind's humor as his critical distance, without heed to which a production dissolves into elements that are at once realistic, surrealistic, fantastic, and grotesque. In a subsequent modification of this opinion, Irmer decides the drama is a comedy or possibly a tragicomedy.

The drama remains a tragedy in the eyes of Best (1975, 73), a work depicting not a central figure but society in general. Following the lead of Feuchtwanger, Natan, and Gittleman, Best analyzes the dramatic structure as a collection of unconnected scenes which offer patterns of cross-reference and contrast (64).

With regard to Wedekind's humor, Kuhn (1981) breaks new ground. Humor and parody of the language of the adolescents achieves distance so that the audience is able to exercise its critical judgment in a detached fashion. When the language exceeds the role of the speaker, it becomes inappropriate and destroys theatrical illusion. In both these respects—the absence of identification and the destruction of illusion—Wedekind is anticipating the alienation effect central to the theater of Bertolt Brecht (79).

Jelavich (1983, 137–38) accepts the argument of Rothe (1968, 8), advanced by Kuhn (51), that the children constitute a collective protagonist, but he points out that they do not act in a unified fashion. Tragedy is not caused by their character faults or by an unavoidable conflict with order but by adult authoritarianism and stupidity, which have monstrous consequences.

It is Pickerodt (1984, 19–20), who is most distressed by the failure of *Frühlings Erwachen* to conform to the traditional concepts of tragedy, including a unified dramatic development. He is distraught by the absence of exposition, rising action, and so on, in what the reader may recognize as Gustav Freytag's time-honored scheme for the five-act tragedy (19). Refining the argument of Jelavich without singling him out, Pickerodt denies that youth acts collectively as a central figure since each young person has his or her own personality and problems. The hero is sexuality, Life, the force of nature, as illustrated by individual cases when this hero comes into conflict with the temperament of youth and social expectations of role.

The configuration Ilse-Moritz-the Masked Gentleman attracts considerable attention among the literary critics. The model, favorite of the artists, offers to let Moritz accompany her in the pursuit of pleasure, but he declines; after committing suicide, he appears in the graveyard with his head under his arm to glorify death before Melchior in a confrontation with the Masked Gentleman.

As Kapp (1909, 114) observes, if Melchior is the victor in life, Moritz is the loser. The latter is the incorporation of Death as Wedekind describes him in 1911, into the mouth of whom the author tells us he has inserted the thoughts of Nietzsche (IX, 424). But Fechter (1920) suggests that Wedekind is being autobiographical in that Moritz expresses the author's own desire for a superior, detached consideration of a world without God, an external view of the behavior of confused mortals (40).

Ilse serves as a prototype for those free-loving women who abound in Wedekind's work, and Fechter first observes that she treads the path of Lulu and will develop into this character in the later tragedy (38–39). Of greater significance is Ilse's allegorical meaning; Fechter notes an allusion, widely overlooked, in which the

Masked Gentleman suggests that if Moritz had chosen to accompany Ilse, he would have embraced Life instead of Death (II, 173); she incorporates Life, which she offers to Moritz, as does the Masked Gentleman to Melchior (38). For nearly fifty years hereafter the critics ignore this link between Ilse and the Masked Gentleman.

Fechter submits that Moritz cannot accept the company and love which Ilse offers because he is too shy and because of the manner in which he has been educated; his suicide amounts to sneaking away from life before he has ever begun it (38–39). And whereas Faesi (1956, 245) argues quite lamely that Moritz is not equal to the burdensome trials of existence, Völker (1965, 28) calls him the most interesting figure in the work since he is at the same time a lofty humorist and the most pitiful of creatures.

It is not until 1966 that the identity between Ilse and the Masked Gentleman is rediscovered by Sokel, with nary a gesture towards Fechter. Sokel argues that Ilse embodies eros and at the conclusion of the drama becomes identical with the Life force since the meaning and core of Life is eros (201–2).

Rothe (1968) notes the identification of Ilse and the Masked Gentleman, and Vinçon (1987, 181) incorrectly attributes to Rothe that original perception of Fechter seized upon by Sokel. The relationship of Ilse to the Masked Gentleman means that they lend something to each other; he gains some of her immediacy, and she a meaning for her bohemian lifestyle (29). Ilse, however, alludes to a drawback in her spontaneous existence when reference is made to its transience with her words, "By the time any of you are fit for anything, I shall be on the rubbish heap" ("Bis es an euch kommt, lieg ich im Kehricht" II, 141).

Gittleman (1969) is thoroughly taken with Ilse, describing her as "a sensual, animalistic, and thoroughly innocent creature" (44). But Wagener (1980) is troubled and returns to the line of hers quoted above; he is the first to suggest that she is pursuing a negative lifestyle, her words constituting an admission that her existence can lead to no good. Taking issue with Fechter without direct reference to him, Wagener argues further that Ilse is not intended as the glorification of the "Freudenmädchen," or woman of pleasure enjoying unrestrained sexuality, since this is not possible within bourgeois society; he cites the *Lulu* tragedy as a basis for this interpretation (32).

The critics have completely overlooked one bond of similarity between Ilse and the Masked Gentleman; she indulges her mathematic wit as does he in that final differential of life, which he propounds as a new morality. When called upon to account for the demise of Moritz, Ilse identifies the cause of death as parallelepipeds ("Parallelepipedon"). The term refers to a six-sided prism, each face of which is a parallelogram. Alone among the scholars, Wagener notes this remark and interprets it as a reference to excessive demands by the school system (1980, 38). The term occurs once previously on that fateful evening when Moritz refuses Ilse's offer of pleasure; the boy provides the excuse that he must turn back since he has parallelepipeds on the conscience.

Kuhn (1981) attributes to Ilse a unique meaning since this character serves as a structural principle of the drama; she poses an antithetical relationship to Wendla—naive, innocent instinct juxtaposed to repressed, prudish morality (23).

Although leading a bohemian life unknown to the children of the drama, Ilse is far from being an outsider according to Jelavich (1983, 141). She exists in a symbiotic relationship to bourgeois society; the artists' colony where she models is supported by the sale of sexually suggestive pictures such as those used for self-arousal by Hänschen Rilow (141).

Boa (1987) turns to that subject considered by Fechter (1920) and Faesi (1956), namely the refusal by Moritz of that pleasure offered by Ilse and his ensuing suicide. With an allusion to masturbation and an association of the gun with a phallus, Boa concludes that Moritz turns "inwards into narcissism" (42).

Women of pleasure abound in Wedekind's works, as noted by Fechter (38–39) and Wagener (1980, 32); the latter denies that they present a positive image. That Ilse distinguishes herself from her sisters is the argument of Diethe (1988), who submits that Ilse is considerably less complex; she is characterized by her "nonchalant tone" and that "unequivocally carefree context" from which it emanates (84).

The language of Wedekind's dramatic figures first becomes the subject of consideration when that of the children is accounted a failure by Elsner (1912), who finds it not childlike but childish and clumsy (22). To the ears of Diebold (1921), however, it sounds different; the young people speak lyrically, prose and poetry being one (70); the words are sung like the stanzas of a ballad (47). With regard to the adults, on the other hand, the language goes beyond the delineation of character and the illusion of naturalism to assume a style which casts the figures as types (45–46). Differentiating among the children and the Masked Gentleman, Kutscher (1922) hears their patterns of speech as follows: Wendla—clear, touching, wavering at times in a tomboyish way; Moritz—enthusiastic but feverish, melancholy, and philosophic; Melchior—clearer, more quiet, inclined to sophisms; the Masked Gentleman—polished and hard as steel (I, 252). Spalter (1967), on the other hand, sides with Diebold in his view that the children speak alike, with a lyrical voice associated with innocence; this is distinguishable only by that rapture which wells from Wendla in the garden at dawn after having become a woman. The adults tend to differentiate themselves; Zungenschlag is recognizable by his stammering, and the Headmaster Sonnenstich identifies himself as a bureaucrat by his "ponderous formulations" (121).

The closest analysis of speech patterns is provided by Kuhn (1981), arguing that the dialogue is subordinate to Wedekind's social-critical and didactic intentions. The language of the adults is not individualized, but stylized, according to a pattern of religious or bourgeois clichés or the jargon of a particular office or occupation. The adults emerge, therefore, as sociological types. Moreover as these figures tend to lose their individuality, they may become caricatures. This specialized language associated with pedagogy, religion, or the law conveys Wedekind's ideological criticism of the bourgeoisie and reveals the egotism of the adults in their treatment of children. The language of the children, on the other hand, serves two purposes: The absence of responsive dialogue underlines their alienation; monologues convey the outpouring of their language expressively and immediately so that they are understood as being at one with nature (79–80). That Kuhn's observations with regard to the language of the children are oversimplified is the argument of Boa (1987, 32); considerable complexity is present in the fluctuation between colloquial and lyrical styles involving naive simplicity and sophisticated irony.

Some scenes of the drama attract particular interest among the critics. This is especially true of those two in which Melchior submits to Wendla's request to beat her physically; they subsequently have sexual intercourse in a hayloft. His moral hackles raised, Elsner (1912) goes to the issue of character and accuses Melchior of irresponsibility and perversity (15). More interesting is the observation of Friedenthal (1914) that the scene where Wendla is taken sexually by Melchior in wild desire bears the shocking scream of truth (55). The two scenes are linked in Rothe's eyes in 1968 because the sadism and masochism which motivate the beating are born of sexuality; sexual instinct transforms the two characters into a marionettelike state of heteronomy; the drive overcomes Melchior and deprives him of his individuality and self-determination (22–23). The beating therefore amounts to a prelude to the encounter in the hayloft (25).

A year later Rothe distinctly changes his tack; he raises the issue of consent in an ambiguous manner and posits Wendla as the conscious initiator. She provokes her own rape in conformity with the tenets of a patriarchal system which permits the woman pleasure only when it is forced upon her from without (37).

Borrowing from early Rothe (1968) the concept of a heteronomous drive, Irmer (1970) notes that sexual intercourse has for Melchior the compulsive quality of a natural event. Denying love and asserting the predominance of self-interest, he expresses cynicism which lends him strength; the copulation of the adolescents is distinguished from that of animals only by the egoism that directs people to embellish it with morality (113).

There is a strong inclination to associate orgasm with self-destruction and death since this is a minor theme in Wedekind's works. One thinks of Lulu, Lisiska in *Tod und Teufel*, and Effie in *Schloß Wetterstein*, where a high sexual libido accompanies a desire for an orgiastic death. Diethe (1988), however, notes a distinction as she points out that the masochism of Wendla Bergmann is born of sexual abstinence and may be understood as a substitute for the sex act itself (83–84).

Two other scenes which are closely related in the criticism and draw considerable attention occur at the beginning of the third act. The pedagogues Affenschmalz (Monkeygrease), Knüppeldick (Cudgelthick), Hungergurt (Starveling), Knochenbruch (Bonebreak), and others gather in conference before the busts of Pestalozzi and Rousseau to consider the complicity of Melchior in the death of Moritz. Melchior is given no chance to speak, and they debate at length the question of how wide the window should be opened. In the following scene the funeral of Moritz evokes the sentiments of the sanctimonious Pastor Kahlbauch (Baldbelly) and the denial of his father.

Both Kapp (1909, 118) and Hofmiller (1910, 88) think that Wedekind's gross exaggeration with regard to these figures causes his point to be lost in vindictiveness. Elsner (1912) goes so far as to describe the view conveyed by the burial scene as not only exaggerated but also inaccurate and disgusting (21). Friedenthal, however, conceding that such caricature in the conference scene is exaggerated, maintains that it is essentially accurate (56). Humor is paramount in the view of Kutscher (1922), who submits that the improbable distortion of the caricature in both scenes is grotesquely comical (I, 251); Gundolf (1948, 193) describes the conference scene as satire while Feuchtwanger (1952, 18) calls the funeral tragicomedy. The grotesque qualities of the adults, submits Natan (1963), reflect Wedekind's repugnance for moral hypocrisy that runs so deep that it causes him to lose his control as a writer (104). Further, the conference scene indicates the inability of the older generation to come to grips with the real problems of life; the quarrel regarding the window, although taking place between members of the same generation, provides a reflection of "the unbridgeable gulf" between the generations (109).

Applying an idea borrowed from Andreas-Salomé (1907, 98–99) with acknowledgment, Völker (1965) observes that the conference scene is not just a caricature but a vision of the children heightened to fantasy; the teacher's behavior is presented as seen through the eyes of children (27). The caricatures of the teachers, according to Gonçalves da Silva (1985), emphasize their "snobbery, pettiness, and sadism" (4), and their names point to their dehumanization (5). The names also render the teachers less threatening by subjecting them to ridicule and scorn as if directed at them by children, suggests Boa (1987, 34), borrowing from Andreas-Salomé and Völker.

The boys in the reform school where Melchior is confined engage in a masturbation contest. Whereas Pissin (1905, 14) describes the scene as the greatest obscenity ("die massivste Schweinerei"), most critics consider the contribution it makes to the drama. Fechter (1920) observes that Melchior is revolted by the vileness of the imprisoned longings of the boys and, presumably for this reason, breaks out (39). Natan (1963), too, uses the scene to reflect favorably upon Melchior when he observes that the institution is unable to harm that which is good and decent in the boy (109). The masturbation represents lewdness and brutality from which Melchior stands aloof, as Best (1975) notes. Wedekind deliberately employs obscenity here as a provocation of those Christian sentiments expressed by Melchior's father, who sent him to the reformatory (78). No redeeming features are evident to Boa in the function of the scene or Melchior's reaction therein. Devoid of any sexual fantasy which would transform it, the activity is "drearily sordid" (43); the boys represent "the brutish and competitive male in his lowest form" (42).

Above the toilet, Hänschen Rilow fantasizes as he masturbates while contemplating pictures of classical female beauty. In another scene, he and Ernst Röbel roll about in the grass in a vineyard, drinking wine and kissing. The autoerotism of Hänschen, unlike the masturbation contest in the reform school, elicits no offense. Hofmiller (1910) regards the scene as one of the most bold and truest in the literature of recent decades (96–97). The critic, however, distinguishes himself from other scholars as he applies a singular criterion to the scene of blossoming, homosexual friendship: Hofmiller dismisses it as completely useless (99). With regard to Hänschen's sexual fantasies, Natan describes the boy as "the valiant knight of romantic illusions, who becomes captive of his own sensuality so willingly" (106). The scene in the vineyard contains the most tender dialogue Wedekind ever wrote (108) and "belongs to one of the outstanding confessions of modern German drama" (107). In a similar vein, Shaw (1970) characterizes their "sterile exchange of kisses" as "one of the most touchingly ironic scenes in all German drama" (57). Hänschen's fantasies as he quotes Othello's farewell speech to Desdemona strike Boa (1987) as humorous; and she characterizes the scene of the homosexual kiss as lyrical (44).

The mothers of Wendla Bergmann and Melchior Gabor—the one prudish, the other enlightened—evoke critical attention. Frau Bergmann is intended to generate social criticism, according to Friedenthal (1914); she refuses to tell her daughter about the origin of babies with the excuse that as a mother she cannot be responsible for such a thing since she would land behind bars. This pretext constitutes what Friedenthal calls Wedekind's accusation directed against the muffled church bells of buried morality (54). Frau Gabor, as Fechter (1920) points out, is enlightened in theory but retreats all too quickly from her principles. Her husband demands that Melchior be sent to a reformatory, and as soon as Herr Gabor reveals the letter which is sexually incriminating, Frau Gabor relents, relinquishing her support of Melchior and agreeing that he should be punished. Without reflecting on her motivation or that of her husband, Fechter observes simply that at this point she becomes more bourgeois and narrow than he (39).

The tragic aspect of Frau Bergmann's silence to the pleas of her daughter is underplayed by Faesi (1956) and Michelsen (1965). Denying that Wedekind is advocating sexual enlightenment, Faesi finds himself in an untenable position. Forced to overlook the fact that Wendla's ignorance was the major factor in her pregnancy and subsequent death, the critic offers the implausible suggestion that Frau Bergmann's inability to talk to her daughter about sexuality constitutes grotesque humor (245). Michelsen refers to the foolish prudery of Frau Bergmann as satire (53).

Whereas Fechter is appalled at the sudden conversion of Frau Gabor to the punitive attitude of her husband regarding Melchior, both Rothe (1969) and Irmer (1970) analyze the source of Herr Gabor's urgency in his sexual attitudes. Rothe explains the stubborn insistence that Melchior be sent to a reformatory as a symptom of jealousy since Melchior competes with his father for the favor of his wife, Melchior's mother (33). Irmer provides an explanation in terms of sexual politics. Frau Gabor tries to instill in her son a sense of responsibility and the ability to make personal decisions; this, according to Irmer's Marxist view, makes her willy-nilly an opponent of bourgeois society. Such independence implicitly undermines Herr Gabor, and when his wife threatens to leave him, he plays the letter as his trump card enabling him to continue to hold her in his power (127). Looking not so much to Gabor as an explanation for his wife's change of heart, Best (1975) interprets her conversion as indicative of an inherent weakness. Her liberal attitudes, he argues, conceal a lack both of sympathy and parental responsibility (72). The critic faults both mothers for their views of their offspring: Frau Bergman treats her daughter Wendla as a child when she is an adolescent, and Frau Gabor treats Melchior like an adult when he is not (69). The view that Frau Gabor is trapped in a moral dilemma is the singular interpretation of Gonçalves da Silva (1985), who detects not a hint that Wedekind is adversely criticizing school, religion, and law and observes that Frau Gabor brings "the conflict between parental love and social convention to a climax" (6). Unlike both Fechter (1920), who does not inquire into the reason for Frau Gabor's change of opinion, and Best (1975), who thinks Frau Gabor is a phony all along, Boa (1987) characterizes what she terms Frau Gabor's "sudden retreat from liberalism" as unmotivated. Sharing with Rothe the view of the relationship between Melchior and his mother, Boa describes her change of heart as the end of her love affair with her son and a return to her husband (39). Both Frau Gabor and Frau Bergmann have idealized conceptions of their children and identify with them as a symptom of "regressive infantilism" (40).

The critics might have made more of the bond between Frau Gabor and Melchior—the importance of a son to his mother, exceeding that of any daughter. Her role as a liberal, anti-authoritarian figure is an egoistic expression of her sexual frustration. Fear strikes into her heart at the revelation of losing him to another woman.

Critics of the theater are eager to place *Frühlings Erwachen* within a literary tradition, and both Fechter (1920, 35) and Elster (1922, 47) do so; they recognize Wedekind's debt to the drama of Sturm und Drang as well as to Georg Büchner (1813–37) and his work *Woyzeck* (published 1879), with what Fechter describes as its thrusting, searching, dull, aimless unconsciousness. However, it is Kutscher (1922) who plants Wedekind squarely in a literary tradition while at the same time arguing that he is unique. Characterizing the dramatist as original and without parallels, Kutscher nevertheless compares him with J. M. R. Lenz (1751–92) and Christian Friedrich Grabbe (1801–36) as well as Georg Büchner. The works of these dramatists dispense with a listing of the dramatis personae and consist of scenes which are closed in form. The language is by turn terse, flowing and lyrical, inclined to caricature and dialect (I, 249). The authors write lively, grotesque comedy and evidence little regard for the limitations of the theater (253). The influence of this analysis by Kutscher is pervasive and extends to numerous subsequent critics.

Although the drama of Sturm und Drang was, of course, deeply indebted to Shakespeare, *Frühlings Erwachen* is seen as particularly Shakespearean, and Friedenthal (1914, 56) notes this especially with reference to the graveyard scene. Benjamin writing in 1929 extends the comparison to reputation; he observes that the work within its lifetime has come to be regarded with a degree of seriousness worthy of Shakespeare (551). Stealthily borrowing an idea from Gundolf (1948, 213), Natan (1963) characterizes the last scene as grandiose, causing one to recall Hamlet addressing the skull of Yorick (109).

Romanticism suggests itself to other critics. Fechter (1920, 41) recalls the spooky romantic horror of the anonymous *Nachtwachen des Bonaventura* (Night Watch of Bonaventura, 1804) in the conclusion. The appearance and comments of the Masked Gentleman, whether played by Wedekind himself or interpreted as a mouthpiece figure serving the dramatist, indicate a strong debt to romanticism; irony and self-irony characterize the epilogue of romantic drama since Ludwig Tieck (1773–1853), as both Benjamin (1929, 552) and Gundolf (1948, 213) recollect.

The critics look not only backwards to place *Frühlings Erwachen* in an earlier literary-historical tradition but forwards to indicate the influence of the work on subsequent drama. Faesi (1956, 241) argues that Wedekind represents a break with naturalism, his grotesque eccentricity providing the precursor of expressionism. Natan (1963, 104) and Ude (1966, 26) write of Wedekind's breakthrough to grotesque symbolism, which in turn leads to expressionism, surrealism, and the theater of the absurd. *Frühlings Erwachen* initiated a revolution in the theater, which, according to Gittleman in 1969, is still continuing (52).

How do the critics evaluate *Frühlings Erwachen*? In an opinion, which finds no resonance in subsequent literary criticism, Paul Goldmann (1908) seizes at an early date the opportunity to damn it. The work is inaccurate with regard to the representation of adults, children, and their language as well as adolescent eroticism (119–20). But this is nothing. There are those shortcomings that go to the very heart of drama: the work is untheatrical; the scenes are not related to each other in a dramatic way (113); and the play is impossible to present on stage (118).

The general appraisal of *Frühlings Erwachen* is overwhelmingly positive, an example of which is provided the same year by another critic. Writing in 1908, the Marxist Leon Trotsky sounds like a proponent of the New Criticism with its penchant for ambiguity, tension, and complexity; he praises the work as moving, helpless, and beautiful in its awkwardness because it is full of possibilities (381). This early work of Wedekind is seen as one of his most mature by Kapp (1909, 112), and Friedenthal (1914, 57) is content to characterize it as a great work of art. Underscoring, perhaps, what Kapp meant by the maturity of an early work, Fechter (1920) describes *Frühlings Erwachen* as the most poetically rich of Wedekind's pieces, the most beautiful in its feeling (34); the warmth of young life illuminates the adolescents as in no subsequent drama of the author's (41). In the plays which follow, love no longer has its beauty and magnificence but manifests itself as lust that leads to ruin (43). Gundolf (1948, 207) shows prudence as he recalls another significant work, calling this drama together with the *Lulu* tragedy Wedekind's best, but Dosenheimer (1949) disregards the qualifiers and throws caution to the wind; in this she is by no means alone. Dosenheimer characterizes this work as the dramatist's most brilliant and most artistically perfect (190). Hill (1960) agrees wholeheartedly; it is Wedekind's most beautiful, "a poetic and tender rendition of the emotional world of young people" (84). A rather peculiar limitation is imposed upon the play by a critic who makes a great demand of the genre. Jelavich (1979) rates the work as social satire that is "truly brilliant." It is, however, held to suffer from severe limitations in its failure to provide a solution to the "problem of humane maturation in an inhuman society" (215). Mennemeier (1980) is unique in that he appraises the work relative to what it reveals about the author; *Frühlings Erwachen* is a masterpiece that illustrates Wedekind's extraordinary critical intelligence (361). Evaluating the drama, in turn, for its position on the landscape, Boa (1987) characterizes it as "a seminal work in the history of modern theater" (26).

Works Cited

Andreas-Salomé, Lou. 1907. "*Frühlings Erwachen*." *Die Zukunft* 58 (19 January): 97–100.

Benjamin, Walter. 1972. "Frank Wedekind: *Frühlings Erwachen*." In *Gesammelte Schriften*, edited by Rolf Tiedemann and Hermann Schweppenhäuser. Vol. 4, Part 1 edited by Tilman Rexroth. Frankfurt am Main: Suhrkamp. 551–52. This essay first appeared in 1929.

Best, Alan. 1975. *Frank Wedekind*. London: Oswald Wolf.

Blei, Franz. 1914. "Marginalien zu Wedekind." In *Das Wedekindbuch*, edited by Joachim Friedenthal. Munich and Leipzig: Georg Müller. 128–50.

Boa, Elizabeth. 1987. *The Sexual Circus. Wedekind's Theatre of Subversion*. Oxford: Blackwell.

Böckmann, Paul. 1969. "Die komödiantischen Grotesken Frank Wedekinds." In *Das deutsche Lustspiel*. Vol. 2 edited by Hans Steffen. Göttingen: Vandenhoeck & Ruprecht. 79–102.

Bullivant, Keith. 1973. "The Notion of Morality in Wedekind's *Frühlings Erwachen*." *New German Studies* 1: 40–47.

Burns, Robert A. 1975. "Wedekind's Concept of Morality: An Extension of the Argument." *New German Studies* 3: 155–64.

Chick, Edson M. 1984. "Frank Wedekind and his *Lulu* Tragedy." In his *Dances of Death. Wedekind, Brecht, Dürrenmatt, and the Satiric Tradition*. Columbia, South Carolina: Camden House. 11–45.

Diebold, Bernhard. 1972. "Wedekind der Narr." In his *Anarchie im Drama*. New York and London: Johnson Reprint Corporation. 43–76. The work first appeared in 1921.

Diethe, Carol. 1988. *Aspects of Distorted Sexual Attitudes in German Expressionist Drama*. New York, Bern, Frankfurt am Main, and Paris: Lang.

Dosenheimer, Elise. 1967. *Das deutsche soziale Drama von Lessing bis Sternheim*. Darmstadt: Wissenschaftliche Buchgesellschaft. This first appeared in 1949.

Elsner, Richard. 1912. "Frank Wedekind. *Frühlings Erwachen*." In *Moderne Dramatik in kritischer Beleuchtung*, edited by Elsner. Heft 1. Berlin-Pankow: Sozialpädagogischer Verlag. 10–23.

Elster, Hanns Martin. 1922. *Wedekind und seine besten Bühnenwerke*. Berlin and Leipzig: Franz Schneider.

Faesi, Robert. 1956. "Ein Vorläufer: Frank Wedekind." In *Expressionismus. Gestalten einer literarischen Bewegung*, edited by Hermann Friedmann and Otto Mann. Heidelberg: Rothe. 241–63.

Fechter, Paul. 1920. *Frank Wedekind. Der Mensch und das Werk*. Jena: Lichtenstein.

Feuchtwanger, Lion. 1952. Introduction to *Five Tragedies of Sex*, by Frank Wedekind.

Translated by Frances Fawcett and Stephen Spender. London: Vision. 7–21.

Friedenthal, Joachim. 1914. "Einleitung." In *Das Wedekindbuch*, edited by Friedenthal. Munich and Leipzig: Georg Müller. 1–121.

Gittleman, Sol. 1969. *Frank Wedekind*. New York: Twayne.

Glaser, Horst Albert. 1974. "Arthur Schnitzler und Frank Wedekind. Der doppelköpfige Sexus." In *Wollüstige Phantasie. Sexualästhetik der Literatur*, edited by Glaser. Munich: Hanser. 148–84.

Goldmann, Paul. 1908. "*Frühlings Erwachen*." In his *Vom Rückgang der deutschen Bühne*. Frankfurt am Main: Rütten & Loening. 111–23.

Gonçalves da Silva, M. Helena. 1985. *Character, Ideology, and Symbolism in the Plays of Wedekind, Sternheim, Kaiser, Toller, and Brecht*. London: Modern Humanities Research Association.

Gundolf, Friedrich. 1948. "Frank Wedekind." *Trivium* 6: 187–217. This appeared posthumously.

Hahn, Manfred. 1969. "Frank Wedekind. Leben und Werk." In *Frank Wedekind. Dramen I*. Berlin and Weimar: Aufbau-Verlag. 7–93.

———. 1969. *Frank Wedekind. Prosa III*. Berlin and Weimar: Aufbau-Verlag. "An einen Kritiker," 452–54. "An Fritz Basil," 580–81.

Hibberd, John L. 1979. "Imaginary Numbers and 'Humor': On Wedekind's *Frühlings Erwachen*." *Modern Language Review* 74: 633–47.

Hill, Claude. 1960. "Wedekind in Retrospect." *Modern Drama* 3.1 (May): 82–92.

Hofmiller, Josef. 1910. "Wedekind." In *Zeitgenossen*. Munich: Süddeutsche Monatshefte. 88–131.

Irmer, Hans-Jochen. 1975. *Der Theaterdichter Frank Wedekind. Werk und Wirkung*. Berlin: Henschelverlag. This originally appeared in 1970.

Jelavich, Peter. 1979. "Art and Mammon in Wilhelmine Germany: The Case of Frank Wedekind." *Central European History* 12: 203–36.

———. 1983. "Wedekind's *Spring Awakening:* The Path to Expressionist Drama." In *Passion and Rebellion. The Expressionist Heritage*, edited by Stephen Erich Bronner and Douglas Kellner. South Hadley, Mass.: J.T. Bergin. 129–50.

Kapp, Julius. 1909. *Frank Wedekind. Seine Eigenart und seine Werke*. Berlin: Hermann Barsdorf.

Kaufmann, Hans. 1969. "Zwei Dramatiker: Gerhart Hauptmann und Frank Wedekind." In his *Krisen und Wandlungen der deutschen Literatur von Wedekind bis Feuchtwanger*. Berlin and Weimar: Aufbau-Verlag. 47–84.

Kuhn, Anna Katharina. 1981. *Der Dialog bei Frank Wedekind*. Heidelberg: Carl Winter.

Kutscher, Artur. 1970. *Frank Wedekind. Sein Leben und seine Werke*. Vol. 1. New York: AMS Press. This is a reprint of the edition appearing in 1922.

Mennemeier, Franz Norbert. 1980. "Frank Wedekind." In *Handbuch des deutschen Drama*, edited by Walter Hinck. Düsseldorf: Bagel. 360–73, 568–69.

Michelsen, Peter. 1969. "Frank Wedekind." In *Deutsche Dichter der Moderne*, edited by Benno von Wiese. Berlin: Erich Schmidt. 51–69. The essay first appeared in 1965.

Natan, Alex. 1963. "Frank Wedekind." In *German Men of Letters*, edited by Natan. Vol. 2. London: Oswald Wolf. 101–29.

Pickerodt, Gerhart. 1984. *Frank Wedekind: Frühlings Erwachen*. Frankfurt am Main, Berlin, and Munich: Diesterweg.

Pissin, Raimund. 1905. *Frank Wedekind*. Berlin: Gose & Tetzlaff.

Rasch, Wolfdietrich. 1969. "Sozialkritische Aspekte in Wedekinds dramatischer Dichtung. Sexualität, Kunst und Gesellschaft." In *Gestaltungsgeschichte und Gesellschaftsgeschichte*, edited by Helmut Kreuzer. Stuttgart: Metzler. 409–26.

Rothe, Friedrich. 1968. *Frank Wedekinds Dramen. Jugendstil und Lebensphilosophie.* Stuttgart: Metzler.

———. 1969. "*Frühlings Erwachen.* Zum Verhältnis von sexueller und sozialer Emanzipation bei Frank Wedekind." *Studi Germanici* 7: 30–41.

Shaw, Leroy R. 1970. "The Strategy of Reformulation. Frank Wedekind's *Frühlingserwachen.*" In his *The Playwright and Historical Change.* Madison: University of Wisconsin Press. 49–65.

Sokel, Walter H. 1966. "The Changing Role of Eros in Wedekind's Drama." *The German Quarterly* 39.2: 201–7.

Spalter, Max. 1967. *Brecht's Tradition.* Baltimore: Johns Hopkins Press.

Stewart, Corbet. 1985–86. "Comedy, Morality and Energy in the Work of Wedekind." *Publications of the English Goethe Society*, n.s., 56: 56–73.

Trotsky, Leon. 1968. "Frank Wedekind." In his *Literatur und Revolution.* Translated by Eugen Schaefer and Hans von Riesen. Berlin: Gerhardt. 366–87. The article appeared in German in *Die neue Zeit* April 1908.

Ude, Karl. 1966. *Frank Wedekind.* Mühlacker: Stieglitz.

Vinçon, Hartmut. 1987. *Frank Wedekind.* Stuttgart: Metzler.

Völker, Klaus. 1965. *Frank Wedekind.* Velber bei Hannover: Friedrich Verlag.

Wagener, Hans. 1979. *Frank Wedekind.* Berlin: Colloquim.

———, ed. 1980. *Erläuterungen und Dokumente. Frank Wedekind. Frühlings Erwachen.* Stuttgart: Reclam.

Wedekind, Frank. 1921. "Was ich mir dabei dachte." In *Gesammelte Werke.* Vol. 9. Munich: Georg Müller. 424–26.

White, Alfred. 1973. "The Notion of Morality in Wedekind's *Frühlings Erwachen*: A Comment." *New German Studies* 1: 116–18.

3: Lulu (1895, 1904)
Female Sexual Liberation and Societal Reaction

In the absence of her husband Goll, the ravishing Lulu throws herself upon the painter Schwarz; when Goll returns to confront them, he dies of a stroke. Schwarz marries Lulu, but when he hears the history of her earlier relationship with Dr. Schön, he kills himself. Although Schön attempts to keep Lulu at arm's length in order to make a socially advantageous marriage, she exercises her sexual domination, and they marry. His son, Alwa Schön, promotes her career as a dancer and is drawn into the circle of men infatuated with her. Discovering males concealed about the apartment, Dr. Schön presses a revolver into her hand so that she may kill herself. Distraught, she shoots him, taking the life of that man she declares the only one she ever loved.

Countess Geschwitz aids Lulu's escape from prison, and Lulu flees with her fourth husband, Alwa Schön, to France. There the procurer Casti-Piani and the circus performer Rodrigo Quast attempt to use her for their purposes at the threat of surrendering her to the police. In London with Alwa and her supposed father Schigolch she serves as a streetwalker. Alwa is murdered by one of her patrons, and Jack the Ripper kills Geschwitz and then Lulu.

In its original manuscript form the *Lulu* tragedy consisted of five acts and was subtitled "Eine Monstretragödie" (A Monster Tragedy). From this emerged both *Erdgeist* (Earth-Spirit, 1895) and eventually *Die Büchse der Pandora* (Pandora's Box, 1904) as the original was divided and additional acts were added. References will be made to the two dramas as Part I and Part II of the *Lulu* tragedy.

In the prologue to *Erdgeist*, Lulu is described by the animal trainer as "the *true* animal, the *wild, beautiful* animal" ("das *wahre* Tier, das *wilde, schöne* Tier"): she is compared to the snake that was created to poison, seduce, and murder and is described further as "*the primal form of woman*" ("*die Urgestalt des Weibes*" III, 8–10). With the notable exception of another pattern in the criticism, which will be considered later, Lulu was interpreted from the outset in the light of the words of the animal trainer as an intrinsically destructive female force. This allegorical representation of autonomous female sexuality posed a threat to masculine hegemony and a challenge to patriarchal misogyny.

When Lulu is described in 1909 as the elemental principle of male destruction, Kapp initiates that line of interpretation which will continue for over half a century (127). Even in the subordinate role of the prostitute in Part II, since Lulu carries syphilis she bears the germ of masculine devastation (130). Male order is threatened by female chaos and the eternally destructive sexual drive, according to Friedenthal (1914, 79). Wedekind's representation of women purely as vessels of pleasure compels Blei (1914) to endow the physiological term 'vaginismus' (a spasmodic contraction of the vagina) with the import of a philosophy; foremost in the critic's mind is the behavior of Lulu, who, he notes, lives with thighs spread so wide as to remind one of the position assumed before a gynecologist rather than a lover (138–39). Male fantasy is inflamed; Fechter (1920) describes Lulu as unreal, a formation in the imagination of those about her (45). Man's inadequacy and weakness cause him to fall victim to Lulu; she is the personification of the female sexual drive that stands in the center of Life and destroys, in the eyes of Kutscher (1922 I, 363–64).

The principle represented by Lulu as the demonic, amoral sex drive is upheld into the years after World War II by Dosenheimer (1949), who gives it an autobiographical twist; she asserts that the *Lulu* tragedy was born of Wedekind's disillusionment engendered by the war of the sexes (193). Faesi (1956) understands Lulu as an incorporation of the demonic power of female sexuality (248), and reference is made to her by Hill (1960) as "the soulless arch-symbol of Woman," representing "pure instinct, lust, desire, flesh" (84–85). Natan (1963) interprets Lulu as "the woman identical with the elemental principle of destruction" (110), and to Irmer (1970) she is the law of female nature seeking revenge in a masculine world (139). Sexual antagonism, however implicit, is identified in this pattern of the criticism by Boa (1987) in her reference to the binary oppositions, or antinomies, which characterize the interpretations (203).

Standing opposed to this prevalent view is that of the work as a hymn to erotic liberation. At the Viennese premiere of *Die Büchse der Pandora* an influential voice was that of Karl Kraus (1905), who directed the play and provided commentary upon it. He characterizes Lulu as a maze of femininity, a labyrinth in which a fellow might lose track of his senses (9). Such an unfortunate man, then, for his own foolish deed repays Lulu with cruelty. Males avenge their own guilt, and masculine immorality triumphs over a woman's absence of morality (12–13).

The extension of Kraus's argumentation is advocacy of radical sexual freedom and the pursuit of pleasure. Gone is the concept of Lulu as an abstraction of any kind when Völker (1965) considers her six decades later. Wedekind is celebrated as a proponent of women's sexual emancipation. He calls for women to have control over their own bodies and asserts that sexual self-realization can be achieved only with the recognition of unrestricted concubinage (36). By interpreting Wedekind as an advocate of full equality for the sexes, Völker causes the dramatist to emerge as more radical than those contemporary defenders of women's rights who were willing to compromise and who sought accommodation within a society ordered by men. Although Völker concedes that Wedekind was little inclined towards socialism, the dramatist is seen to share with Friedrich Engels the view that only when love is freed from economic conditions will the meaning of life be realized in the experience of love (38).

The conception of erotic autonomy is extended when Rothe (1968) seizes upon Blei's misogynistic reference in 1914 to the vaginismus inherent in Wedekind's depiction of female characters. Rothe interprets this disparaging observation as merely an indication that Wedekind attempted to depict nymphomaniacs; Lulu's sexual drive thus becomes conscious and intentional (46).

"Love is egoistic self-satisfaction, the vital core of sex," according to Hahn (1969 I, 44–45). From what is still the German Democratic Republic, the critic borrows and develops, without acknowledging it, that argument made by Völker when he interprets Wedekind in the light of the economic constraints perceived by Friedrich Engels upon the realization of life and love. Lulu's sexual power over men becomes the means of her social self-preservation (51). Consistent with this conception of love, the *Lulu* tragedy illustrates that bourgeois society does not allow the natural pursuit of life to the fullest (53).

Lulu's eroticism originates in her clinical history for Mennemeier (1980), who points out that Lulu was sexually exploited as an adolescent; her desire to gain revenge upon men and at the same time subject herself to abuse by them is an expression of sadomasochism (366).

The school which interprets the Lulu tragedy as a hymn to erotic liberation includes a subgroup with a debt to psychology. Herbert Marcuse's interpretation of Freud provides the explanation of Lulu and her fate in the eyes of both Gittleman (1969) and Glaser (1974). She embodies the pleasure principle of immediate sexual gratification. Gittleman sees her as representative of mankind in an innocent and instinctive state prior to civilization (65). The reality principle requires the restraint of her pleasure. For both critics this restraint is represented by patriarchal society and, additionally for Gittleman, by civilization which is threatened by woman's spontaneous sexuality (73–74).

Without reference to either the pleasure principle or to that of reality, the interpretation of Höger (1981) is, nevertheless, conceptually quite close to that of Gittleman and Glaser. Höger posits an allegorical struggle between two disparate elements. On the one hand are men as representatives of the patriarchal system and of the concept of property; on the other is Lulu as an incorporation of the will to live, the vitalistic principle, which finds its highest pleasure in death (133, 87–88).

Both the interpretations of Lulu as a force of elemental sexual destruction and of erotic liberation summon myth to support their arguments; on the one hand Eve and Pandora, and on the other, hetaerism. In the prologue, the animal trainer presents the beasts of his menagerie, and associates Lulu in these lines with a snake. The serpent is within Eve and makes use of her, the symbol of destructive feminine power, to which sexual drive Lulu acts as a continuous attraction in Kutscher's interpretation (1922 I, 362). Creating slightly more distance between the two women, Irmer (1970) argues that the snake is simply a mythological appellation for the principle that Lulu incorporates (137). Noting the similarity of their names, Irmer associates Lulu with Lilith, Adam's first wife (133). The mythic allusion contained in the title of Part II of the tragedy suggests to Höger (1981) an identity shared by Pandora and Eve since both released evil into the world (192–93, note 1).

The use of myth of the Garden and of Pandora to endorse erotic liberation is an exceptional stance assumed by Schröder-Zebralla (1985). She posits the origin of Lulu during that time before the Fall when Lilith existed (97) and represented a status of equality between man and woman, spirit and eros (109–10). The Greek myth of Pandora and the Judeo-Christian myths surrounding Lilith and Eve commonly treat the theme of rebellion against a god, necessarily male (105); Wedekind recasts these women in the figure Lulu, who brings happiness and love (112).

To the school interpreting the *Lulu* tragedy as an expression of erotic liberation it is the utopian myth of hetaerism which provides the most support. This posits a prepatriarchal society in which independent courtesans exercised self-determination. Only in the hetaera can the woman realize herself sexually to that degree advocated by Wedekind, Völker argues (1965, 36). The concept is fully developed by Höger, who reaches back to sources in ancient history to develop Lulu as a figure standing opposed to the patriarchal system and the concept of property (133); hetaerism reigns in Part I of the Lulu tragedy, and in Part II society attempts to destroy it (136). Lulu's qualities shade off from the hetaeristic to the divine when Schröder-Zebralla characterizes her as a prophet of the religion of sensualism. Dance combines religion and eros as Lulu approaches a divine source and feels the divine within herself (157, 153).

In sharp contrast to that criticism which interprets Lulu as an intrinsically destructive force or the tragedy as a hymn to erotic liberation are those interpretations which attack these widely held positions. In the foreword to Part II, Wedekind speaks of the difference between bourgeois morality, which is protected by the judicial system, and human morality, which transcends all earthly justice and is based in a deeper, more comprehensive knowledge of the nature of the human being and of the world (III, 105–6). The distinction expressed in these lines by Wedekind generated criticism by Emrich (1958) which proved far-reaching it its influence. Emrich conceived of Lulu as representative of an unconditional sphere of human morality or nature that cannot be constrained within the limits of society or envisioned in the mundane, bourgeois imagination (211). Society characterizes her behavior as immoral, and tragedy is engendered by the conflict between the two moral systems (212–13).

The critics rose eagerly to respond to the challenge of Emrich; Michelsen (1965) characterizes Emrich's argumentation as abstract and theoretical. Basing his own interpretation upon the influence of Friedrich Nietzsche and Arthur Schopenhauer, as well as the biographical information of Kutscher (1922), Michelsen argues that Lulu is the product of contemporary masculine prejudices shared by Wedekind. She is the fictitious image of that with which the dramatist saw himself confronted in the opposite sex: "the embodiment, raised to its highest power, of what constitutes the animal-sexual gifts of the species" ("die höchst potenzierte Verkörperung dessen, was die animalisch-geschlechtliche Begabung der Gattung ausmacht"). In a characterization which would elicit howls of protest from subsequent critics, Michelsen describes Lulu as a purely natural being consisting of nothing but flesh and vulva (55). Lulu, Michelsen continues, does not represent a moral claim to be loved as a person or individual as Emrich argues (55). Consistent with the view of Schopenhauer that the value of women lies solely in the propagation of the species (58), the dramatist has created "the female beast of prey" ("das Raubtierwesen Weib") that lurks in the subconscious of male Wilhelmine society; the dramatist betrays its secrets, thus bringing the authorities down upon himself (59).

When Wedekind spoke of the existence of a human morality higher than that known to the bourgeois sphere, according to Rasch (1969), the dramatist envisioned a moral order requiring the recognition of sexuality (414). Although Emrich perceives a conflict between the individual and society, Rasch interprets the work as an indictment of society itself; Rasch asserts that society by its nature restrains sexuality in an immoral and unhealthy way (411). Disagreeing most strongly with Michelsen's characterization of Lulu as a creature consisting of nothing but flesh and vagina, Rasch interprets her as a credible woman, misused and misunderstood (411).

Whereas Michelsen in 1965 looked to contemporary thought to suggest that Wedekind presented his audience with a gross parody of what lurked in the Wilhelmine male subconscious, Hibberd (1984) about two decades later looks to the same source in philosophy to argue that the dramatist earnestly attempted to present an accurate image. The ideas of Eduard von Hartmann, Schopenhauer, Johann Jakob Bachofen, and Nietzsche were widely known and fashionable; these led Wedekind to an idealistic conception of the woman as an irrational and mysterious being. The critical argument continues, then, in two directions: first, that Wedekind found it difficult to reduce the feminine ideal which Lulu represents to something intelligible upon the stage (351); and, conversely, that the dramatist's devotion to accuracy caused him to complicate excessively something that was conceptually simple (355).

The speculation regarding the meaning of Wedekind's lines in the foreword is dismissed by Stewart (1985–86). This critic characterizes as balderdash the reference to human morality beyond earthly justice and bourgeois reality. However impressive it sounds, it is rather too much like the mathematical proposition of the Masked Gentleman in *Frühlings Erwachen*; that is, it "promises more than it delivers," revealing nothing about the metaphysics which supposedly generates this morality (65).

While Hibberd suggests that Wedekind's material got away from him, Boa (1987) credits the dramatist for being a marvelously ambiguous deconstructivist, limited only by his insight into the female psyche. Wedekind exploits sexual fantasies with such adept ambiguity that the plays may be interpreted as advocacy of erotic liberation or a demonstration of patriarchal misogyny, or both, or neither (210–11). Looking to Rothe (1968) for his ability to sustain different, possibly conflicting interpretations simultaneously and Bovenschen (1979) for her understanding of Lulu as a manipulator of roles, Boa concludes that Lulu is "a hopelessly ambiguous heroine hovering between innocent victim and wicked villainess" (120). She may do justice to male sexual longings, but she constitutes what Boa describes as "an inadequate representation of female sexuality, to say nothing of women as full personalities" (75).

A central focus of critical interpretation is the death of Lulu. If she represents a destructive threat to order, then justice demands her end. Her demise subdues sexual anarchy, represses hidden desires, and reaffirms male dominance. These are the arguments of Kapp (1909, 127) and Kutscher (1922 I, 365). Lulu violates the law of society in killing Schön, and therefore society strikes back to defeat her, according to Wagener (1979, 60). Or to put it only slightly differently, as does Gonçalves da Silva (1985), the bourgeois spirit embodied in Jack avenges itself on Lulu and preserves the bourgeois order at "a moment of pathological nihilism" (19). If the work, however, amounts to an indictment of male-dominated society, Lulu's demise is a tragedy. Kraus (1905) interprets Lulu as a victim of male possessiveness (14), and more than seven decades later Lorenz (1976) describes Jack the Ripper as the vengeful representative of patriarchal society (49–50). Lulu does not die; as an abstraction she lives on after death when conceived of as a principle or allegory, as by Gittleman (1969), Irmer (1970), Glaser (1974), and Höger (1981). By casting herself in a role calculated to appeal to men's preconceptions or desires, Lulu initiates her own emotional and psychological self-destruction, and Jack the Ripper completes the process, in the feminist view of Boa (55).

That sexual pleasure and death are closely related in Wedekind's works has not gone unnoticed by Gundolf (1948, 207, 216), Michelsen (1965, 61), and especially Sokel (1966), who coins what appears to be a new Anglicism in his use of the term "lust murder" (203). In Act I of *Die Büchse der Pandora*, Lulu tells Alwa that at one time she dreamed repeatedly of falling into the hands of a rape murderer, and in this light her death may be interpreted as wish fulfillment. Jack satisfies her longings, in the view of Kutscher (1922 I, 366), and both Glaser and Höger interpret death as the highest attainment of pleasure (181–82 and 87–88 respectively). Wish fulfillment is associated with compulsive self-destruction by Rothe (1968) and Hahn (1969). The former sees Lulu's death as the consequence of unlimited lust and the loss of the battle of the sexes to a sadist (56–57), while the latter perceives in Jack the ultimate satisfaction of Lulu's continuous need for sexual possession (I, 45).

Stage directions at the conclusion of the tragedy provide considerable latitude for interpretation. These indicate that Jack follows Lulu into the enclosed area usually occupied by Schigolch, from which she emerges screaming, clothed in dress and slip. The Ripper carries her back into that area, and we hear her cries as she dies under his knife. Her demise lends itself to two interpretations which turn about the concept of consent and are diametrically opposed, but are nevertheless closely related in the criticism. One involves the *Liebestod* associated with Tristan and Isolde and the other involves rape murder as inflicted by the historical figure of Jack the Ripper. Lulu's death constitutes a *Liebestod* in the eyes of Rothe (57), and Hahn confirms this idea (I, 45) but goes on to develop the contrary concept of rape murder (52), an interpretation which is affirmed by Böckmann (1969, 92). That there was no rape since Jack did not have sexual intercourse is the opinion of Schröder-Zebralla (1985, 136), and Boa (1987) maintains that there was no *Liebestod* since this requires a coincidence of death and orgasm, which was not the case here (110). Further,

RITTER LIBRARY
BALDWIN-WALLACE COLLEGE

Diethe (1988) fails to even find intercourse but rather "a grotesque parody of the sex act" in which Lulu receives death as a substitute in the interaction between sadist and masochist (99).

Early versions of the play make clear that with his knife Jack excises Lulu's vagina as a trophy; it is intended for eventual auction before the astonished and impressed members of the assembled London Medical Club. According to Kraus (1905), the knife of Jack serves as a symbol (14), an implicit allusion which becomes more clearly developed in the lines of Rothe (1968), where it is asserted not only that Lulu has Pandora's box in her possession but that she *is* the box (55). Midgley (1985) argues that "Büchse" in the title is a reference to the vagina as is the "Monstre," from the original title, which Jack, the trophy hunter, captures (222). This critic notes that Lulu is the victim of "male anxiety at potentially insatiable sexual demand" (225). Jack remarks several times upon the beauty of Lulu's mouth, which Boa suggests is a metaphor for her vagina and indicative of the male fear of castration or engulfment (104). As a prostitute accessible to all men, Lulu presents a threat to their identity since they become reduced to interchangeable ciphers (104). Jack's bloody excision evokes a pornographic thrill (111).

Wedekind's work lends itself to interpretation in the light of a rich variety of literary and theatrical references, some topical and contemporary, the most derived from the canon. The "Erdgeist" of the title appears in Goethe's *Faust I* (1808), scene 3, where Faust attempts to invoke this power but is rejected by it since he is deemed unequal. The Erdgeist is the spirit of activity and physical energy and is identified by Wedekind scholars with Lulu herself, a figure beyond human comprehension. Schön invokes this Erdgeist since he mistakenly thinks he can dominate it, according to Hahn (1969); and tragedy is engendered by the struggle of the two, the unconscious versus the conscious, sexuality against intellect (I, 49). In that wider societal context perceived by Irmer (1970) it is the males in a patriarchal world who conjure Lulu and are unable to comprehend her defiance of the masculine moral order (138). Lulu remains from the moment of her origin a mystery to men, notes Jelavich (1979, 217), the nature of her incomprehensibility lying in paradox; she is essentially both creative and destructive, Boa argues (1987, 59).

An attempt is made to explain the essence of the earth-spirit from another literary context. The title page of *Erdgeist* (III, [1]) bears a thirteen-line quotation from Friedrich Schiller's drama *Wallensteins Tod* (Wallenstein's Death, 1799), act 2, scene 2, where Wallenstein, commander of the imperial armies of the Hapsburgs in the Thirty Years' War, speaks to the young officer Max Piccolomini. Considering the evil spirit of the earth which attracts him, Wallenstein extols his own worldly experience in lines which are interpreted variously. The term *Erdgeist* may refer to the evil earth-spirit emanated by repressive society, "the seduction and corruption of the human ideal" to which Lulu succumbs (Peacock 1978, 107). It is the dominance of that human materialism which makes moral goodness impossible (Hibberd 1984, 337). The concept constitutes a warning against the corrupting influences of wealth and authority (Chick 1984, 26).

The use of Schiller to explain Wedekind does not stop here, and Schiller becomes the object of parody. In his drama *Kabale und Liebe* (Love and Intrigue, 1784), act 3, scene 6, the devious servant Wurm dictates to the heroine Luise a letter calculated to terminate the relationship to her lover Ferdinand. The male and female roles are reversed in *Erdgeist*, act 3, scene 10, where Lulu dominates Schön and dictates a letter in which he renounces the engagement to his fiancée Adelaide.

Best (1975) distinguishes himself among the critics by indicating quite clearly how the scene, although perhaps to be understood as parody, is considerably more than that; the scene demonstrates the relationship of the performer Lulu to her admirers in the audience. The conventions of the theater both constrain and liberate the male, however emotionally intoxicated by her beauty he may become; the barrier represented by the stage achieves distance and imposes restraint; the conclusion of the performance provides a limitation, at which time the spectator is released from his spell and once again free to rise and leave. When Schön separates himself from those protections provided by the conventions of the theater, he becomes vulnerable; he leaves the audience in order to confront Lulu in her dressing room, where she turns her full seductive powers upon him (89).

Overt references to contemporary theater are evidenced in the prologue to *Erdgeist*. Though opposed to naturalism as a dramatic technique, Wedekind was even more opposed to Gerhart Hauptmann, the leading exponent of this movement, and he used the prologue for an attack upon him. Hauptmann had abused Wedekind's confidence in his drama *Das Friedensfest* (The Coming of Peace, 1890), where Hauptmann depicted the contentious relationship between father and son that actually led Wedekind in the autumn of 1886 to strike his father and leave home (Best, 12). In the prologue to *Erdgeist* the animal trainer vows that the audience will experience something bold and vital by Wedekind and not be subjected to simply more of what was then current in the theater, namely heroes vexed by alcohol consumption or plagued with romantic self-doubt (III, 8). The identity of the dramatic characters meant in these two instances by the animal trainer and Wedekind leaves little room for uncertainty; with only one exception the critics agree universally with that identification of the figures first made by Fechter (1920, 50): Alfred Loth in Hauptmann's *Vor Sonnenaufgang* (Before Dawn, 1889) is concerned with alcohol consumption, and Johannes Vockerat in *Einsame Menschen* (Lonely Lives, 1891) is stricken with self-doubt. Among the critics only Klotz (1979) overlooks this attack upon Hauptmann's drama when he interprets the object of Wedekind's barbs as Wilhelmine theater generally (24).

Pierrot is a comedy character from French pantomime; naive and pathetic, this figure appears with whitened face beneath a black cap and wearing loose, white pantaloons. Lulu sat for her portrait as Pierrot by Schwarz early in Part I, and thereafter the painting plays a contrastive role in the drama. Connotations of the pantomime figure suggest Lulu may be associated with a puppet or a lovely doll; however, Pierrot is masculine, and a tension is therefore posed between male and female identities. An even more significant aspect of the contrastive function of the portrait is to be found in the fact that it follows Lulu throughout the drama, providing a reflection and describing the arc of her career. Kraus (1905) is the first to point out that this painting, as it reappears throughout the tragedy, outlines the decline of Lulu's fortunes and illustrates, especially in Part II, the discrepancy between her former life of glamour and her subsequent misery (12). The current of the criticism runs along a different path, however, as soon as the master biographer Kutscher (1922) discloses the titles of works Wedekind planned to read during his stay in Paris; one title was Oscar Wilde's *The Picture of Dorian Gray* (1891), in which the picture reflects the aging and deterioration of Gray while his physiognomy remains unchanged (I, 263). The temptation to make a connection between this work and Lulu's portrait as Pierrot becomes irresistible; Rothe (1968) looks to the conclusion of Part II where the portrait has become dark and begun to peel, noting the identity of the person and the portrait in both Wilde and Wedekind (45). Of course, aside from the darkening and peeling, the resemblance in the painting of Pierrot to Lulu does not change; so Skrine (1989) rises to the challenge: the painting reacts like that of Dorian Gray, only in reverse, "it remains young while she grows old" (88). Skrine's contribution is not limited to this observation, however, and this critic goes on to break new ground regarding the contrastive role of the portrait when he describes how the frames and settings provided the painting relate successively to the perception and treatment of Lulu by the people about her. Schwarz, the recognized painter of high society, surrounds it with "artistic extravagance" and Dr. Schön, the wealthy self-made man, with gilt; it is set into the wall of a luxurious apartment like a safe when she is treated as a commodity for barter by the procurer Casti-Piani; removed from the frame and rolled, it is preserved lovingly by the devoted Geschwitz at the conclusion (90).

In *Erdgeist* men give different names to Lulu. Goll calls her Nelli in the marriage contract; as his model, Schwarz names her Eva; and Schön refers to her as Mignon. This has been interpreted to mean that the men see different images in Lulu as they project themselves upon her, that she assumes various identities, or both. In act 2, scene 2, Schigolch observes that it is all the same how Lulu is called since the principle remains the same. The unifying concept of this principle recognized by Schigolch appears to Michelsen (1965, 56) as the sex drive and to Böckmann (1969, 88–89) the elemental love of life, regardless of what name it operates under. The Marxists, on the other hand, ignore the principle and emphasize the multiplicity of roles as indicative of the treatment of the human being as an object under capitalism. According to Hahn (1969), Lulu fulfills various social needs: for Goll the necessity to dominate and manipulate her as a tool; for Schwarz the craving to establish moral values, however illusionary; for the African traveler Escerny the delight of morally sublimating himself to her, becoming her object; for Alwa the urge to form a person in a literary manner (I, 47–48). A countryman of Hahn from the former German Democratic Republic, Irmer (1970) attempts to extend the Marxist interpretation; he asserts that the various identities attributed to Lulu reflect the self-alienation of the human being in capitalist society (137).

The different names given Lulu, according to Best (1975), are basic to Wedekind's social criticism. She is surrounded by egocentric individuals who bestow names symptomatic of their "pathological self-delusion" (84). As long as the audience perceives these social outsiders and artists as a community apart from itself, it does not feel threatened. However, Wedekind gradually reveals that there exists little or no difference between the members of the audience and the figures on stage and indeed that society is responsible for the state of these psychological and emotional cripples (25).

As do the Marxists, the feminists emphasize the multiplicity of identities rather than the unifying principle. Lulu is interpreted by Bovenschen (1979) as a bearer of roles, images, and masks of different concepts of female nature which are imposed by culture and by men (44). Lulu is the myth of what the different individual male figures see in her, and she is also a character who destroys these images. She rejects one image just to assume the next one, which will likewise deconstruct (48). Continuing this line of thought, Boa (1987) refers to the dramatist's subversive deconstruction of the roles and clichés associated with the complex of attitudes surrounding women as the object of male desire (210–11). As a figure on a quest for her own identity, Lulu is perceived by Ritter (1991) as a player of a variety of roles in which the portrait of Pierrot represents her alter ego and the only stable constant in periods of flux (127).

In the first scene of Part II, Alwa reveals that he is writing a drama called *Erdgeist* about Lulu, a work devoted to people who have never in their lives read a book and whose behavior is determined by the most simple, animalistic impulses (III, 125–26). The direction which his writing follows, Alwa continues, is that which must be pursued to achieve great art; for it is the curse of German literature that it is too literary and that it deals only with issues that touch authors and scholars. This dramatic moment is characterized as romantic self-irony by Fechter (1920, 49), who refuses to take it seriously. Kutscher (1922), however, accords it considerably more attention as a personal statement of Wedekind's very own views. The dramatist is inclined towards the primitive, at the center of which stands sexuality as the elemental passion; this is the core of the Lulu tragedy (I, 362). The figure of Alwa as Wedekind, working on his play *Erdgeist* right in the middle of the very play, is engaged in tragic futility, according to Emrich (1958); in the act of composition he attempts to reveal to consciousness the sphere of the unconscious that disappears as he sets it to art (226). Best (1975), on the other hand, simply dismisses the remarks of Alwa regarding literature as farce directed against the naturalists (93).

Dr. Schön is described by Kutscher as intellectual, brutal, and without conscience, the incorporation of egoism (I, 372). Emrich sees this character as the self-conscious representative of bourgeois morality, which he is dedicated to defend since it defines his social existence; Schön tries therefore to humiliate and confine Lulu, and she turns upon him to dominate him (220). According to Rasch (1969), Schön is vulgarly oriented towards success; his commercial interests reflect a society which pales before the intensity of the love she bears, and in him Wedekind is criticizing the bourgeoisie of which he is himself a member (412–13). The person of Lulu represents for Schön an object to be used for his satisfaction in what amounts to Hahn (1969) as a satire of the bourgeois marriage arrangement; standing in the reflection of her beauty, Schön gains social esteem by association (I, 49) as well as an illusion of enhanced sexuality, that Best (87) notes, he is able to create about himself.

No critic has a good word for Goll, a dirty old man whose emotional life is spent. Kapp (1909) observes that only in perversity can Goll still find thrills (130). His enjoyment of Lulu lies in her performances and, according to Best, the stimulation these provide for his impotent, sexual fantasies (87). Diethe (1988) scores him for pedophilia (97).

Foremost among the distinguishing qualities of Schwarz is his ignorance of the world. He is timid and unfamiliar with people; never having known a woman's love, he is repressed. His exaggerated idealism causes him to fall easy victim to Lulu's coquetry. Kutscher sees the painter as undeveloped, a lonely, egoistic hypochondriac and moralist, who devotes himself dully to his art (I, 374). Rasch notes his philistine banality (413), and Diethe asserts that the idealized innocence attributed to his wife under the name Eva is an attempt to conceal his own sexual inhibitions (97).

Schigolch is an ageless enigma, the origins of whom Friedenthal identifies as early as 1914 in the realm of Mephistopheles (80); this interpretation prevails with some variations. His evil, according to Emrich, emanates from his position as an outsider; he sees through human machinations and nevertheless affirms what transpires, assuming no responsibility (219). Natan (1963) extends these aspects of his character to include his "satanic pleasure in the destruction of human illusions"; moreover, the rhyme of his name with "Molch" (newt, salamander) suggests his origins in prehistoric, infernal slime (113).

With regard to interpreting the Countess Geschwitz, Kraus (1905) initiates a current in the scholarship which flows strongly down to the present, despite what Wedekind says about the character himself. Kraus first suggests that Geschwitz is accursed (17), describing her as "a demon of sorrow" ("ein Dämon der Unfreude"). The following year in a preface to *Die Büchse der Pandora,* the author held out the Countess as the central tragic figure of the work; she deserves sympathy, Wedekind submits, not that scorn to which the lesbian is often subjected (III, 102–3). Nevertheless, the scholarship holds true to that pattern established by Kraus; and whereas she is not accorded the primary position in the tragedy as Wedekind suggests, she is closely linked to Lulu. Friedenthal (1914) argues that the Countess offers a counterpart to Lulu since they both bear a curse; Lulu to destroy and Geschwitz to be destroyed (82). Although Kutscher (1922) writes that Wedekind told him personally that his words about the importance of Geschwitz were intended as a pretext to avoid confiscation of the new edition by diverting judicial attention from the figure of Lulu (I, 375–76), Gundolf (1948) nevertheless takes Wedekind by the words of his preface and assigns to the Countess the primary role (216).

In the literary criticism after this time, Lulu and Geschwitz remain linked, not by a curse, but by something very similar—prejudicial social attitudes toward their respective sexuality. Emrich (1958) notes that Geschwitz alone among the other characters expresses unconditional love as does Lulu (226). Representing the "intellectual counterpart of Lulu's feminism," Geschwitz is accurately described by Gonçalves da Silva (1985) as a victim of society's sexual discrimination (22). Just like Lulu, according to Boa (1987), Wedekind defines Geschwitz solely in sexual terms; she is a "ludicrous monster created by a male author for whom women have no identity other than the sexual" (75).

In the foreword of 1906, Wedekind describes the circus gymnast and strongman, Rodrigo Quast, as the normal reader, typical of those who scorn the lesbian. Functioning as the opponent of Geschwitz, Wedekind explains, Quast employs wit that becomes increasingly brutal as she experiences torment that elevates her morally, and he is left to appear ridiculous by comparison (III, 103–4). Fechter (1920) goes unheeded when he argues that not Geschwitz, but rather Quast, physical, unintellectual, and masculine, is the counterpart of Lulu (58). But the scholars tend to follow the lead provided by the dramatist. Feuchtwanger (1952) sees Quast as representative of the solid majority, the rabble whom Wedekind opposes (20); and Hahn (1969) describes him as illustrative of the unspiritual, bourgeois norm (I, 51).

Scant attention is accorded the schoolboy Hugenberg. Kutscher emphasizes his idealistic, self-sacrificing nature with regard to Lulu and her happiness (I, 376); and Chick (1984) quite improbably asserts that this character is named after the right-wing politician and film magnate Alfred Hugenberg, whose influence dominated public opinion by means of his controlling interest in newspapers during the Weimar Republic (33).

The distance between characters, their isolation from one another, and that internal void they represent are expressed in dialogue which is unresponsive. Since the figures talk right by each other, the pattern amounts to a series of monologues, a dramatic technique which Ude (1966) characterizes as an original contribution of Wedekind (39–40). What Gittleman (1969) describes as "a kind of surrealistic stream-of-consciousness" (73) reflects to Best (1975) the inner quality of the characters, their "moral and emotional emptiness" (91); inadequate figures fearful and insecure share sex as the single language in common, not "daring" to speak directly to each other since they may receive no answer (83). Hibberd (1984) argues that the dialogue is both characteristic of the figures and their egocentricity and also indicative of a problem which Wedekind failed to solve successfully; this is the reduction of that conceptual abstraction which Lulu represents to the narrow context of human beings employing an intelligible system of communication upon a concrete stage (351).

There are differences of opinion regarding the congruence of Parts I and II of the tragedy. Midgley (1985) argues that they are not coherently related to each other. In *Erdgeist*, Lulu develops an increased sense of her power and independence (217); the social protest is articulate (226). But *Die Büchse der Pandora* does not follow as a consequence; the drama presents a central figure devoted to compulsive sexual promiscuity (225).

Familiar with Midgley's conclusions but disregarding them, Boa (1987) argues that there is a continuity provided by the ultimate dehumanization of Lulu (88–89). Personal relations, human freedom, and individuality are undermined in Part II by an authoritarian state and free market economy (92); male and female sexuality assume destructive, depersonalized forms (105).

Erdgeist was originally described as "burleske Tragödie" (farcical tragedy), and most critics feel comfortable with the designation *tragedy* for Parts I and II together. However, scholars in the last few decades tend to qualify this concept. Böckmann (1969), for example, argues that an ambivalence of tragedy and comedy is achieved in the grotesque (90). And Best, too, emphasizes the features of the grotesque which deprive the characters of their human dignity, thereby rendering the play not tragedy but black comedy (91). Peacock (1978) sees the work as a hybrid, satirical and grotesque as well as tragic (117), to which Chick (1984) adds the element of irony (13). Features of comedy, farce, melodrama, satire, and tragedy are noted by Boa, a combination bound together by the author's peculiar humor (86). The characteristic fashion in which Wedekind unites both horror and comedy simultaneously is emphasized by Skrine (1989, 91–92) when he focuses on the final line of the work, the expression of the dying Countess Geschwitz, "Oh, curse it!" ("O verflucht!" III, 193).

Comparison is made with *Frühlings Erwachen*. Fechter (1920) points out that in the earlier drama the author was putting his own experiences to use in an expressionistic manner, and now he has assumed a more objective relationship to the world (44). In the drama of adolescence, *Frühlings Erwachen,* children and adults, nature and society, confront each other in opposition; now in *Lulu*, Hahn (1969) notes, society and nature are bound up together (I, 46). Boa points out that both plays concern role-playing as dictated by convention and models, with the emphasis in *Lulu* on the woman as a performer before a male audience (54).

The early critics Kapp (1909) and Kempner (1911) express opinions about the *Lulu* tragedy representative of critical judgment which has prevailed since that time. Kapp writes that this work marks the climax of Wedekind's artistic creativity, leaving all his other dramas, with the exception of *Frühlings Erwachen,* far behind (138); and Kempner agrees that the *Lulu* tragedy is by far the most significant of the author's works (27).

Works Cited

Best, Alan. 1975. *Frank Wedekind*. London: Oswald Wolf.
Blei, Franz. 1914. "Marginalien zu Wedekind." In *Das Wedekindbuch,* edited by Joachim Friedenthal. Munich and Leipzig: Georg Müller. 128–50.
Boa, Elizabeth. 1987. *The Sexual Circus. Wedekind's Theatre of Subversion*. Oxford: Blackwell.
Böckmann, Paul. 1969. "Die komödiantischen Grotesken Frank Wedekinds." In *Das*

deutsche Lustspiel. Vol. 2 edited by Hans Steffen. Göttingen: Vandenhoeck & Ruprecht. 79–102.

Bovenschen, Silvia. 1979. "Inszenierung des inszenierten Weiblichkeit: Wedekinds *Lulu*, paradigmatisch." In her *Die imaginierte Weiblichkeit*. Frankfurt am Main: Suhrkamp. 43–60.

Chick, Edson M. 1984. "Frank Wedekind and his *Lulu* Tragedy." In his *Dances of Death. Wedekind, Brecht, Dürrenmatt, and the Satiric Tradition*. Columbia, South Carolina: Camden House. 11–45.

Diethe, Carol. 1988. *Aspects of Distorted Sexual Attitudes in German Expressionist Drama*. New York, Bern, Frankfurt am Main, and Paris: Lang.

Dosenheimer, Elise. 1967. *Das deutsche soziale Drama von Lessing bis Sternheim*. Darmstadt: Wissenschaftliche Buchgesellschaft. This first appeared in 1949.

Emrich, Wilhelm. 1968. "Wedekind, Die *Lulu*-Tragödie." In *Das Deutsche Drama*, edited by Benno von Wiese. Vol. 2. Düsseldorf: Bagel. 209–30. This first appeared in 1958.

Faesi, Robert. 1956. "Ein Vorläufer: Frank Wedekind." In *Expressionismus. Gestalten einer literarischen Bewegung*, edited by Hermann Friedmann and Otto Mann. Heidelberg: Rothe. 241–63.

Fechter, Paul. 1920. *Frank Wedekind. Der Mensch und das Werk*. Jena: Lichtenstein.

Feuchtwanger, Lion. 1952. Introduction to *Five Tragedies of Sex*, by Frank Wedekind. Translated by Frances Fawcett and Stephen Spender. London: Vision. 7–21.

Friedenthal, Joachim. 1914. "Einleitung." In *Das Wedekindbuch*, edited by Friedenthal. Munich and Leipzig: Georg Müller. 1–121.

Gittleman, Sol. 1969. *Frank Wedekind*. New York: Twayne.

Glaser, Horst Albert. 1974. "Arthur Schnitzler und Frank Wedekind. Der doppelköpfige Sexus." In *Wollüstige Phantasie. Sexualästhetik der Literatur*, edited by Glaser. Munich: Hanser. 148–84.

Gonçalves da Silva, M. Helena. 1985. *Character, Ideology, and Symbolism in the Plays of Wedekind, Sternheim, Kaiser, Toller, and Brecht*. London: Modern Humanities Research Association.

Gundolf, Friedrich. 1948. "Frank Wedekind." *Trivium* 6: 187–217. This appeared posthumously.

Hahn, Manfred. 1969. "Frank Wedekind. Leben und Werk." In *Frank Wedekind. Dramen I*. Berlin and Weimar: Aufbau-Verlag. 7–93.

Hibberd, John L. 1984. "The Spirit of the Flesh: Wedekind's *Lulu*." *Modern Language Review* 79: 336–55.

Hill, Claude. 1960. "Wedekind in Retrospect." *Modern Drama* 3.1 (May): 82–92.

Höger, Alfons. 1981. *Hetärismus und bürgerliche Gesellschaft im Frühwerk Frank Wedekinds*. Copenhagen and Munich: Fink.

Irmer, Hans-Jochen. 1975. *Der Theaterdichter Frank Wedekind. Werk und Wirkung*. Berlin: Henschelverlag. This originally appeared in 1970.

Jelavich, Peter. 1979. "Art and Mammon in Wilhelmine Germany: The Case of Frank Wedekind." *Central European History* 12: 203–36.

Kapp, Julius. 1909. *Frank Wedekind. Seine Eigenart und seine Werke*. Berlin: Hermann Barsdorf.

Kempner, Hans. 1911. *Frank Wedekind als Mensch und Künstler*. Berlin-Pankow: Oskar Linser.

Klotz, Volker. 1979. "Wedekinds Circus mundi." In *Viermal Wedekind*, edited by Karl

Pestalozzi and Martin Stern. Stuttgart: Klett. 22–47.

Kraus, Karl. 1958. *"Die Büchse der Pandora."* In his *Literatur und Lüge. Werke,* edited by Heinrich Fischer. Munich: Kösel. 9–21. These are remarks made at the first performance in Vienna on 29 May 1905.

Kutscher, Artur. 1970. *Frank Wedekind. Sein Leben und seine Werke.* Vol. 1. New York: AMS Press. This is a reprint of the edition appearing in 1922.

Lorenz, D. C. G. 1976. "Wedekind und die emanzipierte Frau. Eine Studie über Frau und Sozialismus im Werke Frank Wedekinds." *Seminar* 12.1 (February): 38–56.

Mennemeier, Franz Norbert. 1980. "Frank Wedekind." In *Handbuch des deutschen Dramas,* edited by Walter Hinck. Düsseldorf: Bagel. 360–73, 568–69.

Michelsen, Peter. 1969. "Frank Wedekind." In *Deutsche Dichter der Moderne,* edited by Benno von Wiese. Berlin: Erich Schmidt. 51–69. The essay first appeared in 1965.

Midgley, David. 1985. "Wedekind's *Lulu:* From 'Schauertragödie' to Social Comedy." *German Life and Letters* 38: 205–32.

Natan, Alex. 1963. "Frank Wedekind." In *German Men of Letters,* edited by Natan. Vol. 2. London: Oswald Wolf. 101–29.

Peacock, R. 1978. "The Ambiguity of Wedekind's *Lulu*." *Oxford German Studies* 9: 105–18. This appeared in German also: "Zur Problematik der Lulugestalt." In *Bild und Gedanke. Festschrift für Gerhart Baumann zum 60. Geburtstag,* edited by Günter Schnitzler. Munich: Fink. 343–56.

Rasch, Wolfdietrich. 1969. "Sozialkritische Aspekte in Wedekinds dramatischer Dichtung. Sexualität, Kunst und Gesellschaft." In *Gestaltungsgeschichte und Gesellschaftsgeschichte,* edited by Helmut Kreuzer. Stuttgart: Metzler. 409–26.

Ritter, Naomi. 1991. "The Portrait of Lulu as Pierrot." In *Frank Wedekind Yearbook 1991,* edited by Rolf Kieser and Reinhold Grimm. Bern, Berlin, etc.: Lang. 101–40.

Rothe, Friedrich. 1968. *Frank Wedekinds Dramen. Jugendstil und Lebensphilosophie.* Stuttgart: Metzler.

Schröder-Zebralla, Josephine. 1985. *Frank Wedekinds religiöser Sensualismus. "Die Vereinigung von Kirche und Freudenhaus?"* Frankfurt am Main, Bern, and New York: Lang.

Skrine, Peter. 1989. *Hauptmann, Wedekind, and Schnitzler.* New York: St. Martin's Press.

Sokel, Walter H. 1966. "The Changing Role of Eros in Wedekind's Drama." *The German Quarterly* 39.2: 201–7.

Stewart, Corbet. 1985–86. "Comedy, Morality and Energy in the Work of Wedekind." *Publications of the English Goethe Society,* n.s., 56: 56–71.

Ude, Karl. 1966. *Frank Wedekind.* Mühlacker: Stieglitz.

Völker, Klaus. 1965. *Frank Wedekind.* Velber bei Hannover: Friedrich Verlag.

Wagener, Hans. 1979. *Frank Wedekind.* Berlin: Colloquim.

Wedekind, Frank. 1920. "Vorwort" to *Die Büchse der Pandora.* In *Gesammelte Werke.* Vol. 3. Munich: Georg Müller. 101–7.

———. 1921. "Was ich mir dabei dachte." In *Gesammelte Werke.* Vol. 9. Munich: Georg Müller, 426–28.

4: *Fritz Schwigerling* (1899) and *Der Kammersänger* (1899) The Trick Rider's Magic Potion and the Court Singer's Life for the Stage

Fritz Schwigerling (Der Liebestrank).
Schwank in drei Aufzügen
(Fritz Schwigerling [The Love Potion].
Farce in Three Acts, 1899)

The aged Russian Prince Rogoschin finds his ardor for his nineteen-year-old ward Katharina unrequited; she is almost totally occupied with horses and riding. Rogoschin hires the trick rider Fritz Schwigerling from the circus, ostensibly to tutor his sons but actually to concoct a love potion that will bring Katharina around. Fritz informs the Prince he must drink the potion without thinking of a bear. When the concoction fails to achieve the desired result, Schwigerling concludes that Rogoschin has failed to observe the precaution and must therefore be confined to bed for a twenty-four hour sudorific, or perspiration, cure.

Schwigerling recognizes his first wife Cordelia in the Princess, who was sold to Rogoschin by an American life insurance agent as the Virgin of Colorado River. Nevertheless, Schwigerling turns to Katharina, whom he promises to aid in a circus career of bareback riding, and they escape in the company of two servants as the Princess remains to console the Prince.

Given the bizarre events depicted and the strange people portrayed, in particular the imbecile Prince, Kapp (1909) considers the Russian setting of the drama appropriate and credible in the context of farce. The dramatic technique is masterful as the play moves from an unsuccessful exposition studded with flat jokes to an explosive whirlwind of exuberance and violent comedy (47, 49).

Friedenthal (1914) looks to Wedekind's essay "Thoughts about the Circus" from 1887, where the author suggests that circus performers illustrate an essential quality necessary for a person living at that tempo demanded by modern life, namely elasticity or flexibility (IX, 297). Friedenthal observes that Fritz Schwigerling is the ancestor of a lineage of elastic adventurers, nimble and opportunistic, who run through Wedekind's works; and one thinks immediately of Keith and Hetmann. Another dimension is added to the type when Friedenthal injects the thought of Nietzsche, characterizing the adventurer as a distant, if sometimes degenerate, cousin of the blond beast (51).

Fritz Schwigerling is the most amusing of Wedekind's dramas in the opinion of

Fechter (1920), who points out the literary wit that accounts for the names of characters from the Russian novel of Dostoevski. Wedekind's Rogoschin is named after a character in *The Idiot* and his son Alioscha is identifiable as the youngest of *The Brothers Karamazov* (65–66).

Appearing in 1921 in "What I Was Thinking about at the Time" are words of the playwright indicating that the work is an expression of his enthusiasm for the circus, a passion which held him from his earliest days (IX, 426). Characteristic of that emphasis he placed upon the flesh, rather than upon the spirit, throughout his entire life is his remark that the play is intended as a defense and justification of physical, rather than mental or spiritual, art. And Kutscher (1922) interprets the character Fritz Schwigerling in this light, suggesting that he, albeit grotesque, is the ideal figure of the circus performer, a cavalier and man of the world demonstrating elasticity in its broadest sense (I, 292–93). He is born of Wedekind's love of vitality as is Katharina; and if Schwigerling suggests to Friedenthal a line of male adventurers in the dramas, Katharina in her physical perfection is related to Lulu and is a forerunner of Effie and Franziska (296).

Borrowing both Friedenthal's observation regarding the kinship of Schwigerling to a conception from Nietzsche and that remark of Wedekind regarding the distinction between the physical and the mental, Ude (1966) observes that the dramatic figure is a Superman who defends Life against spirit (32).

A plea for the acceptance of "physical spirituality" is seen in the playwright's words by Gittleman (1969, 57), who provides a biographical note by identifying Wedekind's friend Willy Wolf Rudinoff as the model for Schwigerling (56). With features of melodrama and burlesque and "a delightfully vulgar villain" in the character of Rogoschin, this is Wedekind's "most enduring comic work" (53) and since 1945 one of the most popular in the German repertory (143, note 2).

The elasticity to which Wedekind refers is interpreted by Irmer (1970) as adjustability to all situations in life. Disdaining force in the training of the Prince's sons, Schwigerling makes no distinction between educating a person and training an animal, and Irmer submits that in each case the learning creature is strengthened with regard to its capacity to realize itself under all conditions (118–19).

The most originality in the criticism since that of Friedenthal is shown by Alan Best (1975), who argues that the bravado of Schwigerling is born from his sense of inferiority. This figure employs his background in the circus and the aura associated with this atmosphere to establish and maintain a position superior to the other figures; the circus atmosphere accounts for his appeal to Katharina. Successful within the context of the circus, Fritz extends the circumference of this arena to include everyday reality in the attempt to continue his success in this latter sphere (33, 37).

Both Jelavich (1979) and Wagener (1979) concern themselves with the subjects of circus and the vision of societal change. To Jelavich this comedy amounts to what he curiously terms Wedekind's "aesthetic education of the circus world," a solution that does not prove equal to that "general social regeneration" the playwright is argued to desire (215–16). Echoing Gittleman in describing the work as burlesque,

Wagener shares with Irmer the emphasis on the education of animals and children, an aspect of the drama which reflects upon the attempt to recast the circus world in a utopian light (46–47).

By extending the concept of vitalism, Höger (1981) expands on the dichotomy to which Wedekind refers when distinguishing between physical and mental art. Physical pleasure is understood as the expression of the will to live, which is opposed by the world of the spirit, the world of bourgeois social illusions, which tries to dominate (89).

Der Kammersänger
(The Court Singer, 1899)

The tenor Gerardo must hurry to catch a train since he sings *Tristan* on the morrow in Brussels. In the remaining few minutes he wants to rehearse and leaves instructions that he not be disturbed. Nevertheless, he finds himself besieged by people with requests which would constitute a violation of his contractual obligations as an artist. He turns aside the lovesick teenager Miss Coeurne, the unsuccessful, elderly composer Professor Dühring, and the most beautiful woman in the city, Helene Marowa, with whom he has had an affair. Helene kills herself, and only police arrest can justify Gerardo's detention. Since no officer appears, he dashes out to fulfill his contract.

The play has inspired an imaginative diversity of interpretation which is not suggested by Kutscher (1927). Circumscribing the work in a surprisingly narrow fashion, he overlooks implicit social criticism or commentary on the nature of art and commerce to interpret the work primarily as a reflection upon the person of Gerardo. Believed by his public to pursue an elevated and unrestricted existence, Gerardo is actually engaged in a continuous defensive action against his admirers, expending energy to counteract their obtrusiveness and blind enthusiasm (II, 49).

An autobiographical background suggests itself by generalization to Elster (1922). The three scenes illustrate the fate of the artist as an occupational egoist. All aspects of life, youth and age, happiness and love, woman and child, must be rejected for the sake of art, a statement of Wedekind's attitude toward the life of an artist (57).

The work illustrates for Völker (1965) the price of success; a clear-thinking parvenu draws upon his intelligence and accumulated experience to tell himself that discipline and critical self-evaluation are required for continued good fortune in a society which is inhumane (41). Hahn (1969) says the same thing as Völker, giving it a Marxist twist, namely that success in bourgeois society means money, which opposes, perverts, and destroys art and life (I, 62). Feelings and natural drives only hinder the struggle for existence (58); therefore, the tenor must use his entire intelligence, strength, and inner elasticity to withstand the demands made upon him as a human being and artist (60).

The theme of commercialism is paramount in the minds of several critics. Wedekind's work plays a dual role, according to Rasch (1969); the drama takes aim at the falseness of a contemporary idea and constitutes an expression of social criticism. *The Court Singer* is an attack on the belief in the redeeming and transforming quality of music, and it is a representation of the degree to which art and the artist are corrupted by commercial interests (423). Commercialism serves a somewhat more sophisticated Marxist argument than that of Hahn in the interpretation of Irmer (1970) that capital determines the themes and forms of art consistent with the criterion of salability; artistic merit is converted to commercial value or rendered worthless (94). Although Geißler (1978) does not seem to have thought it through, this is probably what he has in mind with the assertion that the art world is here revealed as being thoroughly capitalistic (156). Borrowing overtly the interpretation of Rasch that the work illustrates the perversion of the arts through commercialization, Jelavich (1979) notes its effect on Gerardo; to obtain success he will be a slave to managers and make a fool of himself on stage (222–23).

Just as Rasch sees the work as a treatment of a prevailing idea of those days, that of the ennobling power of music, Mennemeier (1980) remarks upon the conceptual dialectic of art and life, which was also very popular during Wedekind's time. On the stage Gerardo represents art and the passion of love in *Tristan;* Dühring and Helene incorporate art and love respectively and confront him in turn, and he brushes them aside. For the court singer his art becomes a compensation for life, which no longer bears social significance (368).

The title of the work strikes Skrine (1989) as a satirical reflection on the cultural snobbery associated with the court singer's official title, and this Englishman finds the work peculiarly German since it exploits a concept cherished since romanticism: the view of art and the artist as being sacrosanct (102).

The drama is formed about ten short scenes, and the subtitle "Three Scenes" means more accurately three encounters involving four central characters and hotel personnel in a salon. Elster (1922) is the first to note that the constraints of time—the dwindling minutes before the departure of the train for Brussels—dictate the tempo of the work, underscore the harassment of Gerardo, and enhance the suspense (57).

The repeated reminder of time yet unexpired holds the three encounters together in the absence of a plot or development, as Kutscher (1927) points out. These meetings stand in no necessary relationship to one another and focus upon Gerardo, whose character unfolds in the process. Parallelism dictates that a scene with servants introduces each encounter, and this is interrupted by the entrance of other persons. This interruption is an aspect of structure which reinforces meaning by illustrating the tumult in Gerardo's existence as a chamber singer (II, 54).

Space, too, reinforces meaning in the eyes of Hahn (1969), who notes that the impersonal hotel room conveys a state of human isolation; this is further emphasized by the assurance of the hotel proprietor that catastrophes such as the suicide happen often (I, 63).

Since the death of Helene interjects a grim note into a work widely interpreted as satiric. Some directors took it upon themselves to modify the final scene; their changes call for Helene to rise from the floor after the shot remarking that not even her suicide will evoke a response from Gerardo. Kapp (1909) is the first to protest the altered conclusion with his assertion that the work is more moving when played seriously. Moreover, mock suicide makes the observations about art superfluous and causes the play to become distorted (58–59). In notes composed about 1909, but not published until later, Wedekind observes that Helene's suicide is thus transformed into a joke (IX, 438). The modified ending is an act of violence in the eyes of Friedenthal (1914), who interprets the work as a tragedy rather than a comedy (58–59). But Kutscher (1927) finds both, suggesting that the confusion of the final scene most clearly indicates Gerardo's tragicomic isolation (II, 54). Employing a concept associated with the death of Lulu in the arms of Jack the Ripper and relevant here because of the performance of *Tristan*, Hahn describes Helene's death as *Liebestod*, which Gerardo rushes off to sing about on stage (I, 62).

Both Thomas (1971) and Haida (1973) find that genuine suicide strains the limits of dramatic probability. The former characterizes the death as a farfetched gesture calculated for dramatic effect (190). Moreover, Helene's actual death constitutes a drawback since it unmasks Gerardo's brutal egoism, performing a greater injury to him than he deserves, regardless of his treatment of her (185). Haida concurs, characterizing the conclusion as baffling and unexpected but calculated to demonstrate the brutalization of Gerardo, who has succumbed to the business of art (97–98). But Best (1975) lends credibility to the suicide by pointing out that it was premeditated; Helene had brought the revolver with her, having decided to die in a dramatically grand manner. The effect is a "chilling attraction" achieved by the combination of tragedy and pathos (44–45). Helene kills herself not because of her love affair, according to Mennemeier (1980), but because of confusion; she has been deceived by the amusement industry as she was by Gerardo, the difference being that he knew what he was doing and could not accept her love for economic reasons (370–71).

In a preface to the fourth edition of 1909, Wedekind describes the work as a collision between brutal intelligence and various blind passions (III, 197). And Kapp accepts this view, describing Gerardo as a person of the mind without deep feelings (57). The term *Maschinenmensch* (machine person) occurs to Kempner (1911), who imputes a didactic intention to Wedekind; the playwright holds forth as a frightening example a category of human beings who waste freedom on senseless, joyless ideas (42–43). Returning to the subject of his central figure Gerardo in 1911, Wedekind describes him as a blown-up philistine soul, who because of his success thinks himself an artist as do all who worship fame (IX, 428–29). A dyed-in-the-wool worshiper of success and favorite of the philistines, Gerardo is not a great person, as he believes, but a gnat magnified five thousand times. Overlooking Wedekind's more recent explanation, Friedenthal (1914) reaches back to the author's first assessment, describing Gerardo's brutality and that ready legal morality with which he justifies his existence: "the protective bulwark of contracts" and "contractual slavery." To violate his contract would mean emotional and financial bankruptcy for Gerardo (59–60); he is a fool who degrades himself to a marketable commodity on the balance sheet of values (60–61). Autobiography is detected as Fechter (1920) initiates a vein of interpretation which will become increasingly stronger with the later plays; Gerardo's behavior suggests Wedekind's compulsive relationship to his own production (72). Noting the cool, precise, comic and grotesque logic of Gerardo, Kutscher (1927) finds him undeserving of all the negative qualities ascribed to him by the author; this critic points out that Gerardo gives Miss Coeurne his picture, allows Dühring to play the piano, and adopts Helene's children.

Further, Kutscher perceives a similarity between Gerardo and characters who preceded him: Melchior Gabor, Fritz Schwigerling, and Dr. Schön. They all possess an elastic nature which allows them to be the master of life. Like the bareback rider in the circus, Gerardo is equal to all situations in the successful pursuit of art, albeit with a lack of soul (II, 52–53).

To the Marxists Hahn (1969) and Irmer (1970), Gerardo is an economic animal who perceives the world in terms of quantitative relationships of sound value for exchange. Contracts determine his terms for love; partners are interchangeable; duration is that of the concert engagement. But Gerardo is seen also as a confidence man of the art world, and in this suggestion Hahn may be anticipating the Marquis of Keith (I, 61–62). Since Helene refers to him as Oskar, Irmer surmises that his name is Oskar Gerardo (96).

Wedekind's description of the work as a confrontation between brutal intelligence and a sequence of blind passions strikes Best (1975, 38) as apt, but Wagener (1979) is more discriminating. This critic concedes that Gerardo is a brutal representative of the commercialized art business, but this is not all that is to be said for him. Borrowing the argument of Kutscher (1927 II, 52–53) without acknowledgment, Wagener points out that Gerardo behaves in a considerate and humane fashion in his dealing with Miss Coeurne and is helpful towards Dühring (64). If Gerardo may perhaps be called brutal towards Helene, she is, on the other hand, naive in her estimation of him. There is comic grotesqueness but no brutality in his role as the marionette manipulated by his contract (65). Gerardo is "selfish and patronizing" in his treatment of Helene, according to Diethe (1988), and she is the object of such bitter scorn from Wedekind as to suggest that only feminine sexuality awakens the author's serious interest (103). But the character of Gerardo is considerably more complex in the view of Stewart (1985–86). Considering Wedekind's description of this figure from 1911, Stewart concludes that Gerardo is less crass and more intelligent than the author gives him credit for. He shares with Lulu "a certain honesty and freedom from self-delusion" and behind his ruthlessness lies an element of vulnerability, a fear of himself becoming the prey (67).

What is said of Miss Coeurne? The moral feelings of Kapp (1909, 56) are ruffled and his masculinity apparently threatened. He regards the desirous sixteen-year-old, despite her self-proclaimed moral uprightness, as lower than a prostitute; she represents a type, the groupie, of which this critic fears there are already too many in the metropolis of Berlin in 1909. Unrestrained by the inhibitions of Kapp, Kempner (1911) characterizes the young lady as cute and naive in her proposals of love (42).The scene makes clear, as Rasch (1969) underscores, that the erotic attraction Gerardo evokes in Miss Coeurne is the intended effect of his artistic performance (424). Gittleman (1969) suggests that Isabel Coeurne has a basis in fact and represents a young American woman to whom Wedekind was engaged until she thought better of the idea (95). But reference to the notes accompanying Wedekind's letters collected by Fritz Strich (1924 I, 352) indicates that the dramatist was dilatory, and the young lady returned to the United States and married. Making unacknowledged use of the observation of Rasch (424) that the court singer's person and the effect he elicits are calculated to correspond to preconceptions held by the bourgeoisie regarding an operatic star, Geißler (1978) finds irony: in order to be rid of Miss Coeurne, Gerardo appeals to the claims made upon him by art as a higher world, that is, to these very preconceptions (156–57).

The figure of Professor Dühring is taken very seriously, as is the scene in which this unfortunate gentleman appears, by Kapp, who characterizes the musician as a genius defeated in the hard struggle of life (56). Without having gained anything, Dühring departs proudly, his head held high with an unshaken belief in his estimation of himself as an artist (55). Kapp argues that the scene is a drama in itself and, although bearing elements of caricature, contains valid statements about art and music and justifiable accusations against theater and the theater public (56–57). That these may in fact be Wedekind's opinions is suggested by his remarks about the play from 1911 where he identifies Dühring as himself at age thirty-three as he stood in relation to the theater (IX, 429). The scene is touching, and Friedenthal (1914) finds it embarrassing. Gerardo, in attempting to give Dühring money, makes a mistake; he fails to take the musician's feelings into account and offends him (59–60). That Gerardo serves as Wedekind's mouthpiece to attack hack authors is a function of the character, but he does not remain the single spokesman of the dramatist, Kutscher (1927) notes. Opinions of Wedekind are heard from Dühring too, and the various viewpoints merge (II, 53). Dühring, in the eyes of Völker (1965), corresponds to the popular conception of a true artist; he has a romantic, touching and idealistic conception of art as life and lives exclusively for his art (40–41). Hahn (1969) sees the same figure in a more complex light. Analyzing Dühring as an idealist with an idealistic conception of art, exactly as does Völker, Hahn finds humor. At the same time the artist is unsuccessful and tragic. And to the extent that Wedekind depicts himself in the character, one encounters the element of self-irony (I, 61).

While Friedenthal (59–60) suggests that Gerardo's tactlessness in attempting to give Dühring money is born of insensitivity, Gittleman (1969) submits that the singer is moved by sympathy, indeed to such a degree that he overwhelms the musician and causes him to leave "in a pathetic state of agitation" (82). Dühring is the misunderstood artist, a figure whom Gittleman perceives in Keith, Nicolo, and Hidalla (80). Conceptually similar to the viewpoint of Kutscher (1927) regarding the fact that both Gerardo and Dühring express views of the author, is the contention of Gittleman that the figures represent two spokesmen for the artist; and it is only because of Wedekind's irony that this does not amount to "a black-and-white confrontation of artless cynicism and artistic idealism" (84).

Because he does not consider the irony, Thomas (1971), on the other hand, perceives a black-and-white confrontation which represents Wedekind's conversations with himself: Dühring is the misunderstood genius and idealist who is conscious of his mission, and Gerardo is the ambitious individual who knows how to achieve success (187–88). This juxtaposition amounts to Wedekind's reckoning with an art world that has denied him recognition (185). Gerardo emerges as the superior of the two because of his sharper insight and ambitious dedication (190). There is, however, an unresolved contradiction when Gerardo, the interpreter of Wagner, advises the musician to plagiarize this composer (188–89).

In his dialogue with Miss Coeurne, Gerardo emphasizes the idealistic nature of art, a position now propounded by Dühring, notes Haida (1973); and Gerardo must advance the opposite position, stressing the market value of art and the status of the artist as a luxury article of the bourgeoisie (97). Geißler (1978) perceives the operation of fate in the marketplace. Dühring represents a person who comprehends the capitalistic mechanism of the art world but refuses to adjust himself to it (157). Gerardo can offer no help since singing an unknown role would reduce his market value. Thus the market poses a vicious circle of irrationality: without acceptance of the composer's role by a star there is no performance; without public recognition of the composer, no singer would assume his role. Gerardo stresses the performance, Geißler continues, rather than the music, emphasizing the means rather than the end as the sine qua non of economic success. It is the star and not the work which attracts the public, and it is only entertainment that achieves the economic effect of art (158); there is no such thing, therefore, as an unrecognized musical genius (159). Wagener (1979) emphasizes the musician's uncompromising obstinacy as a spokesman for pure art (64), and Mennemeier (1980) his naïveté as an artist of the old school adhering to the belief that an art work is transformed to the realm of the illusionary and abstract (369). The high regard of Stewart (1985–86) for Gerardo causes him to dismiss Dühring as "a fumbling and ineffectual figure for whom no great respect is solicited" (67). The most refreshing treatment of the musician is that by Skrine (1989), whose description conveys the contagious quality of the humor. The sight of Dühring at the piano, fumbling through his music and playing the wrong parts, comprises one of Wedekind's funniest scenes; "the inept presentation is ludicrous." The interchange between the two about whether the music is modern or old-fashioned constitutes a commentary on what is happening in German music at the time (103).

With regard to Helene Marowa, Völker (1965, 41) sounds rather condescendingly masculine when he observes that she has a romantic conception of love, ridiculous but touching. The female is not taken seriously; her plea to be allowed to live is lent no credence until she shoots herself. The most beautiful woman in the city through her alliance with Gerardo provides promotional advertising during the period of his guest performance; and consistent further with his analysis of human behavior in economic terms, Hahn (1969) perceives that at the conclusion of Gerardo's concert series Helene becomes a liability and threat to his contract and livelihood (I, 61). Unlike Tristan, the turn-of-the-century prototype of the lover who would sacrifice himself for love, Gerardo stands ironically adamant, submits Rasch (1969, 425). But Gerardo, as well as Helene, are absolved of blame by Best (1975), who focuses on the concept of volition and suggests that the relationship concerns more than just the two of them; he describes them as "victims of a conspiracy in which they are willing partners" (43). Gerardo is described similarly by Geißler (1978) as a prisoner of his occupational image obliged to accept all favors of his feminine admirers willy-nilly (159).

In the light of Wedekind's description of the drama, Mennemeier (1980) characterizes Helene as Life, a blind passion who collides with Gerardo. She is a victim of illusion and functions in another world; her use of the name Oskar for the tenor is an indication that she is out of touch with reality (370).

Helene stands to Gerardo in a dialectic relationship of love to art. Vinçon (1987) observes that she uses art to gain access to his love, and he appeals to the immediacy of his next performance to extricate himself from her influence (206).

It is generally agreed that the work is tragicomedy. In 1914 Friedenthal emphasizes its grotesque nature including traces of irony and satire; the play offers a fluctuation between brutality and passion (58–59). According to Fechter (1920, 68), it is a tragicomedy which is similar in dramatic mood and construction to *Erdgeist*, where human wills are opposed to one another, instead of values as is here the case (71–72). Elster (1922, 57), Kutscher (1927 II, 54), and Pamela Wedekind (1959) interpret the three main figures, Gerardo, Dühring, and Helene, as both tragic and comic at the same time. Subjectively these characters are right, that is, from their own viewpoint; however, from the objective viewpoint of the other partner in dialogue, they are wrong. Therefore, the audience may sympathize with them and laugh at the same time. The roles require absolute seriousness; only in this way can the intended double effect of tragicomedy be achieved (65–66).

Placing emphasis upon direction, Völker (1965) notes that a comedic fact must be treated seriously, namely that every piece of furniture conceals a female admirer (40). Rasch (1969) ignores the explicit rejection by Pamela Wedekind (1959, 65) of the work as farce. He remarks that Wedekind is himself one of those figures who is here subjected to social criticism; this accounts for features in the work which are farcical and grotesque (423). Irmer (1970), on the other hand, finds nothing funny. The work does not deal with the fate of individuals or amount to a conversation about a virtuoso; Wedekind presents his early, eerie foreshadowing of our contemporary practice of dealing with stars of stage and screen as commercial properties (95).

Haida (1973) distinguishes himself by his opposition to the term *tragicomedy*, a characterization which he finds inaccurate and unhelpful; use of the term amounts to a solution reached by resort to an auxiliary concept that allows disparate elements to be joined. *Der Kammersänger* is in fact a comedy, which achieves humor by repetition; while trying to practice his music, Gerardo is interrupted time after time. The absence of a happy ending, however, provides a variation of the genre (95).

Siding with Rasch in opposition to Pamela Wedekind, Mennemeier (1980) calls the work a farce, grotesque and ridiculous (371). Brechtian features are evident in didacticism and alienation (372, 369). The conclusion of the work presents an open dialectic like the laugh of scorn which accompanies the comedy of the absurd (368).

The critics like the work. Pissin (1905, 38) calls it a brilliant example of Wedekind's pointed irony; and Kapp (1909) cites it, curiously, for the accuracy with which the characters are drawn and their verisimilitude. The work lends itself to the theater more easily that any other of Wedekind's plays, given the small number of actors required and the minimum of staging (56). Hofmiller (1910, 107–8) finds the long, cynical speeches boring, but then he would. Elster (1922, 57) calls it one of Wedekind's most artistic works and unlike other critics sees the conclusion as closed. With Olympian condescension, Hill (1960) dismisses *The Court Singer* as "a mere trifle— but rather clever and convincing as a study of character" (86). In light of his high regard for the work, Völker (1965) refuses to see the drama limited to classification as a satire of the bourgeois art business (41). Noting the success the drama has achieved, Hahn (1969 I) remarks that Wedekind as no writer before him shows how a successful *Lebens-Künstler,* or artist of life, behaves under the conditions of capitalism as these apply to art and life (60). *Der Kammersänger* is, for Mennemeier (1980, 367), one of Wedekind's most characteristic works.

Works Cited

Best, Alan. 1975. *Frank Wedekind.* London: Oswald Wolf.

Diethe, Carol. 1988. *Aspects of Distorted Sexual Attitudes in German Expressionist Drama.* New York, Bern, Frankfurt am Main, and Paris: Lang.

Elster, Hanns Martin. 1922. *Wedekind und seine besten Bühnenwerke.* Berlin and Leipzig: Franz Schneider.

Fechter, Paul. 1920. *Frank Wedekind. Der Mensch und das Werk.* Jena: Lichtenstein.

Friedenthal, Joachim. 1914. "Einleitung." In *Das Wedekindbuch,* edited by Friedenthal. Munich and Leipzig: Georg Müller. 1–121.

Geißler, Rolf. 1978. "Kunst und Künstler in der bürgerlichen Gesellschaft. Wedekinds *Der Kammersänger.*" *Literatur für Leser* 7.2: 156–60.

Gittleman, Sol. 1969. *Frank Wedekind.* New York: Twayne.

Hahn, Manfred. 1969. "Frank Wedekind. Leben und Werk." In *Frank Wedekind. Dramen I.* Berlin and Weimar: Aufbau-Verlag. 7–93.

Haida, Peter. 1973. *Komödie um 1900. Wandlungen des Gattungsschemas von Hauptmann bis Sternheim.* Munich: Fink. 92–107.

Hill, Claude. 1960. "Wedekind in Retrospect." *Modern Drama* 3.1 (May): 82–92.

Hofmiller, Josef. 1910. "Wedekind." In *Zeitgenossen.* Munich: Süddeutsche Monatshefte. 88–131.

Höger, Alfons. 1981. *Hetärismus und bürgerliche Gesellschaft im Frühwerk Frank Wedekinds.* Copenhagen and Munich: Fink.

Irmer, Hans-Jochen. 1975. *Der Theaterdichter Frank Wedekind. Werk und Wirkung.* Berlin: Henschelverlag. This originally appeared in 1970.

Jelavich, Peter. 1979. "Art and Mammon in Wilhelmine Germany: The Case of Frank Wedekind." *Central European History* 12: 203–36.

———. 1983. "Wedekind's *Spring Awakening:* The Path to Expressionist Drama." In *Passion and Rebellion. The Expressionist Heritage,* edited by Stephen Erich Bronner and Douglas Kellner. South Hadley, Mass.: J.T.Bergin. 129–50.

Kapp, Julius. 1909. *Frank Wedekind. Seine Eigenart und seine Werke.* Berlin: Hermann Barsdorf.

Kempner, Hans. 1911. *Frank Wedekind als Mensch und Künstler.* Berlin-Pankow: Oskar Linser.

Kutscher, Artur. 1970. *Frank Wedekind. Sein Leben und seine Werke.* Vols. 1 and 2. New York: AMS Press. This is a reprint of the editions appearing successively in 1922 and 1927.

Mennemeier, Franz Norbert. 1980. "Frank Wedekind." In *Handbuch des deutschen Dramas,* edited by Walter Hinck. Düsseldorf: Bagel. 360–73, 568–69.

Pissin, Raimund. 1905. *Frank Wedekind.* Berlin: Gose & Tetzlaff.

Rasch, Wolfdietrich. 1969. "Sozialkritische Aspekte in Wedekinds dramatischer Dichtung. Sexualität, Kunst und Gesellschaft." In *Gestaltungsgeschichte und Gesellschaftsgeschichte,* edited by Helmut Kreuzer. Stuttgart: Metzler. 409–26.

Skrine, Peter. 1989. *Hauptmann, Wedekind, and Schnitzler.* New York: St. Martin's Press.

Stewart, Corbet. 1985–86. "Comedy, Morality and Energy in the Work of Wedekind." *Publications of the English Goethe Society,* n.s., 56: 56–73.

Strich, Fritz, ed. 1924. *Gesammelte Briefe.* Vol. 1. Munich: Georg Müller.

Thomas, Klaus Wolfram. 1971. "Gerardo-Dühring: Ein Selbstgespräch Wedekinds." *German Quarterly* 44.2 (March): 185–90.

Ude, Karl. 1966. *Frank Wedekind.* Mühlacker: Stieglitz.

Vinçon, Hartmut. 1987. *Frank Wedekind.* Stuttgart: Metzler.

Völker, Klaus. 1965. *Frank Wedekind.* Velber bei Hannover: Friedrich Verlag.

Wagener, Hans. 1979. *Frank Wedekind.* Berlin: Colloquim.

Wedekind, Frank. 1909. "Vorrede zu *Oaha.*" In *Gesammelte Werke.* Vol. 9. Munich: Georg Müller. 436–51.

———. 1921. "Was ich mir dabei dachte." In *Gesammelte Werke.* Vol. 9. Munich: Georg Müller. 426, 428–29.

———. 1921. "Zirkusgedanken." In *Gesammelte Werke.* Vol. 9. Munich: Georg Müller. 293–305.

Wedekind, Pamela. 1959. "Mein Vater Frank Wedekind." In *Der Kammersänger,* by Frank Wedekind. Stuttgart: Reclam. 57–66.

5: *Der Marquis von Keith* (1901)
A Slick Operator Meets His Match

Set in Munich at the turn of the century, the drama deals with the speculative activities of Keith, a self-centered impresario, who is attended by Molly, faithful and unassuming, as well as by his beauteous mistress, Countess Anna Werdenfels. Keith founds a project centering upon the "Feenpalast" (Magic Palace) to enhance his finances and promote Anna's career as a singer; coincidentally he attempts to dedicate the born moralist Ernst Scholz to a life of hedonism. The financial project collapses upon the discovery that Keith keeps no business records. After Scholz is rejected by Anna, he breaks with Keith because of his amorality and seeks refuge in an insane asylum. Molly commits suicide, and Keith is forced by the financier Casimir to withdraw from the financial negotiations, which he does by accepting a banknote as he casually puts aside a revolver.

From the very first, *Der Marquis von Keith* (The Marquis of Keith, 1901) has caused critics to look beyond the masks of the two central male characters. Behind Keith and Scholz, the confidence man and the moralist, they see the single, unified countenance of Wedekind. Kapp (1909) establishes this pattern in the criticism with his perception of a polarity reflected in Wedekind's personality. The critic then extends this duality beyond the dramatist to apply it to all human beings. Kapp comes then to a curious conclusion: within everyone the qualities of the moralist, who would improve the world, struggle against the swindler, and the qualities of Scholz must be overcome before those of Keith may be realized (59). The path which scholarship would follow is marked further by Fechter (1920) as he adopts Kapp's conception of the two souls of the author in dialogue (73), underscoring a connection to Faust, which will be discussed further below.

In notes published in 1921 Wedekind makes clear that the drama is intended as a treatment of ideas and principles for living, presented in the interplay between these central characters (IX, 429); Keith is the Don Quixote of hedonism, who will employ morality to reach his pleasurable ends, and Scholz is the Don Quixote of morality, for whom hedonism serves his ethical purposes. Both are ultimately unsuccessful in the means they employ as well as in the attainment of their ultimate aims.

Although Wedekind's words were heard by critics, they looked beyond his commentary. The identity between Wedekind and his two dramatic characters is intensified by Kutscher (1927), who notes the qualities and features they share (II, 64–65). Since the two figures provide a poetic symbolization of the person of Wedekind, according to Dosenheimer (1949), the work offers an insight into the author and is confessional in nature (201). That Keith and Scholz are *not* mouth-pieces of the author is the position of Völker (1965), the solitary naysayer, who sees the two figures as interrelated objects employed in a dramatic demonstration (44). Spalter (1967) perceives "the individual above all eager to affirm his animalism and the individual wholly afraid of life" (133–34). While preserving the emphasis on the drama as autobiography, Kuhn (1981) moves the focus from both Keith and Scholz to the former character alone. In Keith, Wedekind has a dramatically integrated mouthpiece, and the work represents a turning point towards later, even more clearly autobiographical, dramas (221).

The name and title of the central figure, which lend themselves to that of the drama, is of central interest as it establishes a pattern of nationalities, writes Boa (1987, 131). The French title *Marquis* is coupled with *von* indicating German aristocracy, and the name Keith would seem to be from the English. Considering the German preposition in a linguistic context indicative of geographical origin, the critic identifies a small town in Scotland.

The surname, according to Hibberd (1987), evokes particular historical associations for Germans, an assertion, which if accurate, goes strangely unnoted in the critical literature. Hibberd points out that Keith was the family name both of an intimate, German-born friend of Frederick the Great of Prussia in the eighteenth century and of two aristocratic Scottish émigré brothers who served this king at that time (521, note 20). More probable is the information provided by Erhard Weidl (1990) suggesting that the dramatic figure bears the name of Minor Cooper Keith (1848–1929), a Central American railroad magnate (II, 782, note 50).

Keith may be seen as an outsider, a confidence man or adventurer, and a bourgeois entrepreneur. In act 1 Keith characterizes his marginal social status when describing himself as the bastard son of a gypsy by a mathematically inclined, intellectual father; he calls himself a cross between a philosopher and a horse thief, who was born into the world a cripple and a beggar. Faesi (1956) employs the term *Outlaw* for this man without an occupation, class, or country (248); and the interpretation of the outsider is sustained by Völker (1965, 43) and developed by Maclean (1968), who emphasizes that Keith has disassociated himself from the past by abandoning his first name and adopting a title (174). Motivation defines his outsider status for Nolting (1982): Keith is singular because he holds foremost in his mind the concept of the Magic Palace, in accordance with which he shapes his life (201).

As a confidence man or adventurer Keith lives by his wits. Extrapolating a term from comments by Wedekind made in reference to the figure Gerardo in *Kammersänger*, Kutscher (1927 II, 59) endorses the quality of brutal intelligence ("brutale Intelligenz"); he characterizes Keith as a person of the intellect who despises feelings. With a biographical connection, Kutscher provides a substantial contribution to the body of interpretation of Keith as a confidence man; the critic suggests that Keith's limp indicates his relation to a close acquaintance of Wedekind, Willy Grétor, the art dealer and forger to whom *Erdgeist* had been dedicated (60). Dosenheimer (1949, 200) recognizes the mark of the swindler in Keith's retort when warned by Molly that there is no money in the house for bread: "then we'll eat in the Hotel

Continental" (IV, 15). The need of the confidence man to successfully create illusion in order to deceive suggests to Wysling (1973) a connection between him and the artist (49). Finding more than a similarity between Willy Grétor and Keith, Jelavich (1979) interprets the central figure not as a mere reflection of this person but as an intended tribute to him; an individual such as Grétor, who with his art forgeries had successfully defrauded Wedekind's hated publisher Albert Langen, was probably highly admired (226).

Keith reveals himself as a bourgeois entrepreneur when at the beginning of act 5 he outlines his commercial philosophy to Hermann, who is about to leave for London. Keith emphasizes that the only way to properly exploit people consists of taking advantage of them conscientiously while in the right. This is his philosophers' stone: "the most brilliant business in the world is *morality* (IV, 84)." Recognizing that good business is to be done among the company of the bourgeoisie, Keith attempts to integrate himself, as Völker (1965, 43) notes. Keith is willy-nilly bourgeois, whether he knows it or not, according to Michelsen (1965, 64), but Rothe (1968) argues that Keith's attempts to imitate the middle-class citizen by conformance are undertaken in order to conceal his true nature (69). While at the same time attempting to refute Wysling (49), who perceives a cofidence man or adventurer, Kuttenkeuler (1977) advances an interpretation of Keith as a bourgeois entrepreneur. Kuttenkeuler argues that Keith's schemes do not allow him to enjoy the moment; he does not define his own behavior but instead responds in conformance with capitalistic economic modes (594, note 65).

What, then, accounts for Keith's failure? Friedenthal (1914) proposes two answers: Keith's shortsightedness and the poor quality of his work. This critic contends that Keith fails to recognize that his own well-being is inextricably related to that of others about him (66), a moral argument that evokes little resonance in the scholarship. Much more influential is Friedenthal's further observation that Keith performs below the standards of a swindler (67). Kutscher (1927) characterizes Keith as a victim of his excessive optimism and self-deception. Moreover, the operator is not true to his lights; he fails to pursue his precept of morality as business (II, 62). Keith falls victim to bourgeois dignitaries from whom he is no different except that they act in accordance with the law and have learned the business of deception better than he, submits Michelsen (1965, 64). Borrowing Kutscher's conception of Keith's self-deception, Rothe (1968, 100) and Hahn (1969 I, 64) enlarge upon it, suggesting that he deludes himself either with his faith in vitalism or with the ideology of free enterprise or both. Because of his low regard for the bourgeoisie, according to Bayerdörfer (1973), Keith is negligent with regard to details, such as financial accounts, and underestimates his competitors (350). The source of Keith's difficulties is traced to his physical appearance by Best (1975) and to his psyche by Boa (1987). In support of the idea of Michelsen that Keith is outsmarted by those he sought to exploit, Best argues that the attempt to convey or preserve authority is undermined by his appearance (100); his movements with their "restless jerkiness" create a handicap for him in the presence of those who judge only on a superficial basis

(102–3). One might add, however, that since the stage directions do not describe such movement, Best must have inferred it from Keith's limp. Boa becomes deeply psychological when she indicates that Keith's problems emanate from a split personality; he is a socially alienated individual as well as a representative of free enterprise (16).

Scholz is another story. He puts himself in Keith's hands in order to learn hedonism, but his conscience is never at rest; he feels a moral obligation to justify his existence by proving himself a useful member of society. Unlike Keith, who lives at ease with himself, Scholz intentionally complicates his existence; he finds meaning only in a life which is directed against himself, Fechter observes (1920, 74). Scholz behaves, Kutscher (1927) notes, as if he were atoning for something or working off a punishment (II, 65). Keith and Scholz stand as principles unmodified throughout the course of the drama, contends Rothe (1968). The two figures incorporate a polarity: Keith is an intransigent egoist representative of vitalism, and Scholz is the figure sickly denying this Life force (65). Maclean (1968) develops the idea of Kutscher that Scholz is atoning and punishing himself, while recognizing and cultivating a side of his being that he has always denied and repressed (171).

During the spectacle of the fireworks in act 3, widely understood as a metaphor for Keith's dazzling deception, Scholz is injured by an explosion and begins to limp like Keith. The two are identified at this point as Doppelgänger by Fechter (79). Hartwig (1965) speaks of the doubling of the central character (97) and Best writes of Keith's "mirror-image" (107).

Scholz evokes a range of humorous responses. It is amusing that he rejects his title to assume a bourgeois name for philanthropic reasons, while Keith invests himself with a title for acquisitive purposes, as Kapp observes (1909, 62–63). Unable to enjoy life or understand women, Scholz is sad and deadly earnest in the eyes of Friedenthal (1914), and at the same time funny in his martyrdom to his feeling of duty (65). The moralist is intended as a caricature, says Diebold (1921), since Wedekind considered morality both a restriction of human freedom and cowardice in the face of life (47–48). At the same time the glorification of bourgeois morality inherent in the pontificating of Scholz reveals itself as romantic humanitarian nonsense when subject to the unscrupulousness of Keith, writes Völker (1965, 44). Wedekind is mocking himself in Scholz, according to Spalter (1967), who assumes the positivistic, biographical approach of Kutscher; Spalter observes that Wedekind, in his fight against the censors, personally demonstrated much of the uncompromising, self-sacrificial attitude of Scholz (134). Consistent with the remarks of Friedenthal and Völker, the naive altruism of Scholz is cited by Gonçalves da Silva (1985) as the source of the humor in this character; "he speaks an alien language and becomes ridiculous in the eyes of society" (25).

The shortcomings of Scholz are evident. He is seen as a victim of his inhibitive conscience (Diebold 1921, 50), of his inferiority complex (Faesi 1956, 249), and of his inflexibility regarding compromise (Hahn 1969 I, 65). Bayerdörfer (1973) identifies the source of his pathologically internalized concept of duty in his failure to have ever known economic hardship (350). Further, Best (1975) describes a quality lacking in Scholz as "the inner mental equilibrium to see things as they really are" (101).

Scholz decides to enter a sanitarium. Such action amounts to flight from life and an abnegation of responsibility in the eyes of Friedenthal, but since Scholz is such a sorry figure, the idea of declaring himself insane is eminently reasonable and sound (65). Friedenthal is not alone in emphasizing the rationality of Scholz; Fechter (1920) writes that this character voluntarily assumes what he as a moralist would have imposed upon a person such as himself (76); and Natan (1963, 117) describes as sane the idea of Scholz to have himself declared mad. Best assumes and develops the view of Bayerdörfer (350–51) that society drives Scholz into final isolation; Best writes that Scholz chooses the asylum "as a place where he will be able to refashion the world to suit his own needs without opposition" (108). More than six decades after Friedenthal's statement regarding Scholz's flight from life, Höger (1979) appropriates this idea in his reference to the resigned attitude of Scholz and his death wish (99).

The action of the drama turns about a central object which is the focus of Keith's entrepreneurial efforts: the projected "Feenpalast" (Magic Palace) of the arts. The Deutsches Theater, constructed in Munich in September 1896, serves as a model for this undertaking, states Kutscher (1927 II, 64). Best and Kuttenkeuler (1977), on the other hand, associate the Feenpalast with the Glaspalast, opened in Munich in 1883 and intended as an experimental theater for Richard Wagner (118, note 21; and 588 respectively). If, however, the Deutsches Theater stands behind the Magic Palace, as maintained by Kutscher, then the latter edifice is intended as an object of parody, according to Jelavich (1979), since the theater represented to Wedekind's contemporaries the commercialization of culture (226, note 65). Hibberd (1987) remarks that the Deutsches Theater complex, including a theater with two thousand seats, restaurants, bowling alleys, gardens, and shops, survived only a year before going into bankruptcy (520); he asserts that Wedekind simply borrowed the term *Palast* (519).

Keith characterizes Consul Casimir as the greatest German financial genius, and the Consul responds by describing himself as the most highly regarded man in Munich and at the same time one who might expect to find himself behind iron bars the very next day. Consistent with this assessment, the critics see Casimir primarily as a confidence man or entrepreneur or both. As a businessman Casimir is, unlike Keith, the product of those successful commercial undertakings he has already accomplished (Fechter 1920, 75). That the real swindlers in this work are Casimir and the circle of financiers referred to as the caryatids is an interpretation of Diebold (1921 51–52), which received wide agreement. Casimir keeps abreast of the law by circumspection and the quiet self-assurance of his speculation (Kutscher 1927 II, 67). He is knowledgeable and frankly divulges that success is simply a matter of competition, that every gain is temporary, and that any person might run afoul of the law (Kuttenkeuler 1977, 586). Boa (1987) points to the measure of Casimir's prominence as both a swindler and an entrepreneur. In the list of dramatis personae the men are named before the women among the main characters; the position of Consul Casimir at the very top of this list is a reflection of the dominance of money over art and gender (131).

The widow Countess Anna Werdenfels is Keith's female counterpart. Feeling taken for granted and sensing his impending misfortune, she deserts him for that rich pillar of society represented by Consul Casimir, who thereby scores a success denied to Keith; it is Casimir who will bask in the reflection of her beauty. Described by the critics as cool, egoistic, and passionate, Anna is desirous of life (Fechter 1920, 75). She, like Keith, is a fortune hunter and social climber but is more careful, persistent, and intelligent than he (Kutscher 1927 II, 67). What binds her to Keith initially and then causes them to separate is her instinct for success and distrust of his inability to compromise (Hartwig 1965, 107). Hartwig is, however, inaccurate in his perception of her as a courtesan and swindler in one (107), an observation that suggests her identity with the women of Schwabing such as Simba; the Countess is clearly distinguished by the very absence of fraudulent motives. Best (1975) is more directly on point when he remarks that Anna has parlayed her beauty, an equivalent currency to wealth, into a sound social position (100). That she does this causes the feminists to split ranks: Lorenz (1976) takes Werdenfels to be self-assured and emancipated; Wedekind, who has always granted women sensuality, now concedes them good sense in that Anna will marry for security (51). Boa, on the other hand, scores Anna's feminine capitulation to patriarchal family order (163). The beautiful Countess from the moment of her concert appearance is no longer Keith's, writes Nolting (1982); she is comparable to the idea of the Magic Palace in that Keith deems both of them to be his product and property, and they are lost to him as soon as they are revealed publicly (186).

The figure of Countess Werdenfels suggests parallels to Lulu. Anna is characterized by Kutscher as the original image of feminine perfection ("ein Urbild weiblicher Vollkommenheit" II, 66), a description similar to that of Lulu provided by the animal trainer in the prologue, who refers to Lulu as the primal form of woman ("die Urgestalt des Weibes" III, 10). Just as Schön attempted to increase the public value of Lulu by promoting her theatrically, the impresario Keith fashions the Countess as an artist and speculates upon her success. In both cases that effect which the women have on men is associated with music (Hartwig 1965, 106). Just like Lulu, Anna is able to be all things to all men (107): suitable to every partner (Keith, Scholz, Hermann, and Casimir), and knowledgeable of every role; (sales clerk, countess, lover, artist, and maternal friend). And Maclean (1968) expands upon this idea when he remarks that with "a mixture of intuition and practicality" she adapts herself to the personality of individual men; for Keith, conscious of his red hands and limp, she stands for beauty and self-assurance, for Scholz social advancement, and for Casimir parental authority (170).

Rothe (1968) assumes a biographical approach in a comparison with the *Lulu* tragedy and concludes that Wedekind has become resigned. In *Erdgeist* this critic sees an expression of the idea that the pleasure principle might sweep aside the bourgeois order (71); Lulu loves as a part of living. Now, however, women offer their sexual favors for something in return. The Countess Werdenfels strikes a deal; she sells herself as expensively as possible to Casimir for wealth and prestige (72).

At the opening of act 1 Anna tells Keith that for a while she has entertained from time to time thoughts of suicide engendered by the pleasure of living (IV, 10). In drawing a parallel to *Erdgeist*, one might recall that this expression of the peculiar combination of pleasure and self-destruction echoes the confession of Lulu to Alwa in Part II that she once dreamed repeatedly of falling into the hands of a sex murderer (III, 142).

In act 2 Werdenfels converses with the young Hermann. She discloses to him that she divides all men into the categories overly fastidious ("ethe-petete") and alert and lively ("hopp-hopp") (IV, 36). On the basis of this singularly insignificant remark some critics have constructed their interpretations of the work. Diebold (1921) argues that Wedekind here groups characters according to what he calls the tempo of their temperaments and poses the categories in opposition to each other (50). Michelsen (1965) makes the terminology central to his argument that the difference between Keith and the financiers is more apparent than real (63). And Diethe (1988, 67) thinks the two types reflect the contrast between the energy of the trapeze artist and the lethargy of the tightrope walker from the essay "Thoughts About the Circus."

Anna urges Hermann to reconcile himself with his father and pay him respect. In the eyes of Boa (1987), Anna at this dramatic moment reinforces the power of money, of men over women, and of fathers over children (163). Hibberd (1987), on the other hand, interprets these lines of Anna as a statement of Wedekind's belief in a morality that is both egotistic and unselfish (526).

At the age of fifteen Molly Griesinger ran away from her parents in Bückeburg to follow Keith to America and as a consequence has led a life of insecurity about the globe. Knowing that Keith belongs to her only as long as he is in difficult straits, she gloats over his misfortune and seeks it. Torn between her bourgeois background and her love for Keith, Molly demands that he abandon his elegant lifestyle and spendthrift ways and move with her back to her parents in Bückeburg. The town name evokes overtones which strike Boa (132) as "oppressive," and the place is ridiculed by Keith for its petty bourgeois provincialism. His attitude is justified, and art is related to life when Hibberd indicates that this town located in lower Saxony has entertained a reputation for narrow-minded insularity dating back to at least the middle of the nineteenth century and is described in this light in the writing of Heinrich Heine (522, note 22).

In act 4 Scholz makes reference to Molly as Keith's wife; her legal status remains, however, somewhat unclear. Friedenthal (1914) describes her as Keith's spouse and loving Cinderella (66), but Best (1975) contends that they are not married and that she is simply held out as his wife (104). A middle position is offered by Boa, who characterizes Molly as a "quasi-spouse" as well as a surrogate mother (150).

Molly's presence is unsettling to Keith, a fact which elicits wide comment. Fechter (1920, 73) observes that beyond her role as a household servant she is ignored by Keith and her self-sacrificing love is fully unrequited; moreover, she represents a contradiction in his life since she does not desire his happiness. Subservient and masochistic, according to Kutscher (1927 II, 69), Molly is anxious, mistrustful, and easily angered; seeing Keith as the noble victim of those who would exploit him, she fears at the same time impending good fortune for him and the alienation of his affections (63). That masochism attributed to her by Kutscher is tempered by Maclean (1968), who notes that she possesses "a real, but perverse, pleasure in the indignities which poverty brings" (170); she denies herself self-indulgently, longing for a limited, narrow, bourgeois existence (178). If Kutscher emphasizes Molly's vision of Keith as the victim, her premonitions of disaster justify Best in describing her as "a clear-sighted observer and commentator on the fruitlessness of his efforts" (104). Molly is unsettling for Keith since her bourgeois qualities undercut the image he holds of himself and attempts to project (103–4); moreover, she provides a visible reminder of the history of his failures (100). Nevertheless, Keith bears a sentimental bourgeois sense of responsibility for her (104). Molly takes her life out of fear that the success of Keith will deprive her of him, in the view of Kutscher (II, 630) supported by Best (104). Others such as Dedner (1975, 501) and Stewart (1985–86, 70) simply describe her death as a consequence of her fanatic possessiveness.

Consistent with her feminist interpretation, Boa (1987) gives Molly considerable attention and importance. The uneasiness which the woman evokes stems from the threat her love poses to Keith's freedom-loving male psyche (150). Although self-effacing (138), Molly is seen to assume an impressive stature; in her unyielding struggle with Keith, her suicide is an expression of defiance (162). Her tragic status constitutes a paradox, "the heroic assertion of servility" (164).

Simba is a girl of Schwabing, sensual and promiscuous, who seeks pleasure for its own sake. When Scholz in act 3 attempts to persuade her that she is a martyr of civilization, she is dumbfounded and uncomprehending. She derides the Social Democrats and their moralistic attempts to better mankind. Hartwig (1965, 112) argues that Simba's lifestyle contradicts her status as a victim of civilization; her naive search for pleasure and satisfaction constitute her affirmation of existing society. Her political remark is taken, moreover, as a hint that Wedekind thought this society beyond the help of modern political ideology.

The resemblances between Ilse in *Frühlings Erwachen* and Lulu and Simba are clear enough. But the attitude of the dramatist towards these characters may have changed. Rothe (1968) asserts that Wedekind has adopted a new view towards this latter figure as he abandons his advocacy of the natural, spontaneous life of vitality and beauty (60). When Keith tells Scholz at the beginning of act 2 that the term *sin* is a mythological designation for bad business, Rothe sees Keith quite seriously adopting a bourgeois attitude towards vice, which is in turn imputed to the author. Whereas Wedekind in earlier plays had openly despised the middle class for its hostility to vitalism, here the author shares its rejection of sensuality as a self-destructive waste of resources (71).

Hermann, the fifteen-year-old son of Consul Casimir, consists of a trouser role like that of Sascha, the messenger. The boy borrows money from Keith to travel in artists' circles and longs for the great worlds of London and Paris. Similar to the adolescent figures in *Frühlings Erwachen*, Hermann is distinguished, as Hartwig (109–10) notes, by being the single character in this drama who evokes sympathy and hope, in part, since he alone rejects the bourgeois society of his father.

The two most significant moments in the drama are confrontational and related to one another. The first occurs in act 5 when Keith and Scholz face each other for the last time; the other moment appears at the conclusion when Casimir presents Keith an ultimatum.

Scholz refuses the pleas of Keith for money and begs him to free himself from his illusions and withdraw to an insane asylum. Referring to this scene as his own, Thomas Mann (1914, 31–32) alleges that Wedekind confided that he had written the drama for the sake of it. Mann describes having seen Wedekind play Keith in Munich and characterizes the encounter with Scholz as the most terrible, most moving, and most profound scene that this deep person, the tormented Wedekind, ever wrote (38). While Keith holds himself against the crossbar of the window, immovably and as if crucified, Scholz beckons and pleads with him in a soft voice. He tempts like the devil; perhaps he is the devil, writes Mann (35). Gittleman (1969) refers to the theatrical moment which Mann describes as "harrowing" (86), and Hahn (1969) speaks of tragicomedy erupting into the grotesque (I, 80). But Nolting (1982) points out that Mann is indulging in literary showmanship: he does not explicate the text critically in order to facilitate understanding of the scene but simply bestows his personality upon it by claiming it as his own (195); he then gains authority over it by asserting his acquaintanceship with Wedekind (199).

Two scholars telescope this scene of confrontation into the final conclusion of the work. Here Casimir demands that Keith leave Munich and tenders ten thousand marks. Clutching Hermann's revolver in his left hand and the money in his right, Keith looks indecisively at each in turn; then he puts the revolver aside while retaining the cash and exclaims with a grin that life is a slide ("Das Leben ist eine Rutschbahn . . .") (IV, 98). Keith here makes a choice, which according to Höger (1979, 113) amounts to that reached earlier in response to the demand of Scholz to accompany him to the asylum or remain penniless; the refusal to join Scholz is a decision against the revolver. In a generalization bare in detail and possibly borrowed from Höger, Gonçalves da Silva (1985) simply asserts that the debate between Keith and Scholz serves as an illustration of the conclusion (23).

Frühlings Erwachen has been employed widely to reflect upon Keith's final metaphoric comparison of life to a slide. A voice representative of this vein in the criticism is that of Spalter (1967), who points out that the aphorism of Keith amounts to an affirmation of Life not unlike that made at the conclusion of the drama by Melchior at the behest of the Masked Gentleman (134). If, however, as

Rothe (1968) notes, Consul Casimir is the equivalent of the Masked Gentleman, Wedekind's statement as an expression of vitalism has become less sure; Casimir represents the dominant bourgeoisie, and continuing to live poses for Keith the problem of adaption to that society (73). That Wedekind's concept of vitalism has changed is likewise noted by Kuhn (1981): whereas Melchior affirmed the instinctive and erotic, Keith now opts for something more adventurous, aimless, and ambiguous (163, note 5; 219–20).

Aside from interpretation in the light of vitalism, how do the scholars understand the final aphorism of Keith? At an early date Fechter (1920) sets the tone for one critical school: the positive conclusion. With spirits revived by the money in his hand, Keith shrugs off any sense of defeat and begins the climb anew (77). Further adventures beckon elsewhere (Kutscher 1927 II, 64); the game will begin again (Dosenheimer 1949, 202). Keith refuses to surrender (Feuchtwanger 1952, 11) for he may yet experience success (Kaufmann, 1969, 75; Gittleman 1969, 86). The ultimate in a rosy ending is provided by Best (1975), who practically sends Keith into retirement; the money amounts to more than he has ever known and will suffice to build his dream house (109). Wagener (1979) perceives a triumph of the will to live (66).

Not nearly as sanguine are the scholars first represented by Maclean (1968), who argues that Keith's prospects are hopeless and that he must create another illusion as the price of preserving his sanity (187). Rothe (1968) points out that the giant slide of life leads in only one direction, down (74). Keith has been utterly destroyed by excessively powerful economic interests (Hahn 1969 I, 64), and his quasi-heroic remark is an attempt to allay his fears regarding the instability perceived in society (Mennemeier 1980, 367). Tragedy must repeat itself again and again (Nolting 1982, 202).

Then, of course, some scholars see the conclusion as neutral or ambiguous, which it is. When Keith is revealed as a criminal, he is rejected and shown once more his place without bourgeois society, surviving unscathed and with a sizable check in hand (Völker 1965, 42–43). The slide is ignored by Ude (1966), who expects that Keith will simply continue his life (69). In his accustomed state of insecurity he will once more play cards against that beast, the world, according to Bayerdörfer (1973, 352). Borrowing the image of Bayerdörfer and developing it, Kuttenkeuler (1977) describes Keith as the modern gambler who consents to an existence which has its entire meaning in rise and fall, gain and loss; not fatalistic but frivolously opportunistic, this person submits to competitive economic conditions (587). The conclusion is ambiguous, asserts Hibberd (1987, 529) as does Boa (1987), since the grin specified in the stage directions can be played one way or the other; life is aimless and absurd (165). A failure to read the stage directions closely vitiates the argument of Skrine (1989), who maintains that the conclusion is unclear since the audience does not see Keith grasp the money (98); this is, of course, inaccurate.

One wonders about the concept of the "Rutschbahn" as understood by some of the English language critics. Disregarding the fact that the slide goes in only one direction, Hill (1960) observes that it represents a metaphor for life: one day you are up, and the next day down (86). Retaining the metaphor and applying it to a roller coaster, Spalter (1967) reaches the false conclusion that "one may as well continue to ride" (134). Gittleman (1969) appropriates Spalter's image of the roller coaster (86), whereas Best (1975) has no regard for the slide or chute and reconstructs it as a bowling alley (109). Borrowing without acknowledgment from Hill, Skrine (1989) translates Keith's final aphorism thus: "Life is full of ups and downs" (98).

What is *Der Marquis von Keith* all about? The early voice of Kempner (1911) waxed uniquely metaphysical regarding the meaning of the drama and evoked a special resonance six decades later. The conclusion of the work, he argues, presents an uplifting moral message; here a positive illustration is provided of how one should play out one's life within the bounds granted by providence rather than struggle against these limits (55–56). Less philosophical and more allegorical are Fechter (1920) and Kutscher (1927), who perceive the drama respectively as the struggle with Life (73) and the struggle for power and Life (II, 59). Like Spalter and Rothe (1968), who interpret the play in the light of *Frühlings Erwachen*, Hahn (1969 I, 65) reads the work as Wedekind's final reckoning with vitalism; a compromise with bourgeois society is reached in the principle "keep on muddling" ("Weitermachen"). The ambiguity of human existence is reflected for Böckmann (1969) in a distinctly contemporary interpretation; characters with mottled backgrounds and a variety of names suggest that identities are not what they seem and figures live in a contradiction with themselves (94). The contention of Kempner that one must pursue that path which is one's lot is turned inside out by Wysling (1973) as he applies a principle of Greek tragedy: Keith's career illustrates the myth of the mortal who deems himself equal to the gods and because of his hubris falls, only to rise once more at the conclusion (60).

That Wedekind is autobiographically involved in problem solving is the perception of Diebold (1921), who recognizes the dramatist's own attitudes towards morality (47–48); the work reflects to Michelsen (1965) the author's experience that one is defeated by Life if he takes it too seriously (64); and the choice between resignation or continued struggle as an outsider falls to the dramatist upon defeat, according to Gittleman (87).

The field of social criticism predominates in the interpretations. Traditional values were losing their worth during the Wilhelmine period, and to Natan (1963) the conclusion of the work "underlines the moral and social process of corrosion" at that time (115). An unscrupulous, domineering hero pays with his downfall for treading upon social conventions during the period of late imperialism, submits Völker (1965, 44–45). A bourgeois society in which money is the first principle of morality illustrates the problem of human existence to the Marxist Hahn (I, 63), and Kuttenkeuler (1977) borrows a term usually associated with Bertolt Brecht to characterize the work as a *Lehrstück,* or didactic work, which shows how the idolatry of money pervades society and corrupts the individual (588). A reflection of Wilhelmine reality—a chaotic, decaying society that is sexually and financially promiscuous—and a reflection of the dramatist's contradictory feelings of pleasure and anxiety towards this society are perceived by Mennemeier (1980, 367). The dominant social conditions exposed are accepted affirmatively by Keith and with resignation by Wedekind, Kuhn argues (1981, 214–15), and Gonçalves da Silva (1985, 25) recognizes in the survival of the social system an implicit contradiction inherent in bourgeois ideology, namely a "hypocritical compromise of using morality to do business, and business to shape morality."

Unique among the interpretations is criticism of the artist. Just as Schön in *Erdgeist* attempted to increase the market value of Lulu by writing reviews of her public stage performances, Keith composes an article about a painting by the artist Saranieff which Keith is trying to sell; his promotion of the musical career of Countess Werdenfels is blatant. Boa (1987) interprets Keith, therefore, as an impresario and emphasizes Wedekind's criticism of the relationship between the artist and his or her public (157).

Generally Wedekind's dramatic dialogue is admired for its style. Kapp (1909) notes the rich diversity presented by contrasts, antitheses, dislocated logic, and, of course, humor; moreover, the dialogue is by turns terse, bold, and startling in its effect upon both the dramatic characters who respond to it and the theatrical audience (62). Goldmann (1910), by contrast, takes objection to Wedekind's language for its implausibility; the dialogue employs the imperfect and pluperfect tenses and is marked by complexity befitting a written text. This critic faults the dramatist further for the absence of responsive conversation, suggesting that he was unable to write anything but lines in which the characters talk by each other (111–12).

Goldmann's views do not bear much persuasive weight with Fechter (1920), who recognizes human dialogue that distinguishes itself from the language of the earlier plays, where the speech consisted of monologues which were fitted together and closely compressed (78). Kutscher (1927) points to the elements of wit, irony, sarcasm, paradox, and sophism (II, 69). Linguistic forms catalogued by Hartwig (1965, 114) include colloquialisms, clichés, biblical metaphors and phrases, and allusions to classical literature and trivialisations thereof; the audience hears foreign accents, regional dialect, and standard German, a diverse pattern in light of which it is curious that Rothe (1968, 60) should note a unified conversational style.

Various critics remark upon the effect of the startling dialogue to which Kapp refers. Rothe finds a chaotic impression achieved by witty punch lines in rapid succession (61–62). Such language is characterized by Gittleman (1969) as "breathtakingly concentrated" (87). Bayerdörfer (1973) detects a tension and describes a dynamic movement back and forth between pure conversation and intellectually formulated didactic or argumentative language (352–53).

In treating the subject of wit, Best (1975) perceives that Keith uses it to maintain his authority; he preempts the response of his partners, thereby sustaining his "precarious survival" (101). As compared with the language of the earlier dramas, that of *Keith* is less inclined to verbose grandiosity and includes non sequiturs and what Best terms "throw-away lines" that reflect a lack of communication (102).

Keith's language gives him away, according to Dedner (1975, 505); his aphorisms are the utterances of a country bumpkin in that terms he employs such as sin, higher values, and the like are not references to something concrete and therefore have no meaning to the cosmopolites about him.

The effectiveness of the dialogue is emphasized by Kuhn (1981, 164) as she allies herself with Fechter against Goldmann and shares with Bayerdörfer the regard for movement. She describes the aphorisms as self-contained, highly stylized items of rhetoric embedded in the conversation; they impede the dynamic forward motion of the dramatic development by working in an alienating and retarding fashion (215–16). The aphorisms serve the ends of social criticism not because they are intended negatively by Keith, for he embraces the society and is eager to play by its rules, but in their effect on the consciousness of the audience (214–15).

From the very first the wit suggests parallels to a work from the English stage. The aphorisms remind critics of Oscar Wilde's *The Importance of Being Earnest*, published in 1899, about the time Wedekind completed this work. A distinction is noted, however, by Kapp (1909) since Wilde's logical subtleties, bold witticisms, and anti-philistine spitefulness are integrated ironically and paradoxically within his material; with Wedekind the characters talk merely in order to execute the author's brilliant mental somersaults (63). A parody of the conversational comedy of Wilde suggests itself to Irmer (1970, 100). Kuhn (207) distinguishes between the dramatists' intentions: Wilde meant his aphorisms as a demonstration of wit, while Wedekind is didactic.

At a time when Nietzsche was fashionable, Keith's aphorisms lent him the air of a philosopher. And indeed these were collected and published in the journal *Die Jugend* in 1902 under the title "Thus spake the Marquis of Keith." Removed from their context in dramatic dialogue the aphorisms appeared to Wedekind's contemporaries, according to Dedner, as paradoxical truths (511).

Although the early critics Goldmann (1910, 111) and Kempner (1911, 56) fault the work for an absence of organic development, finding only a series of events, Kutscher (1927) overlooks this objection (as do subsequent critics) since he perceives a more well-defined structure here than in any of the earlier dramas (II, 69). That "station drama" characteristic of expressionism and represented by a structure describing a path from point to point as the work unfolds is recognized by Böckmann (1969, 99). Bayerdörfer (1973) observes a development which effects a tension on two planes coincidentally: on one level the property-owning bourgeoisie versus the shady characters of the demimonde; and on the other plane Keith and the financiers versus Scholz (349).

The form of the drama is described as closed by Rothe (1968) since Casimir, who may find himself in jail the next day, is subject to, and threatened by, the forces which cause Keith's downfall (72). Form closes conclusively behind Scholz upon his departure (Höger 1979, 173, note 43). But it is open form that leaves Keith to his further adventures (Bayerdörfer, 355; Höger 1979, 173, note 43; Hibberd 1987, 530).

Considerable difference of opinion is expressed regarding genre. Although Goldmann goes so far as to deny that the dramatist even had comedy in mind, he observes that Wedekind has willy-nilly attained the status of a humorist and satirist by virtue of writing not even intended to be funny (105). Fechter (1920, 73) relegates the work to a subgenre in comedy, namely that of the confidence man and swindler (*Hochstaplerkomödie*). A satire of bourgeois society is identified by Hartwig (1965, 15) whereas Rothe (1968, 60) recognizes the witty "well-made play." The deceived deceiver and the marriage dictated by social and financial considerations are conventions of the comedy singled out by Bayerdörfer (351). More sophisticated is the argument of Kaufmann (1969) that this drama represents a new type of comedy where the thinking and behavior of the hero are conditioned by a world which needs and desires people of his type in order to recognize itself in him; not the swindler, but this world is revealed as comical and ridiculous (75). It is no doubt the presence of witty lovers, elegant dialogue, and an atmosphere of cynical refinement that lead Boa (1987, 133) to perceive the traditional comedy of manners, although she does not reveal her grounds for doing so.

In the case of the characters Molly and Scholz the drama would seem to represent unequivocally a tragedy. But Kutscher is not of one mind; at first he characterizes the work as a comedy with a mixture of tragic features (II, 63); he finally denies, however, that it is a comedy and relegates it instead to the genre of tragicomedy (70). Dosenheimer (1949) rejects the concept of tragicomedy advanced by Kutscher, although she concedes that the work contains both comic and tragic features (201). This critic sees tragedy in the collapse of Keith's scheme; this is, however, unfortunately diluted by the introduction of Molly's corpse at the conclusion, a dramatic mistake of the author compounded by the fact that Keith is innocent of her death (202). Scholz experiences tragedy in a classical sense, according to Hartwig (97), since he recognizes contradiction in his despair; further, the critic sides with Dosenheimer in citing both comic and tragic aspects of the work but refusing to characterize it as a tragicomedy. The most unique interpretation is that of Rothe grounded in the principle of vitalism: the concepts of comedy and tragedy lose meaning when associated with the experiences of a hopeless and blind adventurer; he trusts himself to Life which moves endlessly without direction like a wave (74–76).

Der Marquis von Keith is rich in its literary relations. From an early date Goethe's *Faust I* (1808) provides a model wherein two souls beat within one breast; these are that of the moralist Scholz and the swindler genius Keith; and Kapp (1909, 59) first unifies the two personalities in Wedekind. The critic makes further use of Goethe's materials when he establishes the identity of Scholz as Faust: helpless, sentimental, exaggeratedly moral, and philosophical. Keith is Mephistopheles: ironic, egoistic, exploitative, and aggrandizing (62). This pattern prevails with Kempner (1911, 51), Kutscher (1927 II, 69), and Faesi (1956, 249). Hitherto unrecognized complexity inherent in the figures of Keith and Scholz is first pointed out by Maclean (1968), who notes that the two are interrelated and interdependent; both share features of

Faust and Mephisto, especially regarding "the quality of insatiability" (165). With an allusion to the limp of Keith, Rothe (1968) extends the identity of this character to Lucifer (65–66). Irmer (1970, 201) sees the reversal of those roles assigned to Keith and Scholz by Kapp in that scene where the two confront each other for the last time; and Boa (1987) echoes agreement (143).

The parallel to *Faust I* is extended to that scene at the beginning of act 5 where Keith provides suggestions to the young Hermann who is about to set off for London; this scene is identified by Rothe (1968, 70, note 13) with that in which Mephistopheles advises the student, an observation repeated by Wysling (1973, 59–60) without acknowledgment.

Literary associations are even extended to Scholz; he is seen as a caricature of the dramatist Gerhart Hauptmann, best known as an exponent of naturalism and the object of Wedekind's scorn in the prologue to *Erdgeist*. Scholz provokes ridicule of Hauptmann's unworldliness in Völker's opinion (1965, 44); and Kuhn (1981) argues further that Wedekind's drama operates as a criticism of naturalism in that it undermines the precepts and conventions of this dramatic style (162–63).

The figure of the confidence man represents a literary current in itself. This vein of the picaresque is continued in the novel by Thomas Mann *Die Bekenntnisse des Hochstaplers Felix Krull* (Confessions of Felix Krull, Confidence Man, 1954); Mann, as stated above, saw Wedekind playing the central role of Keith. And Carl Zuck-mayer's *Der Hauptmann von Köpenick* (The Captain of Köpenick, 1930) provides a dramatic successor, as Skrine (1989, 101) indicates.

Social comedy and satire demonstrating the fragility of the bourgeois citizen and his moral problematics leads directly to Georg Kaiser, according to Dosenheimer (1949, 203). And it does even more clearly to Carl Sternheim, a son-in-law of Wedekind, who wrote eleven plays in the series *Aus dem bürgerlichen Heldenleben* (Scenes from the Heroic Life of the Middle Classes) dating from 1911; this is noted by Dosenheimer (203) and Kaufmann (1969, 75). *Der Snob* (The Snob, 1914) is Sternheim's satire of bourgeois-capitalist society, at the center of which stands the confidence man Christian Maske, described by Boa as a "direct descendant" of Keith (140). Skrine, too, sees Wedekind as the forefather of Sternheim (101).

The influences of Wedekind reveal themselves in the drama of Bertolt Brecht in the figure of the adventurer (Natan 1963, 117) such as the crook Mackie Messer from *Dreigroschenoper* (The Threepenny Opera, 1928); similar is the caricature of Hitler as a gangster in *Der aufhaltsame Aufstieg des Arturo Ui* (The Resistible Rise of Arturo Ui, 1957), as pointed out by Kaufmann (75). When religion is equated with commerce, and sin is merely bad business, Keith, in the view of Spalter (1967), "speaks with a Brechtian voice" (134); or rather, as Spalter should have said, Brecht, in *The Threepenny Opera* for example, speaks with a Wedekindean voice. According to Boa (1987, 144–45), the cynical aphorisms of Keith and his deluded belief in free enterprise and his ability to manipulate the power of money lead to the central figure of *Mutter Courage und ihre Kinder* (Mother Courage and Her Children, 1941).

The play is a precursor of modern drama. The sanity of Scholz and the idea of asylum prefigure *Die Physiker* (Die Physicists, 1962) by Friedrich Dürrenmatt (Natan 1963, 117). When laughter combines with fear, comedic grotesquery with tragicomic effect, the audience finds itself on the borders of paradox and the absurd (Böckmann 1969, 79, 94).

For at least a decade after its premiere in 1901 *Der Marquis von Keith* enjoyed no popular or critical success. The work presents bloodless characters which are intellectual constructions (Kapp 1909, 63); and the absence of an organic dramatic development and closed form make it difficult for the audience to follow, causing the viewer to lose perspective (Kempner 1911, 56–57). In notes written in 1911 to accompany the play, Wedekind states that he considers it his most artistically mature and intellectually rich work and that the character Keith is the best role he ever wrote (IX, 429); but it was not until 1914 that the public and critics came to support his view. Friedenthal (1914) describes the figure of Keith as aesthetically vital and fully formed (67). The drama, according to Fechter (1920), shimmers between reality and symbol with a quality characteristic of the author; next to *Erdgeist*, it is the boldest and most mature (72–73), the most concentrated and concise drama he had written (78). Kutscher (1927) calls *Keith* Wedekind's most perfectly complete work, with a more defined structure than any of the earlier dramas (II, 69–70).

A long period of silence ensued, and it was not until the postwar period that Dosenheimer (1949) rediscovers *Keith* as perhaps Wedekind's best since it is his most poetic (202). Given a producer equal to it, the work, according to Natan, can be "one of the most essential and significant dramas of our times" (117–18). Ude (1966), however, does not agree: a production of the work provides, at best, simply an interesting evening in the theater; the figures are threadbare, the financial negotiations are not credible, too much is reported as having occurred offstage, and the plot is disjointed (69–71).

Serving as literary historians years later, some critics attempt to account in retrospect for the negative reaction the work evoked during the early years: this amounted to confusion and irritation elicited by Wedekind's "uneasy mixture of cynicism and idealism"; the audience suspected it was being laughed at (Maclean 1968, 173). It is suggested further that misunderstanding was conveyed by actors who failed to comprehend their roles and employed a naturalistic acting style (Höger 1979, 95–96).

With the exception of that dissent expressed by Ude, *Der Marquis von Keith* has been highly regarded from the time of Friedenthal (1914) until the present day. Kuhn (1981) describes it as a high point (221), and Boa refers to it as "Wedekind's most elaborate and intellectually challenging exploration of individualist values" (4).

Works Cited

Bayerdörfer, Hans-Peter. 1973. "Non olet—altes Thema und neues Sujet. Zur Entwicklung der Konversationskomödie zwischen Restauration und Jahrhundertwende." *Euphorion* 67: 323–58.

Best, Alan. 1975. *Frank Wedekind.* London: Oswald Wolf.

Boa, Elizabeth. 1987. *The Sexual Circus. Wedekind's Theatre of Subversion.* Oxford: Blackwell.

Böckmann, Paul. 1969. "Die komödiantischen Grotesken Frank Wedekinds." In *Das deutsche Lustspiel.* Vol. 2, edited by Hans Steffen. Göttingen: Vandenhoeck & Ruprecht. 79–102.

Dedner, Burghard. 1975. "Intellektuelle Illusionen. Zu Wedekinds *Marquis von Keith.*" *Zeitschrift für deutsche Philologie* 94: 498–519.

Diebold, Bernhard. 1972. "Wedekind der Narr." In his *Anarchie im Drama.* New York and London: Johnson Reprint Corporation. 43–76. The work first appeared in 1921.

Diethe, Carol. 1988. *Aspects of Distorted Sexual Attitudes in German Expressionist Drama.* New York, Bern, Frankfurt am Main, and Paris: Lang.

Dosenheimer, Elise. 1967. *Das deutsche soziale Drama von Lessing bis Sternheim.* Darmstadt: Wissenschaftliche Buchgesellschaft. This first appeared in 1949.

Faesi, Robert. 1956. "Ein Vorläufer: Frank Wedekind." In *Expressionismus. Gestalten einer literarischen Bewegung,* edited by Hermann Friedmann and Otto Mann. Heidelberg: Rothe. 241–63.

Fechter, Paul. 1920. *Frank Wedekind. Der Mensch und das Werk.* Jena: Lichtenstein.

Feuchtwanger, Lion. 1952. Introduction to *Five Tragedies of Sex,* by Frank Wedekind. Translated by Frances Fawcett and Stephen Spender. London: Vision. 7–21.

Friedenthal, Joachim. 1914. "Einleitung." In *Das Wedekindbuch,* edited by Friedenthal. Munich and Leipzig: Georg Müller. 1–121.

Gittleman, Sol. 1969. *Frank Wedekind.* New York: Twayne.

Goldmann, Paul. 1910. "Der Marquis von Keith." In his *Literatenstücke und Ausstattungsregie.* Frankfurt am Main: Rütten & Loening. 103–14.

Gonçalves da Silva, M. Helena. 1985. *Character, Ideology, and Symbolism in the Plays of Wedekind, Sternheim, Kaiser, Toller, and Brecht.* London: Modern Humanities Research Association.

Hahn, Manfred. 1969. "Frank Wedekind. Leben und Werk." In *Frank Wedekind. Dramen I.* Berlin and Weimar: Aufbau-Verlag. 7–93.

Hartwig, Wolfgang. 1965. "Materialien zum Verständnis des Textes." In *Der Marquis von Keith,* by Wedekind. Komedia 8. Berlin: de Gruyter. 92–120.

Hibberd, John L. 1987. "The Morality of Wedekind's *Der Marquis von Keith.*" *Deutsche Vierteljahrschrift* 61.3 (September): 510–30.

Hill, Claude. 1960. "Wedekind in Retrospect." *Modern Drama* 3.1 (May): 82–92.

Höger, Alfons. 1979. *Frank Wedekind. Der Konstruktivismus als schöpferische Methode.* Königstein: Scriptor.

Irmer, Hans-Jochen. 1975. *Der Theaterdichter Frank Wedekind. Werk und Wirkung.* Berlin: Henschelverlag. This originally appeared in 1970.

Jelavich, Peter. 1979. "Art and Mammon in Wilhelmine Germany: The Case of Frank Wedekind." *Central European History* 12: 203–36.

Kapp, Julius. 1909. *Frank Wedekind. Seine Eigenart und seine Werke.* Berlin: Hermann Barsdorf.

Kaufmann, Hans. 1969. "Zwei Dramatiker: Gerhart Hauptmann und Frank Wedekind." In his *Krisen und Wandlungen der deutschen Literatur von Wedekind bis Feuchtwanger.* Berlin and Weimar: Aufbau-Verlag. 47–84.

Kempner, Hans. 1911. *Frank Wedekind als Mensch und Künstler.* Berlin-Pankow: Oskar Linser.

Kuhn, Anna Katharina. 1981. *Der Dialog bei Frank Wedekind.* Heidelberg: Carl Winter.

Kutscher, Artur. 1970. *Frank Wedekind. Sein Leben und seine Werke.* Vol. 2. New York: AMS Press. This is a reprint of the edition appearing in 1927.

Kuttenkeuler, Wolfgang. 1977. "Der Außenseiter als Prototyp der Gesellschaft. Frank Wedekind: *Der Marquis von Keith.*" In *Fin de siècle. Zu Literatur und Kunst der Jahrhundertwende,* edited by Roger Bauer. Frankfurt am Main: Klostermann. 567–95.

Lorenz, D. C. G. 1976. "Wedekind und die emanzipierte Frau. Eine Studie über Frau und Sozialismus im Werke Frank Wedekinds." *Seminar* 12.1 (February): 38–56.

Maclean, Hector. 1968. "Wedekind's *Der Marquis von Keith*: An Interpretation Based on the Faust and Circus Motifs." *Germanic Review* 43.3 (May): 163–87.

Mann, Thomas. 1953. "Eine Szene von Wedekind." In his *Altes und Neues. Kleine Prosa aus fünf Jahrzehnten.* Frankfurt am Main: Fischer. 31–38. This essay first appeared in 1914.

Mennemeier, Franz Norbert. 1980. "Frank Wedekind." In *Handbuch des deutschen Dramas,* edited by Walter Hinck. Düsseldorf: Bagel. 360–73, 568–69.

Michelsen, Peter. 1969. "Frank Wedekind." In *Deutsche Dichter der Moderne,* edited by Benno von Wiese. Berlin: Erich Schmidt. 51–69. The essay first appeared in 1965.

Natan, Alex. 1963. "Frank Wedekind." In *German Men of Letters,* edited by Natan. Vol. 2. London: Oswald Wolf. 101–29.

Nolting, Winfried. 1982. *Literatur oder Kommunikation.* Münster: Aschendorff.

Rothe, Friedrich. 1968. *Frank Wedekinds Dramen. Jugendstil und Lebensphilosophie.* Stuttgart: Metzler.

Skrine, Peter. 1989. *Hauptmann, Wedekind, and Schnitzler.* New York: St. Martin's Press.

Spalter, Max. 1967. *Brecht's Tradition.* Baltimore: Johns Hopkins Press.

Stewart, Corbet. 1985–86. "Comedy, Morality and Energy in the Work of Wedekind." *Publications of the English Goethe Society,* n.s., 56: 56–73.

Ude, Karl. 1966. *Frank Wedekind.* Mühlacker: Stieglitz.

Völker, Klaus. 1965. *Frank Wedekind.* Velber bei Hannover: Friedrich Verlag.

Wagener, Hans. 1979. *Frank Wedekind.* Berlin: Colloquim.

Wedekind, Frank. 1921. "Was ich mir dabei dachte." In *Gesammelte Werke.* Vol. 9. Munich: Müller. 429–30.

Weidl, Erhard, ed. 1990. *Werke.* Vol. 2. Munich: Winkler.

Wysling, Hans. 1973. "Zum Abenteurer-Motiv bei Wedekind, Heinrich und Thomas Mann." In *Heinrich Mann 1871/1971. Bestandsaufnahme und Untersuchung. Ergebnisse der Heinrich-Mann-Tagung in Lübeck,* edited by Klaus Matthias. Munich: Fink. 37–68.

6: *König Nicolo* (1901)
Loneliness and the Search for Recognition

King Nicolo of Umbria is deposed for his extravagance, and the master butcher Pietro Folchi succeeds to the throne. He banishes Nicolo under the penalty of death should he return and claims his daughter Alma as a ward of the state intended for Folchi's son Filipo. Escaping from a convent, Alma joins Nicolo, who remains in the country disguised first as a swineherd, then a tailor's apprentice. When heard to curse the king who hinders him from being a human being like everyone else, Nicolo is seized and tried for lèse-majesté. Upon his guilty plea he is first imprisoned and then banished under penalty of death should he return. At Elendenkirchweih, where theater and circus performers audition for employment, Nicolo declaims the tragic fate of the unrecognized sovereign, a presentation which elicits laughter as comic parody and gains him employment by a theater owner. A second performance before King Pietro earns him an appointment as court jester. Refusing the king's order to prohibit the marriage of his daughter and Filipo, Nicolo is banished under penalty of death. Such irony causes Nicolo to identify himself, and he is taken for crazy. Threatened while dying with the curse of seeming ridiculous, Nicolo exclaims resignedly "Such is life!" ("So ist das Leben!"). Pietro orders that he be buried in the royal crypt lest history report that Pietro had employed a king as court jester.

Wedekind returned from exile to face imprisonment on the charge of lèse-majesté in conjunction with the *Simplicissimus* affair. This sentence was a wound to his dignity matched only by that inflicted by the critical reception accorded the premiere of *Keith* in October 1901. Shortly thereafter, and as a response to both, Wedekind wrote *König Nicolo* (King Nicolo, 1902). As a frontispiece to the first edition he adopted a line by the critic Julius Hart asserting that there is nothing in contemporary German literature as ordinary as the art of Frank Wedekind.

From the very first, that is, beginning with the attention of Pissin (1905, 59), the critics interpreted the work as an allegory regarding the unrecognized greatness of Wedekind and his fate. Employing the method usually adopted by subsequent critics, Pissin attempts to look beyond the author's personal history and interpret the drama as a generalized statement, here a treatment of the struggle of the artist against the philistines (61).

That such an attempted generalization may not stray markedly from the personal case is illustrated by Kapp (1909), who also perceives the enemy as the philistines; but in his interpretation it is not the artist generally who must strive against such a foe, but Wedekind himself. He is the king in the realm of literature who is driven out because he refuses to make hypocritical concessions or retractions and therefore wanders about his country with lute in hand (68–69).

Kapp is the first to consider the subject of lèse-majesté, arguing that Nicolo's curse of the king is directed at himself (66). The courtroom scene, in which Wedekind opposes punishment for this crime, develops naturally from the plot and is not forced upon it; the scene increases our sympathy for what the dramatist has suffered. Nevertheless, the courtroom scene, like that of the conference of pedagogues in *Frühlings Erwachen*, is crass caricature and constitutes a flaw in the drama (70).

In notes from 1911, Wedekind freely concedes that the work is a reaction to the scorn with which *Keith* was received in Berlin (IX, 430); and Kempner the same year observes that it is no wonder that a person as sensitive and impulsive as Wedekind should react with such bitterness (80–81). Although the work is very personal according to Friedenthal (1914), it is allegory that is sufficiently objective to constitute literature (74–75). *Nicolo* is Wedekind's somber message which, in the words of Blei (1914), amounts to a characterization of himself: "a king in my art, I die an unknown beggar; a prophet of ethics, I am engaged as a clown" (144–45). Quick to concede that the work is confessional and about Wedekind as an author, Fechter (1920) notes that, at least indirectly, all Wedekind's works deal with himself and his relation to the world (84, 90); the fate of the king is to be sure that of the author unjustly disregarded (87), but the work extends also to the subject of human dignity and of the small king and great fool contained in every person (88–89). Diebold (1921) perceives not bitterness but resignation in the phrase "Such is life!"; this utterance expresses the dramatist's capitulation to the public, theater directors, censor, and state (69). As does Fechter, Elster (1922) finds more than confession in a moving drama of the fate of the artist in the world of commoners (73).

A variation on the theme takes shape from Kutscher's (1927) reading of the play; it is the tragedy of a person who is so greatly an artist in his fantasy world that he alienates the philistines and earns their hostility (II, 97). Endorsing the view of Kapp that the courtroom scene constitutes caricature recalling that of the conference of pedagogues in *Frühlings Erwachen* (101), Kutscher interprets the subject of lèse-majesté as part of a process of transformation which takes place in Nicolo. The king within prevents him from being a human being like everyone else, satisfied simply with preserving his social status and defending his property; therefore Nicolo curses the king, committing the crime of insulting one's own majesty. Now Nicolo sinks to his lowest depths, gradually rising by the confession of guilt, repentance, and the reenactment of his experiences; pain and self-contempt are overcome so that Nicolo is ultimately able to hold up with pride once more the royalty within. As a human being he must abdicate in death, but the future brings him recognition and his daughter an inheritance (97–98).

Dosenheimer (1949) compares Wedekind to Friedrich Nietzsche in his loneliness and need for belonging, both seeking a community at the cost of injuring their innermost being (205). While emphasizing the theme of evanescence and attributing to this baroque motif more importance that it merits (205), Dosenheimer considers the internal development of an individual from extreme egocentricity to a sense of responsibility as Nicolo comes to see that he had misused his position as king to the disadvantage of his people (203).

The playwright's audience is the focus of Völker (1965); although Nicolo is both Wedekind and the figure of the artist generally, the people in the play bear no generalized role; they represent the stupid, childish mass identified as the German theatrical public around 1900 that rejects Wedekind's works as vulgar and immoral (48). Wedekind's conviction that success and vulgarity go hand in hand is cited by Spalter (1967) in this context, the point being made that "to be noble is to be isolated and impotent" (132).

In an interpretation which is quite unique, Böckmann (1969) argues that Nicolo represents neither Wedekind nor the figure of the artist but rather the human being on the stage of life, bereft of human dignity and the object of ridicule when he takes himself seriously (99).

Wedekind in this work avoids self-pity in the view of Gittleman (1969, 98); but Kaufmann (1969, 77) reads the play as an expression of excessively sentimental self-sympathy as does Maclean (1969), who observes that the drama was written when the author was "suffering from a particularly severe attack of his recurring feeling of martyrdom." (23). The quotation from Julius Hart on the frontispiece is falsified and taken out of context (22); Wedekind is charged with "hugging the insult to himself in a purely masochistic fashion" (23).

Sharing with Kutscher (1927) the idea of a transformation of Nicolo, Maclean argues that the work is not an allegory of Wedekind's failure and persecution but "a voyage of self-discovery" (23). The "king" stands for the "barren, inward looking personality" of Nicolo, which is ultimately overcome (24). Lèse-majesté amounts to an expression of resignation regarding the tyranny and helplessness of the self (27). Behind the mask of the fool, Nicolo acquires freedom and a release from himself and finally "responsibility and transcendence" as he gains an insight into Pietro's mind (24).

Whereas Gittleman (88) asserts that it is understandable that the travesty of justice which Wedekind experienced should have gone into the drama, Best (1975) makes a distinction more imagined that real; he denies that the work is confessional and characterizes it as dramatic employment of the author's own attitudes and experiences (110). The personal and autobiographical nature of the drama is underscored by Wagener (1979) when he points out that the courtroom scene includes language taken directly from the records of Wedekind's trial in Leipzig (70).

Loving towards his daughter, Nicolo is willful and temperamental, intellectual and egoistic; he is incapable of work and indulgent of splendor. Proud and arrogant, he is contemptuous of others. Additional qualities of Nicolo may be shared with Wedekind himself; Kutscher mentions his emotionalism, sentimentality, despondency, and despair (II, 99–100). Nicolo first becomes a human being when he loses his throne, first a king when he is no longer one, in the view of Dosenheimer (1949, 205). Völker (1965, 48) contends that Nicolo fails as a king because the people are not familiar with his concept of human dignity. But there are contradictions inherent in him and his circumstances: in Pietro he recognizes a better ruler, but no king; the banishment of Nicolo brings improved conditions to Umbria, but the change of rulers is represented as a farce and a political swindle. Gittleman (90) mentions that the identity of Nicolo and Wedekind is closest in the courtroom trial scene and the episodes involving the clown as a tragic figure, but the egotistical figure evokes an initial impression that is "distinctly unsympathetic."

The daughter Alma, dragged about by her father, serves as the poet's muse, observes Friedenthal (1914, 74–75). Kutscher (1927 II, 100) asserts that she is clever, industrious, courageous, and filled with love for her father. Without a personality or life of her own, she reminds Ude (1966, 88) of the third and youngest daughter of Shakespeare's King Lear. Her innocent trust in her father evokes his feeling of responsibility, in Maclean's view (1969, 33); and by perceiving what he has not noticed himself, she reflects that internal development he is unconsciously experiencing (29).

Pietro is a man of order, well-versed in the practice of life, writes Diebold (1921, 68). A sympathetic figure, Pietro is cautious, strong-willed, brave, peace-loving, just, and pious, according to Kutscher (II, 100). Wedekind resisted the temptation of making a caricature of the former butcher; Pietro tries to do right and provides Nicolo a model of what he should have been, Dosenheimer maintains (204). With the king's "warm sensitivity," Gittleman (1969, 90) finds that Pietro stands in sharp contrast to Nicolo.

The scene at Elendenkirchweih is a favorite of the critics, characterized by Friedenthal (75) as one of the most poetic of our time and by Kutscher (II, 104) as one of Wedekind's most effective. The latter critic considers the stylistic reasons for this effectiveness in the nature of Nicolo's monologue; this is a combination of tragedy and comedy, wherein his deepest grief evokes laughter, an aspect of romantic self-irony. The form of the scene also contributes to its effectiveness; the chorus provides the prologue and the epilogue in a framework embracing the contents and constituting a play within a play. Kutscher observes further that Elendenkirchweih amounts to a turning point in Nicolo's life. After this time his continued existence is made possible only by pride in his internal royalty; the recollection of his storied success serves as payment for his years of suffering (95). The spookiness of the scene, in which the auditions of entertainers take place under a gallows at night, is emphasized by Ude (88) and Gittleman (89). The name for the scene refers to the dedication of a church for "die Elenden"; and Maclean (29) goes to the etymology of this term, revealing that it refers in its older sense to people who are uprooted or exiled as is Nicolo. These vagrants wander from country to country and meet once a year to be hired, constituting what Maclean terms "the community of the inverted world."

Another favorite scene of the critics is that in which Nicolo recounts before King Pietro the tragic fate of the unrecognized sovereign; this is known as "the king's farce" ("Die Königsposse"). It is, according to Kutscher (II, 97), the high point of the tragedy; the irony of ordinary life and the curse of ridicule break Nicolo's heart.

Pietro appoints Nicolo court jester because the king recognizes Nicolo's wisdom and nobility of mind. When Alma then confirms his royal status, Pietro grants burial in the royal crypt because he feels himself despised (95–96). Burial in the royal crypt constitutes, at least in part, the recognition denied Nicolo in life, Gittleman notes (90). Without a doubt the most peculiar observation made in the secondary literature regarding Nicolo's role as court jester is that of Pickerodt (1984, 6), who submits that Wedekind uses sentimentality and sarcasm in this context to express his regret at the functional change which art is undergoing as it becomes a medium for mass entertainment.

In his comments on the play from 1911, Wedekind writes that *Der Marquis von Keith* was based largely on dialogue and was misunderstood word for word (IX, 430). For that reason, he continues, *Nicolo* is a work in which dialogue is of no importance and every possible misunderstanding is avoided by simplicity and directness. That Wedekind was successful in this regard is not conceded generally. Kutscher (1927) maintains that the dramatist's avowed intention to foster clear simplicity is achieved more successfully in the central character than in the language; Nicolo lacks the dialectic contradiction present in the figure Keith (II, 99); however, the language of *König Nicolo* is more complex and lacks uniformity. The language is cold and matter-of-fact in the first half of the work; thereafter, lines of pathos and pure poetry are followed by those so difficult in their construction that no actor can deliver them (101–2). Völker (1965, 48) observes that despite the author's assertion that the dialogue is of little importance, the work is quite loquacious.

The structural features of the work draw attention from various perspectives. Kapp (1909, 64) notes that this play distinguishes itself from Wedekind's others by its closed dramatic form, and Diebold (1921, 68) is taken by the play within the play represented by the performance for audition at Elendenkirchweih. The employment of numerous scenes and the indistinct division of acts point to a structural technique borrowed from the period of Sturm und Drang, and first employed by Wedekind in *Frühlings Erwachen*, Kutscher notes (II, 98–99). Dramatic unity is achieved by the repetition of motifs; these include the marriage of Alma and Filipo and banishment under the threat of death (103). Without deference to the literary-historical term *baroque* or acknowledgment of the prevalence of such themes during that period, Maclean (1969) describes the dramatic structure in terms of the "classic reversal" of monarch to swineherd and back (21) and the "traditional inversion" whereby master becomes servant and fool becomes king (24). Best (1975, 114) conceptualizes in a more abstract fashion; he perceives that dramatic movement is generated by sustained opposition between the concepts of human dignity and majesty, on the one hand, and the escapism of illusion and fairy tale, on the other.

The work is most prevalently recognized as a fairy tale ("Märchen"), bearing features of romanticism, and perhaps as a tragedy in addition. The early critic Kapp (64) characterizes it as a tragedy as does Fechter (1920, 84), who also supports the prevailing view that it is a fairy tale (87). Observing that Wedekind feels comfortable with romantic melancholy and describing the work as a "romantic self-portrait"

(67–68), Diebold attacks the interpretation of the work as tragedy by noting that the salient features of this mode are missing: Nicolo wavers unsurely between irony and pathos; serious moments become lost in sentiment; and even Pietro vacillates between earnestness and comedy (68–69). The relationship to romanticism is suggested by Elster (1922, 74) in the resemblance of dramatic style to that of the ballad, a form closely associated with that literary period.

Noting the historical and geographical context provided by the background of the Italian Renaissance in 1499 in the Umbrian city of Perugia, Kutscher (1927 II, 96–97) characterizes the work as a tragedy but refuses to limit his choices. He also calls it a fairy tale and notes that a lack of continuity allows months or more than a year to elapse between scenes, a feature of romanticism (102). Considering the historical garb as well, Völker (1965, 48) detects a contradiction since the author is not alluding to any historical personality but himself; this critic aligns himself with the majority, characterizing the work as a lightly sentimental fairy tale with grotesque and highly artistic theatrical effects (48). Historical costume, according to Skrine (1989, 108–9), was a concession to popular theatrical taste at the turn of the century. Moreover, when the work was played during the Third Reich, it lent itself to the ends of what has been termed the "Inner Emigration" by allowing contemporary political figures to be portrayed behind the masks of historical personalities; historical distance prevented censors from identifying Hitler behind the master butcher Pietro and his silenced opponents behind Nicolo. That this observation is speculative is suggested by reference to Seehaus (1964), which fails to confirm a production of *König Nicolo* during the Third Reich.

As befits drama critics who are also literary scholars, the writers place Wedekind's work in a theatrical tradition and indicate that it serves as a precursor for later developments. The movingly tragic final act strikes Kapp (1909, 64) as nearly equal to something by Shakespeare, with lines reminiscent of *Hamlet*. Unlike writers who attempt to create a distance between themselves and their literary figures, as for example Goethe with regard to Torquato Tasso, Wedekind does just the opposite, argues Diebold (1921, 67), writing himself into roles and then putting his ego into costume by playing them. Wedekind does not release himself figuratively into his writing in the process of creation but in fact projects himself from a figure in his work into the auditorium.

The fairy tale suggests to Kutscher (II, 96) the Cinderella drama *Aschenbrödel* (1835) by Christian Friedrich Grabbe (1801–1836) as a possible source of motifs, and *Nicolo* recalls Shakespeare to Dosenheimer (1949, 203) as it does to Kapp. Gittleman (1969, 91) considers the tradition of the "artist's drama," whereby the solitary figure is alienated from a public unable to comprehend artistic truth. While the work reaches back historically to this tradition, it sustains at the same time a pivotal position anticipating the future; Wedekind and Nicolo will be followed by other authors, such as Hanns Johst, Georg Kaiser, and Georg Trakl, who similarly represent the artist giving voice to feelings of isolation and misunderstanding. While Gittleman in his reference to the vein of artist's drama includes by implication those numerous examples from the nineteenth century and before, Irmer (1970, 171) confines his comparison to two authors who treat this theme in the twentieth century, namely Thomas Mann and Hugo von Hofmannsthal.

The prologue in which the audience is bid to look within itself for the dialogue between father and daughter, the petty king and the great fool, is cited by Best (1975, 113) as a technique which foreshadows that to be adopted by Bertolt Brecht. One thinks of the epilogue to *Der gute Mensch von Sezuan* (The Good Woman of Setzuan, 1942), where before the closed curtain the audience is presented with an open ending; spectators are asked to determine how the good person can provide for himself in our society, or as Eric Bentley phrases it, how "to help good men arrive at happy ends."

As *Nicolo* does to Kapp and Dosenheimer, the play recalls Shakespeare to Wagener (1979, 70), and as fourteen years earlier in Ude's interpretation of Alma, *King Lear* comes to mind with Nicolo as the aged father. While Böckmann (1969, 100) argues that Wedekind anticipates the theater of the absurd in his conception of tragicomedy, Mennemeier (1980) submits that the dramatist does so in another respect: Wedekind creates a particular tension characteristic of such theater (especially that of Luigi Pirandello), a dialectic of normality and abnormality in the light of which a figure interacts with society in a manner suggesting madness (363–64).

Nicolo is accorded a place relative to Wedekind's other works. A continuation of the theme of *Lulu* suggests itself to Gittleman in the representation of a predatory society set upon destroying the solitary, wild creature (91). The line of comparison runs between *Nicolo* and *Keith* as far as Dedner (1975, 512) is concerned; he perceives a thematic parallel as both works deal with art, life, and society, or in a translation of his words, "the subjective problematics of the artist in the age of capitalism." The overview of Wagener (71) borrows from Gittleman, changes the proposition slightly by eliminating society as a predator, and applies the generalization to both *Keith* and *Frühlings Erwachen*: Nicolo embodies the person pursued, as was Melchior Gabor, Lulu, and Keith.

Nicolo is also placed in an autobiographical spectrum. Although Fechter (1920, 84) comments upon the prevalence of autobiographical traces in all of Wedekind's works, Kutscher (1927, II, 106) describes the playwright's concern with himself as a weakness and forewarns his reader of subsequent dramas where this deficiency is not overcome and the audience is subjected to Wedekind's complaints and demands. But Gittleman (1969, 88) sees the author's tendency towards autobiography as well under way, having begun much earlier with *Kammersänger* and continuing in *Keith*, *Nicolo*, and then *Hidalla*, as Wedekind moves increasingly towards identifying with the protagonist; the artist shown earlier leading a precarious and energetic life is represented now with irony and almost self-pity.

The merits of the work evoke some difference of opinion among the critics. The early criticism of Kapp (1909) is most generous in its praise. He describes the play as rich in poetic beauty and particularly moving, especially in the first scene of act 3 between father and daughter; this is the best that Wedekind ever wrote, a poem in prose (64). The drama is technically perfect and is, theatrically speaking, eminently presentable. With reduced emphasis upon the courtroom scene, which is flawed, the play lends itself to any theater with literary aspirations and has provided the most valuable productions yielded by recent German literature (71). Fechter (89) is less effusive, characterizing Wedekind's previous dramas as more forceful; the play *Nicolo* reveals the anxiety and weakness that lay beneath the hard cynicism expressed earlier. Agreeing with Kapp that the courtroom scene amounts to caricature, Kutscher parts ways regarding the merits of the work; he selects the courtroom scene as an artistic high point of the drama (II, 103). Although Hill (1960, 87) thinks *Nicolo* ambiguous and contradictory with regard to details, in atmosphere the drama is the most poetic next to *Frühlings Erwachen*, a contention with which Ude (1966, 88) seems to agree. In comparison to *Keith*, *Nicolo* is a step backwards, and a lachrymose one at that, according to Wagener (1979, 71). And, finally, Skrine (1989, 109) describes *Nicolo* as "extravagant neo-Romantic make-believe."

Works Cited

Best, Alan. 1975. *Frank Wedekind*. London: Oswald Wolf.

Blei, Franz. 1914. "Marginalien zu Wedekind." In *Das Wedekindbuch*, edited by Joachim Friedenthal. Munich and Leipzig: Georg Müller. 128–50.

Böckmann, Paul. 1969. "Die komödiantischen Grotesken Frank Wedekinds." In *Das deutsche Lustspiel*. Vol. 2, edited by Hans Steffen. Göttingen: Vandenhoeck & Ruprecht. 79–102.

Dedner, Burghard. 1975. "Intellektuelle Illusionen. Zu Wedekinds *Marquis von Keith*." *Zeitschrift für deutsche Philologie* 94: 498–519.

Diebold, Bernhard. 1972. "Wedekind der Narr." In his *Anarchie im Drama*. New York and London: Johnson Reprint Corporation. 43–76. The work first appeared in 1921.

Dosenheimer, Elise. 1967. *Das deutsche soziale Drama von Lessing bis Sternheim*. Darmstadt: Wissenschaftliche Buchgesellschaft. This first appeared in 1949.

Elster, Hanns Martin. 1922. *Wedekind und seine besten Bühnenwerke*. Berlin and Leipzig: Franz Schneider.

Fechter, Paul. 1920. *Frank Wedekind. Der Mensch und das Werk*. Jena: Lichtenstein.

Friedenthal, Joachim. 1914. "Einleitung." In *Das Wedekindbuch*, edited by Friedenthal. Munich and Leipzig: Georg Müller. 1–121.

Gittleman, Sol. 1969. *Frank Wedekind*. New York: Twayne.

Hill, Claude. 1960. "Wedekind in Retrospect." *Modern Drama* 3.1 (May): 82–92.

Irmer, Hans-Jochen. 1975. *Der Theaterdichter Frank Wedekind. Werk und Wirkung*. Berlin: Henschelverlag. This originally appeared in 1970.

Kapp, Julius. 1909. *Frank Wedekind. Seine Eigenart und seine Werke*. Berlin: Hermann Barsdorf.

Kaufmann, Hans. 1969. "Zwei Dramatiker: Gerhart Hauptmann und Frank Wedekind." In his *Krisen und Wandlungen der deutschen Literatur von Wedekind bis Feuchtwanger*. Berlin and Weimar: Aufbau-Verlag. 47–84.

Kempner, Hans. 1911. *Frank Wedekind als Mensch und Künstler*. Berlin-Pankow: Oskar Linser.

Kutscher, Artur. 1970. *Frank Wedekind. Sein Leben und seine Werke.* Vol. 2. New York: AMS Press. This is a reprint of the edition appearing in 1927.

Maclean, Hector. 1969. "The King and the Fool in Wedekind's *König Nicolo.*" *Seminar* 5.1 (Spring): 21–35.

Mennemeier, Franz Norbert. 1980. "Frank Wedekind." In *Handbuch des deutschen Dramas,* edited by Walter Hinck. Düsseldorf: Bagel. 360–73, 568–69.

Pickerodt, Gerhart. 1984. *Frank Wedekind: Frühlings Erwachen.* Frankfurt am Main, Berlin, and Munich: Diesterweg.

Pissin, Raimund. 1905. *Frank Wedekind.* Berlin: Gose & Tetzlaff.

Seehaus, Günter. 1964. *Frank Wedekind und das Theater.* Munich: Laokoon.

Skrine, Peter. 1989. *Hauptmann, Wedekind, and Schnitzler.* New York: St. Martin's Press.

Spalter, Max. 1967. *Brecht's Tradition.* Baltimore: Johns Hopkins Press.

Ude, Karl. 1966. *Frank Wedekind.* Mühlacker: Stieglitz.

Völker, Klaus. 1965. *Frank Wedekind.* Velber bei Hannover: Friedrich Verlag.

Wagener, Hans. 1979. *Frank Wedekind.* Berlin: Colloquim.

Wedekind, Frank. 1921. "Was ich mir dabei dachte." In *Gesammelte Werke.* Vol. 9. Munich: Georg Müller. 430.

7: *Karl Hetmann, der Zwerg-Riese (Hidalla)* (1904)
A Morality for the Rich and Beautiful

The minigiant Karl Hetmann has developed a new morality dedicated to the rich and the beautiful and represented by the International League for the Propagation of Thoroughbred Humans, for which the ugly, misshapen Hetmann serves as the secretary. He recruits members who abide by the statutes of the league that require members to readily exchange sexual favors. The beautiful Fanny Kettler is a member and loves Hetmann, who cannot belong since he is a cripple; therefore, he feels morally obliged to reject her love.

The businessman Rudolf Launhart, primarily interested in financial gain from the league, publishes Hetmann's article "Love in Middle-class Culture Compared to that of Our Domesticated Animals." When outraged authorities confiscate Launhart's newspaper, he allows the manuscript to fall into the hands of the police, thereby ensuring publicity for the league and a prison term for Hetmann.

Upon release the minigiant finds the movement in disarray and concedes that he was mistaken in thinking that anything was important to the rich but wealth. He declares his opposition to the feudalism of love as embodied in the prostitute expelled by society, the old maid defrauded of her love life, and the untouched young maiden preserved for an advantageous marriage. Inciting his audience with rage in the attempt to provoke it to take his life, Hetmann is frustrated by the outcry of the Grand Master Morosini that the orator is insane. The minigiant begs Fanny to stand by him. Offered employment by the circus as a clown, Hetmann realizes that he is the object of ridicule and hangs himself. Glimpsing one last opportunity for gain, Launhart seizes Hetmann's most recent manuscript for publication.

Most interpretation of the drama *Karl Hetmann, der Zwerg-Riese* (Karl Hetmann, the Dwarf Giant, 1904) centers upon the figure of Hetmann, the nature of his struggle, and his eventual disillusionment. According to Kempner (1911, 64), who endows the goals of the league with an air of seriousness, the play illustrates that the time is not yet propitious for realization of an ideal of beauty such as that of the minigiant. But Friedenthal (1914) overlooks the appropriateness of this character's goals and borrows the terminology of Wedekind to describe him. Employing a reference made by the dramatist to his two central figures in *Keith*, Friedenthal contends that Hetmann demonstrates the German quality of Don Quixote. As long as Hetmann does not know that he is striving against something irresistible, his struggle is comic and grotesque; but when he recognizes impossibility and continues nevertheless, he rises to the level of a spiritual hero (73–74). Considerably less heroism and more resignation are noted in the behavior of Hetmann by other critics.

Dosenheimer (1949) argues that he becomes disillusioned upon realizing that he is not equal to the banality and philistinism which he must endure (205–6). Reveling in vitalism, Rothe (1968, 83) observes that Hetmann proves himself unequal to Life; the attempts to overcome it and change it might have been expected to fail, given the realities of society. And a Marxist nuance is given to this line of interpretation by Hahn (1969 I, 87–88), who asserts that the nature of bourgeois society dictates that ideals such as nature and humanity must be incapable of achievement. A slant only slightly different is assumed by Kesting (1970), who characterizes the new morality as the erotic cult of the beautiful, an ethic ultimately recognized as false and utopian when the world is revealed as unchangeable; therefore the ideas and goals of Hetmann appear as nonsense, and he is left with nothing but his boredom (192–93).

Arntzen (1971) marks a definite shift in the current of interpretation. Employing the term *science* somewhat generously in reference to the aims and ideals of Hetmann, Arntzen argues that the work illustrates how, under the influence of capitalism, science becomes an ideology and commercial interests assume control. Jelavich (1979, 231), too, sees cultural and social values manipulated by the operation of capitalism. And Klotz (1979) merely elaborates on Arntzen; the ideology wrought by capitalism from science is a strange one not readily comprehensible to the public (33). Hetmann's promise to the rich of membership in an elite league reflects the capitalist social order (31), but this elitism is not to be achieved until the rich adapt themselves to the phenomenon of mass entertainment and the marketing techniques of capitalism (36).

Although the play *Karl Hetmann*, or *Hidalla*, is by no means in need of autobiographical interpretation to make it comprehensible, much is made in the critical literature of the correspondence between Hetmann and his creator, especially since Wedekind played the role on stage. Perhaps the least discriminating critic is Kapp (1909), who interprets the work as confessional and Hetmann and his attitudes as a direct reflection of the author. The audience, Kapp submits, is confronted with "candid dilettantism" when Wedekind acts the part in an absolutely natural manner without posing; the dramatist plays out his own fate in a self-ironic caricature before the eyes of spectators (80–81).

Hofmiller (1910) is less charitable, returning to the theme of unrecognized greatness widely perceived in *Nicolo*. The play *Hidalla* illustrates the tenet close to Wedekind's heart that immorality prevails when genius is not rewarded with success (105). The dramatist has successfully deceived his audience for so long that he now believes in Hetmann, the projection of himself, and fools himself (107).

Kempner (1911, 84) describes seeing Wedekind play Hetmann as one of the strongest impressions of his life. Although the performance was not without weaknesses attributable to the technique of oral delivery, the failure to recall lines, and physical clumsiness, Wedekind's acting is not dilettantish, as people like Kapp suggest, and surpasses that of the professionals in versatility, emotion, and force.

Blei (1914, 144–45), too, joins the chorus of critics who characterize the drama as autobiographical, but the very next year in an article, where Wedekind describes his meeting with the actor Josef Kainz, the playwright denies ever putting his own views into the words of a figure in any of his dramas (IX, 373). Fechter (1920), for one, pays the article no heed. Exercising considerably more discernment than Kapp, for example, Fechter indicates just what elements of Hetmann's theory are shared with his author, namely antipathy towards the women's movement, an inclination towards beauty and breeding, and skepticism regarding the value of virginity (97). To this extent the work is a confession of the morality Wedekind once believed in, and fought for, in his dramas (90).

Diebold (1921, 61) and Elster (1922, 83–84) echo Kapp's view that Hetmann is a spokesman for Wedekind's moral precepts, but Kutscher (1927 II, 169–70) contributes more to the debate by focusing upon the element which generates confusion among the critics, that is, Wedekind's peculiar combination of autobiography and self-irony. Both Hetmann and his creator reject the women's movement and oppose the feudalism of love, but the resemblance ends here. Wedekind does not adhere to a theory combining morality with race and beauty; the league and its statutes are intended as parody. Kutscher points out that Wedekind tries to hold Hetmann at a distance from himself by the use of contradiction and paradox: Hetmann's ugliness engenders his hunger for beauty; his physical constraints find compensation in ideology; the poor man founds a morality for the rich.

Such a distinction between autobiography and self-irony is lost on Dosenheimer (1949, 208), who characterizes Hetmann as Wedekind's mouthpiece. But Spalter (1967) and Hahn (1969) recognize that combination pointed out by Kutscher. Spalter suggests that when Wedekind mocks the "messianic zeal" of Hetmann, he is making light of his own struggle against the censors of his expressed sexual attitudes (134). And Hahn interprets the work as confessional in that the author draws an ironic and tragic balance to the goals he had pursued throughout his life (I, 86). Subtlety holds no attraction for Kaufmann (1969), who, in an observation characteristic of Hofmiller, states that the confusion of Hetmann is a direct reflection of Wedekind's own (77).

Gittleman (1969, 92–93) reworks Kutscher, drawing closer the parallels between the character and the author: Hetmann's state of being crippled carries over to Wedekind's limp; both the dramatic figure and his creator reject women's emancipation and repudiate contemporary sexual attitudes. Attempting to refute Kutscher, Gittleman attributes to Wedekind a belief in the morality of physical beauty. Self-irony undercuts, however, both Hetmann and the author: an aggressive, ugly, pathetic being is excluded from his own morality; Wedekind, too, saw himself as a prophet wasting his words before an audience that could not, or would not, hear him and even heaped derision upon him (93–94).

An unexpected turn in the criticism appears in the lines of Wagener (1979), who looks to the motivation of Wedekind. Wagener argues that the playwright presents his views about sexuality, eroticism, and compulsion in an ironic fashion in order to provoke refutation and ridicule (72); this strategy is employed since the playwright wants to represent himself on stage as a tragic prophet (74–75).

Basing her interpretation on an early version of the work, Schröder-Zebralla (1985) argues that Wedekind assumes for himself the role of Christ and employs Hetmann as his messianic mouthpiece for the expression of views regarding virginity and the liberation of sexuality from social convention; this proselytizing is done in the attempt to extend traditional morality and religion (165, 160, 167). Echoing Hahn (1969), Schröder-Zebralla describes the work as a confessional drama in which Wedekind takes stock in a tragically ironic way of his earlier utopian views (159).

The perception of Diethe (1988) is unique in the secondary literature. She maintains that Wedekind shares with Hetmann an ambivalence regarding sexuality. Both the author and his character recognize sexuality for the generating force of physical desire associated with vitalism, but in turn both can view sexuality in a cool, detached manner (107).

What insights do the critics provide into the nature and character of Hetmann? Kapp (1909, 79) finds him comically touching and at the same time loftily idealistic while Diebold (1921, 60) considers the paradox he embodies: he is a giant of the spirit and a dwarf of the body; his appearance as a cripple denies that beauty which he advocates; he represents the idea of a morality transcendent to his own flesh, but he fails to see the absence of spirituality in human bodies that are nothing but beautiful and lustful. Elster (1922, 81) describes Hetmann as a creative moralist, and Kutscher (1927 II, 170) compares him to Christ since he is destined to offer his life. Employing Wedekind's own words used to describe his figures in *Keith*, Völker (1965) characterizes, as did Friedenthal, the minigiant as Scholz merged into the grotesque; Hetmann is a Don Quixote of morality, who seeks greater pleasure in life but fails since he does things backwards (50–51). To Hamann and Hermand (1966), Hetmann with his ironic morality of beauty is the characteristic outsider of the period of impressionism (118); he illustrates the unbridled, aristocratic individualism of the day, bereft of a sense of obligation to others (34–35). Hetmann is seen variously by those around him, Gittleman (1969) observes, as a great prophet, a mad man, and a source for making money (92); it is this latter role which Kesting (1970, 192) focuses upon when she describes him as a tragic fool whose ideas are used for commercial purposes.

Exploring the paradoxical concept of *minigiant* as does Diebold, Irmer (1970) contends that Hetmann's desires and ideas are gigantic, his achievements minimal; he is a perceptive social critic and a narrow utopian thinker (154). The Marxist Irmer describes Hetmann as wise in his criticism of capitalist society and foolish for trusting the representatives of capitalism and his own words, rather than power, to topple this political system (155–56, 172–73). The reader may be led to remark, however, that there is no hint that Hetmann ever harbored this latter goal.

In contrast to Arntzen (1971, 8), who attributes to Hetmann a complex ideology, Rasch (1979) sees a prophet whose doctrine is so insignificant as to amount to no program at all; his doctrine is simply a means to an end (67). It is the role of the prophet which provides self-fulfillment; the sexually repressed Hetmann finds erotic satisfaction in his effect on the masses (65–66); a climax would be achieved in the intoxication of death as a martyr to the fury of a mob (68).

The name Hetmann is derived by Schröder-Zebralla (1985, 164) from the English *headman* and by Vinçon (1987, 218) from the Russian designation for the leader of Cossack troops.

As does Rasch (1979), Diethe occupies herself with Hetmann's sexuality, perceiving a death wish and a streak of masochism which leads him to torment himself both by founding a league he cannot join and by theorizing about sex when he is terrified of it and probably impotent (106–7). Less concerned with Hetmann as a dirty old man, Skrine (1989, 105) notes his "sardonic humor tinged with pathos." And Dowden's (1992, 260) interpretation of Hetmann as a deformed dwarf, "Wedekind's image of the alienated artist in late-nineteenth-century Germany," is absolutely unique.

Fanny brings suit to gain Hetmann's favor, and Fechter (1920, 97) establishes the precedent that subsequent interpretation follows when he argues that Fanny is partially successful, causing a distant belief in the possibility of love to dislodge Hetmann's obsession with his moral system.

Diebold (1921) has never been one to concede Wedekind's contention that the flesh has its own spirit, and the critic employs this context to point out that Wedekind's hated dichotomy of spirit and flesh persists and prevails. When the beautiful Fanny Kettler offers herself to the ugly dwarf, his spiritual beauty and idealism have exerted an appeal upon her that overcomes the appearance of his repugnant flesh, including Wedekindean spirit and all (61).

Articulating an idea more appropriately applied to *Der Kammersänger*, Elster (1922) interprets Hetmann's rejection of Fanny's love as an expression of Wedekind's personal belief that the poet, for the sake of his art, may not aspire to such happiness. If this reading of the play seems inaccurate, it is rivaled only by that of Dosenheimer (1949, 206), in her vitalistic interpretation. She argues that the most tragic aspect of the work lies in Hetmann's abandonment of his beliefs in response to Fanny's love; he allows the victory of Life over principle and succumbs to resignation. In the light of Dosenheimer's perception of Hetmann's surrender, it is ironic that Völker (1965, 50) finds the source of Fanny's love for Hetmann in those ideological convictions for which he would throw away his life. Fanny has beauty, spiritual qualities, and intellect; and it is the latter that dictates her disassociation from the membership, according to Schröder-Zebralla (1985, 163); like Mary Magdalene she throws herself at the feet of the messiah Hetmann (180). A degree of masochism is detected in Fanny's love for Hetmann by Diethe (1988, 104), and his acceptance of her suggestion that he should have a group of young girls as playmates for diversion evidences his hypocrisy regarding reform as it does hers in regards to feminism (105–6).

The plot line dealing with Rudolf Launhart is a version of the author's experience with the publisher Albert Langen, whom Wedekind never forgave when poems about the Kaiser earned a prison term for him and increased sales and publicity for *Sim-*

plicissimus. Emphasizing Launhart's cowardice and faithlessness, Pissin (1905, 40) notes that on six occasions he feigns concern for his wife in order to extricate himself from some difficult situation.

The figure of the speculator and cunning businessman is exaggeration amounting to caricature, yet a comparison to another dramatic figure of Wedekind, who is more credible, suggests itself: Launhart has something in common with Keith. Kapp (1909) notes that both are rascals, but Launhart is a scoundrel for whom nothing is too low, and Keith is a gentleman and aristocrat among swindlers (79–80). Friedenthal (1914, 69) echoes Kapp's characterization of Launhart as a lower form of Keith. And Kutscher (1927 II, 170–72) explains the differences in the two characters by the historical personalities that stood as models: Willy Grétor inspired Keith, and since Wedekind regarded Grétor with sympathy, Keith became an ironic figure; Albert Langen stood behind Launhart, on the other hand, and because Wedekind felt aversion for Langen, this character is an angry caricature. Both figures are unscrupulous, egoistic, cynical, and lucky; but Keith is ingenious and an aristocrat of the spirit; and Launhart is a cunning, petty businessman and philistine (171). Both figures avail themselves of the witty or cutting quip, Gittleman (1969) points out, but Keith is Wedekind's "last sympathetic capitalist," and Launhart is a "villainous moneymaker" (94).

Launhart and Hetmann are considered in relation to each other. Irmer (1970, 154) notes that the moralist is a tool in the hands of the businessman and borrows without acknowledgment Faesi's observation (1956, 253) that idealism falls victim to cynically brutal selfishness. Launhart is the manipulator of capital who, unlike Hetmann, realistically appraises his situation in commercial society, argues Arntzen (1971, 14). Nef (1979) seizes upon this ability of realistic appraisal to define Launhart as the "Insider" in comparison to the "Outsider" Hetmann, whose ideology is brought into conformance with society by Launhart's adjustments for profit (52–53). Launhart's triumph is emphasized by Klotz (1979, 36–37) and Stewart (1985–86, 72).

In the final scene, director of the circus Cotrelly, who bears old-fashioned ("altfränkisch") Mephistophelian facial features, offers Hetmann employment as a clown. When the director's words cause the minigiant to convulse as if from an electric shock, Cotrelly asks him to repeat this effective gesture. Since Hetmann does not know why the public laughs at him, Cotrelly maintains that he will surpass the chimpanzee which sings the C major scale as a circus attraction. This insult drives Hetmann to hang himself.

When Kapp (1909, 76) terms the scene a moving, dramatic accomplishment, he effectively sets the tone for the criticism to follow. Kempner (1911, 64) describes the scene as tragically gruesome, the most tragically gruesome scene Wedekind ever wrote, and Diebold (1921, 66) calls it comically gruesome, the grotesqueness of which lies in its negation of dignity and self-worth. Kutscher preserves a minor theme in Wedekind's writing when the critic suggests that Hetmann's convulsion is occasioned by the insight into the curse of his ridiculousness; this convulsion is comparable to the cry of a creature mortally wounded. The demonic Cotrelly scorns Hetmann to death in a scene which Kutscher calls the most artistically valuable aspect of the work (II, 166, 170, 173).

The metaphor of the circus is extended to the sphere of the entire work by Irmer, who suggests that Hetmann has played the clown in a world which is a circus and of which Cotrelly is the director (153). Cotrelly represents the world of capitalism as well as a Mephistophelian aspect or feature of Hetmann; when Hetmann refuses the director's offer, he is ruined by capitalism as well as by himself (202).

Neither Arntzen (1971) nor Klotz (1979) are too proud to help themselves generously to a portion of Irmer's thinking, without bothering to give credit. Arntzen argues that Hetmann confronts himself in Cotrelly, and a monologue ensues (20). The element of Mephisto suggests a pact with the devil, circumstances which are not mythical but suggest that Hetmann stands in an irrevocable relationship to the circus world of society that can be terminated only by death (21). Similarly, Klotz argues that Cotrelly serves as an alter ego of Hetmann, who appears as a vision to turn him upon himself; the offer of employment as a clown causes Hetmann to realize he has always played this role in the circus of bourgeois capitalist society (39–40).

At least Stewart (1985–86, 71) is original, if tentative and unsure of himself. He asserts that the metaphor of the circus used heretofore in the author's writing to suggest vitalism is now called into question by distortion when associated with Cotrelly; the aspect of Mephistopheles causes Hetmann to be reflected by contrast as a "pathetic Faust-figure." His convulsion at the moment of insight into his ridiculousness amounts to an enhancement of his qualifications for the position as clown, to which Stewart comments, "a nice touch this."

Diethe (1988, 107) observes, with considerable inaccuracy, that the suicide of Hetmann is generally seen as precipitated by the Mephistophelian aspects of Cotrelly and his suggestion that Hetmann become a clown. She suggests further that the suicide provides both escape from a promise to consummate his love for Fanny and refuge after the collapse of his reform plans and the loss of his voyeuristic pleasure in the mating of members of the league. The full measure of what Diebold refers to as the negation of dignity and self-worth in this scene is expressed with regard to Hetmann's convulsions when Skrine (1989) writes that the minigiant is "seared to the core by the implicit equation between himself, an ugly little human being with noble aspirations, and an ape with the ability to mimic a man"(106).

What accounts for Hetmann's failure? The critics look by turn to Hetmann's audience and the dwarf giant himself. Pissin (1905) maintains that Hetmann's idealism is defeated by stupidity, meanness, and intrigue within the league (23). Kapp (1909), on the other hand, faults Hetmann for acting wrongly and fanatically in the belief that he is able to surmount all (72). The immaturity of the masses and the lack of understanding thereof are cited by Kempner (1911, 63). Kutscher (1927), in turn, focuses on the central figure; Hetmann is wrong in thinking that he is normal, that he does not love Fanny, and that his ideas are correct; he does not fail because of his convictions, however, but because of his intolerable ridiculousness as a dwarf giant (II, 169). Dosenheimer (1949) places the blame on those about Hetmann, noting the inferiority of his supporters, the narrow-mindedness of the opposition, and the crudeness of the mob (206).

The attitudes expressed by Rothe (1968) and Hahn (1969) are quite original. The former considers aspects usually associated with Cotrelly and addresses himself to the nature of Mephistopheles; his attitudes are described as arbitrary, and Hetmann's failure is attributed to the arbitrary application of his ideology to others (82). Hahn contends that, like Hetmann, Wedekind applied ideological and utopian concepts to his contemporary world and saw that antibourgeois attitudes and vitalism had failed (I, 86).

Hetmann is caught in a tension between abstract reflection and blind activity, according to Arntzen (1971, 14). His ideology consists of a syncretism of various views which tend to be contradictory (8). Based on these ideas, Hetmann interprets social reality arbitrarily and unrealistically, argues Arntzen (13) as did Rothe before him.

Hetmann, according to Best (1975), is a victim of "misplaced selflessness" since he serves an organization from which he is excluded (54). In the views of Rasch (1979, 65) and Schröder-Zebralla (1985, 185), Hetmann's failure stems from his relationship with Fanny and his inability to unite the spirit and the flesh. Carrying to its limits a minor theme in Wedekind, Schröder-Zebralla argues that Hetmann puts too much emphasis on the mind, thereby sublimating his sexuality; his sacrificial death becomes a spiritual act of erotic satisfaction akin to the concept of *Liebestod* (174–75).

At an early date Kapp (1909, 78) notes the influence of Nietzsche in Hetmann's attitudes and theories. The philosopher's concepts are applied in the statutes of the league to physical aspects of the human being and to breeding, observes Friedenthal (1914, 70), and Hahn (I, 86) specifically emphasizes Nietzsche's antibourgeois attitudes. Rasch strikes a parallel between the men and their thought: sickly and unstable, Nietzsche affirmed Life and the will to power and served as the model for Hetmann, ugly, crippled, and dedicated to human beauty. Moreover, the content of Zarathustra's doctrine is reflected in the concept of voluntary death (60–61). The motif of insanity, the idea of a prophet before his time, and the theory of the superman suggest themselves to Wagener (1979, 74), but Vinçon (1987) reminds the reader that Hetmann is a parody of Zarathustra or Nietzsche himself (217).

Goldmann (1908) is the first to address Hetmann's eugenics, and the critic's nose becomes worked severely out of joint. He describes Hetmann's theories as ridiculous (103); freeing beautiful people from morality will not guarantee the reproduction of more beautiful children, Goldmann snorts (104); only moral procreation promotes the reproduction of beautiful babies (105). Moreover, the laws of heredity defy prediction (107). Characteristically, Kutscher (1927) is more scholarly and detached; he simply identifies the sources of racism and eugenics in the thought of Willibald Hentschel and Karl Immermann (II, 167).

Postwar criticism is neither puritanical like Goldmann nor aloof like Kutscher: Hitler comes to mind. Rasch (1979) finds a parallel in Hetmann's compulsive need to evoke a response from the masses; this serves as compensation for personal failure and social humiliation. Josef Goebbels with his club foot links the cripple Hetmann with Launhart, the propagator of information (65). Assuming a historical view, Rasch recalls that a social phenomenon contemporary to Wedekind consisted of prophets of various kinds who developed the master-disciple relationship among their adherents. Wedekind illustrates how the phenomenon may be commercialized and exploited (62), and it lasted long enough to produce Hitler (72). Since Hitler's time, Arntzen (1971) suggests, it is no longer possible to find the name of the league funny (18); parallels to the dictator suggest themselves in the power of public oratory and the enlistment of members, Hetmann's charismatic effect upon women, his abstinence from alcohol, and sexual continence (19).

Rasch and Arntzen do not take the subject lightly, but the American Chick (1984, 36) is less earnest. Citing that historical figure mentioned by Kutscher, Chick emphasizes that Wedekind is ridiculing prophets like Willibald Hentschel, who advocated eugenics to achieve a super-race. The dramatist illustrates that eugenicists, like everyone else, may be impelled by selfish hedonism to employ *Realpsychologie*—what Chick describes as anti-idealistic power psychology or applied egoism.

Postwar Europeans such as Rasch and Arntzen remain wary. Vinçon (218–19) sees a political propagandist and prophet who embodies prejudices and employs mass psychology in a way that prefigures Hitler. And the Englishman Skrine (1989) hears ideological overtones, "disturbing prophetic implications" for the Nuremberg race laws of 1935, in "this ugly little man's incongruous obsession with thoroughbred racial purity" (107).

Various features of the work, such as dialogue and structure, receive particular attention. Pissin (1905) considers the antithetical manner in which the play is constructed; it reflects the ridiculous coexistence of the tragic and comic in life; it illustrates the fusion of the essential and the insignificant in everyday reality. Pissin describes the humor of the work as grotesque and cynical (41). Goldmann (1908), on the other hand, denies Wedekind any humor whatsoever; the dramatist has no satiric intent. What the public takes to be the dramatist's satiric humor is unintentionally funny; one laughs at the distortion of an inept writer (101–2). The dialogue, moreover, is language from the printed page, or literature, not sentences which are spoken. The figures pronounce monologues, talking right by each other rather than in a responsive fashion (109). Hofmiller (1910), too, faults the dialogue, describing it as inartistic and undramatic (102) and calling it a monster of bloodless abstraction and dry didacticism (105). The language of the drama, in the view of Kutscher (1927 II, 174), lacks uniformity; it follows in tone, rhythm, and rapidity the moods of Hetmann, sometimes becoming quite abstract as, for example, in his reference to a woman's chastity as "idolization of self-contempt" ("Vergötterung der Selbstverachtung") (IV, 253).

Klotz (1979) concerns himself with both imagery and dramatic form when he borrows an idea from Irmer (1970, 153) and posits a *Circus mundi* about which Wedekind creates his play; the metaphor of the circus reflects the turbulent arena of society where individuals jostle each other for gain in the free market. Klotz infuses this metaphor with concepts borrowed from economics, vitalism, and Nietzschean thought (26, 28). Analogous to the *Theatrum mundi* of the medieval and baroque periods, the concept of the Circus mundi is, however, clearly distinguishable in a manner which Klotz fails to acknowledge since it is not ordered by a divine power with individuals in their designated roles according to a hierarchical system which reinforces the status quo. The critic does point to an anachronistic fallacy in the analogy between the economic marketplace and the circus since capitalism by the late nineteenth century had already reached the monopoly stage, and those days had been left far behind when the daring, heroic individual could demonstrate his initiative (27).

As does Kutscher, Stewart (1985–86) considers the language of the work and concludes that the dialogue lacks "vitality" and bears a "heavy and laboured quality" (72).

According to the prevailing view, the play is a tragicomedy. Although Goldmann (103) will not concede that the work is the tragedy of a genius as the author thinks, in Kapp's mind (1909, 71) it is a genuine tragedy. Hofmiller refuses to allow himself to be pinned down; the work presents a grotesque variety including comic and circus amusement, philosophy, and psychological character sketches (105–6). This tragicomedy attains its climax, in the opinion of Friedenthal (1914, 72), when Grand Master Morosini publicly declares Hetmann insane. It is the tragicomedy, writes Völker (1965, 49), of a moral prophet, who wants to bless the world with happiness since he deeply despises this very world. Kesting (1970, 193) concurs, and Irmer (154) submits that the combination of tragic and comic aspects creates a ghastly joke. Considering the remark of Kutscher (II, 175) that characters enter and leave the stage like doves to and from a cote, Arntzen (1971, 12) characterizes the drama as one of amusement and comic situations ("ein Boulevardstück"). Best (1975, 40) points out that Hetmann's league promotes what its members already have, namely health and beauty; the members therefore are engaged in self-justification and the pursuit of their own self-interest under the guise of social progress. To the extent that this attitude reflects that of contemporary social movements, the work constitutes satire.

In the attempt to gain the attention of the audience, Wedekind distorts traditional dramatic concepts, Klotz (1979, 32) contends. The subtitle "drama in five acts" arouses expectation in the audience of the traditional closed form with the unities of space, time, and development as well as Gustav Freytag's prescription for exposition, rising action, climax, and so on. Far from traditional, the play in its treatment of Hetmann's program for a more beautiful race constitutes a parody of the drama constructed about a central concept or principle ("Ideendrama").

The literary tradition in which *Hidalla* is to be considered is first suggested by Hamann and Hermand (1966). They address the change undergone by the concept of free love since the literary historical period of naturalism when it was associated with female emancipation. In this work it is understood as unrestricted enjoyment of membership in a cult of Priapus tending, however ironically, towards the orgiastic (40).

Observing that Hidalla is the name given the central figure in Wedekind's novel fragment *Mine-Haha*, Hahn (1969) traces the origin of the name to *The Works of Ossian* (1765) by James Macpherson (I, note 715); Hahn is here referring specifically to the English language edition and not a German translation, and the title and date he provides are not entirely accurate.

In the eyes of Jelavich (1979, 232) Wedekind is guilty of a distortion of classical values which demonstrate that beautiful people are created by aesthetic education, not by physical breeding; the author casts a grotesque light upon the ideal of "a new ethical wholeness based upon sensual and spiritual fulfillment."

The literary tradition of the prophet at the turn of the century is outlined by Rasch (1979) in works by Gerhart Hauptmann, Thomas Mann, Carl Sternheim, Alfred Döblin, and Hugo von Hofmannsthal (60). Nef (1979) suggests another figure from literary history, namely the hero or central figure who represents a moral and ideological view; he is familiar since the time of Henrik Ibsen and appears here for the first time in the corpus of Wedekind's works (48).

The critics likewise consider the heritage of Wedekind left to his successors. When Hetmann comes to the conclusion that the rich would sacrifice their lives for their wealth, rather than vice versa, Dosenheimer (1949) identifies a satirical characterization of the bourgeoisie which returns in works by Georg Kaiser and Carl Sternheim (208). Mockery of bourgeois values is an attitude that Spalter (1967), too, singles out together with cynicism, emphasis on animal instinct, and antisentimentalism which fell to the share of Bertolt Brecht (135).

Gittleman (1969, 93) points out that Keith, Nicolo, and Hetmann are all accused of being insane; and in these respective dramas Wedekind becomes the first German writer to make the insane asylum "a major motif" in his work. This tradition will be followed by Erich Maria Remarque, Peter Weiss, Friedrich Dürrenmatt, and Günter Grass among others (144, note 10).

Dürrenmatt's *Die Ehe des Herrn Mississippi* (The Marriage of Mr. Mississippi, 1952) extends, Kesting (1970) notes, Wedekind's conception of an ideal which is relegated to human Don Quixotism by the economic and technical influences of society (193–94).

And the connection to Brecht is taken up again by Höger (1979) in reference to *Der aufhaltsame Aufstieg des Arturo Ui* (The Resistible Rise of Arturo Ui, 1942), the parody of Hitler as the gangster Al Capone in Chicago (177, note 61).

Hidalla enjoys a mixed reception among the critics. Pissin (1905, 23) remarks carefully that it is by no means Wedekind's most significant work, but it does mark a new step in the development of that irony with which the author confronted life. Goldmann (1908) is more explicit: the work is boring and confused (97); the figures are lifeless and without form; a lack of taste is evident in making a human stud farm the subject of drama (108–9). Citing a lack of clarity in *Hidalla*, its stilted quality, and its absurdity, Kapp (1909) quotes another critic in a way as to suggest that he agrees with that person's description of the work as a mixture of originality and ineptitude (81). Hofmiller (1910) calls the drama the most well constructed and clearly closed of all Wedekind's works (103); nevertheless, the acts conclude in an undramatic manner (105), reinforcing the impression that the author is unskilled as an artist and dramatist (102).

The first positive words are those of none other than Fechter (1920), who demonstrates that he is not afraid to go out on a limb; he writes that as an expression of human suffering the drama is perhaps Wedekind's most moving work (96). And Elster (1922), pointing out that the characters are fully rounded and developed, says that it belongs among Wedekind's best (82). However, Kutscher (1927) takes issue specifically with Fechter and impliedly with Elster with the assertion that the figures are not independent, human characters, but marionettes (II, 271).

Rothe (1968) sides with Fechter and Elster, describing *Hidalla* as one of the author's great dramas (83), and Kaufmann (1969, 77) calls it "moving." Viewing this drama against the backdrop of Wedekind's other works, Stern (1979) finds it marks a transition from the author's utopianism to the sarcastic resignation of his later plays (4). Ever mindful of the Christian implications of Wedekind's work, Schröder-Zebralla (1985) hails *Hidalla* as evidence of a turning point where the author's interest moves from sensuality to spirituality in the attempted synthesis of the spirit and the flesh (161). And Boa (1987), being the political animal she is, finds it "typically ambivalent"; eugenics is presented as a solution, but it fails; opposition is expressed towards a double moral standard and male oppression of women, but female intellectuality is only partially accepted; and political feminism is rejected (186). Skrine (1989) concludes upbeat with his reference to the drama's "verve, grotesque humor and ludicrous yet grippingly moving *dénouement*" (108).

How does *Hidalla* stand in relation to Wedekind's other works? The morality of beauty is a theme which is also treated in Wedekind's *Mine-Haha*, Kapp (71) observes. Moreover, *Hidalla* preserves a thematic continuity from *Nicolo* perceived by a number of critics: Kempner (1911) points out that the prominent central figure in each case is revealed as a fool (64); Fechter (1920) notes that both pieces focus upon a character who complains about his failure with bitter scorn; on the other hand, like Gerardo in *Kammersänger*, Hetmann is a slave to his calling and bound by dedication to a mission which denies him the life and love others enjoy (96). Elster joins *Nicolo* and *Hidalla* by the theme of unrecognized greatness (81) and Kutscher the two plays by the treatment of the fool who dies from the curse of ridiculousness; *Keith* also suggests itself to Kutscher in the figure of the crippled outsider who contends with bourgeois society (II, 160).

The parallels between *Nicolo* and *Hidalla* are emphasized by both Dosenheimer (1949) and Faesi (1956), the former since struggle in both cases results in disappointment and resignation (207) and Faesi because he notes a transition: the central figure is no longer disguised but actively engaged, the subject no longer of self-pity but self-irony; as a consequence *Hidalla* is more moving (251).

In the view of Gittleman (1969) the four plays *Kammersänger, Keith, Nicolo,* and *Hidalla* provide "one of the most complete autobiographical statements to be found in all of German literature" (96). Nevertheless, Hetmann is more closely identifiable with Wedekind than the central figures in the other plays (93). The tragic fault of Dühring in *Kammersänger* as well as of Nicolo and Hetmann lies in the excessive seriousness with which they regard themselves, and Keith is almost guilty of this. This shortcoming conceals a virtue, however; the figures demonstrate "exaggerated pathos" that prevents the confessional plays from becoming "morbid expressions of a self-pitying artist" (96).

Gittleman asserts further that Keith, Nicolo, and Hetmann all assume the role of the clown, however briefly, and that this accounts for the tragedy befalling the latter two (93). There is a similarity between them and Dühring in their obstinate dedication to their cause at the risk of the curse of ridicule.

Hidalla is evaluated by Irmer (1970) relative to the *Lulu* tragedy and to *Keith*, and he finds *Hidalla* no match since it rivals the others only in the figure of Hetmann and in the final two scenes (151).

Wagener (1979, 72) stresses the connection to *Nicolo* because the king is appointed a fool and Hetmann is to be employed as a clown; in both works the author appears autobiographically as the misunderstood prophet who becomes ridiculous. Further, the link to *Keith* is noted in the theme of the individual versus society and the handicap of Keith's limp is compared with Hetmann's ugliness. Wagener overlooks the fact that Hetmann, too, is a cripple.

Works Cited

Arntzen, Helmut. 1979. "Der Ideologe als Angestellter." In *Viermal Wedekind*, edited by Karl Pestalozzi and Martin Stern. Stuttgart: Klett. 7–21. This first appeared in 1971.

Best, Alan. 1975. *Frank Wedekind*. London: Oswald Wolf.

Blei, Franz. 1914. "Marginalien zu Wedekind." In *Das Wedekindbuch*, edited by Joachim Friedenthal. Munich and Leipzig: Georg Müller. 128–50.

Boa, Elizabeth. 1987. *The Sexual Circus. Wedekind's Theatre of Subversion*. Oxford: Blackwell.

Chick, Edson M. 1984. "Frank Wedekind and his *Lulu* Tragedy." In his *Dances of Death. Wedekind, Brecht, Dürrenmatt, and the Satiric Tradition*. Columbia, South Carolina: Camden House. 11–45.

Diebold, Bernhard. 1972. "Wedekind der Narr." In his *Anarchie im Drama*. New York and London: Johnson Reprint Corporation. 43–76. The work first appeared in 1921.

Diethe, Carol. 1988. *Aspects of Distorted Sexual Attitudes in German Expressionist Drama*. New York, Bern, Frankfurt am Main, and Paris: Lang.

Dosenheimer, Elise. 1967. *Das deutsche soziale Drama von Lessing bis Sternheim*. Darmstadt: Wissenschaftliche Buchgesellschaft. This first appeared in 1949.

Dowden, Steve. 1992. "Frank Wedekind." In *Twentieth Century German Dramatists, 1889–1918*, edited by Wolfgang Elfe and James Hardin. Dictionary of Literary Biography

118. Detroit and London: Gale. 252–63.

Elster, Hanns Martin. 1922. *Wedekind und seine besten Bühnenwerke*. Berlin and Leipzig: Franz Schneider.

Faesi, Robert. 1956. "Ein Vorläufer: Frank Wedekind." In *Expressionismus. Gestalten einer literarischen Bewegung*, edited by Hermann Friedmann and Otto Mann. Heidelberg: Rothe. 241–63.

Fechter, Paul. 1920. *Frank Wedekind. Der Mensch und das Werk*. Jena: Lichtenstein.

Friedenthal, Joachim. 1914. "Einleitung." In *Das Wedekindbuch*, edited by Friedenthal. Munich and Leipzig: Georg Müller. 1–121.

Gittleman, Sol. 1969. *Frank Wedekind*. New York: Twayne.

Goldmann, Paul. 1908. *"Hidalla."* In his *Vom Rückgang der deutschen Bühne*. Frankfurt am Main: Rütten & Loening. 97–110.

Hahn, Manfred. 1969. "Frank Wedekind. Leben und Werk." In *Frank Wedekind. Dramen I*. Berlin and Weimar: Aufbau-Verlag. 7–93.

Hamann, Richard and Jost Hermand. 1966. *Impressionismus*. Berlin: Akademie-Verlag.

Hofmiller, Josef. 1910. "Wedekind." In *Zeitgenossen*. Munich: Süddeutsche Monatshefte. 88–131.

Höger, Alfons. 1979. *Frank Wedekind. Der Konstruktivismus als schöpferische Methode*. Königstein: Scriptor.

Irmer, Hans-Jochen. 1975. *Der Theaterdichter Frank Wedekind. Werk und Wirkung*. Berlin: Henschelverlag. This originally appeared in 1970.

Jelavich, Peter. 1979. "Art and Mammon in Wilhelmine Germany: The Case of Frank Wedekind." *Central European History* 12: 203–36.

Kapp, Julius. 1909. *Frank Wedekind. Seine Eigenart und seine Werke*. Berlin: Hermann Barsdorf.

Kaufmann, Hans. 1969. "Zwei Dramatiker: Gerhart Hauptmann und Frank Wedekind." In his *Krisen und Wandlungen der deutschen Literatur von Wedekind bis Feuchtwanger*. Berlin and Weimar: Aufbau-Verlag. 47–84.

Kempner, Hans. 1911. *Frank Wedekind als Mensch und Künstler*. Berlin-Pankow: Oskar Linser.

Kesting, Marianne. 1970. "Frank Wedekind." In her *Entdeckung und Destruktion*. Munich: Fink. 189–203.

Klotz, Volker. 1979. "Wedekinds Circus mundi." In *Viermal Wedekind*, edited by Karl Pestalozzi and Martin Stern. Stuttgart: Klett. 22–47.

Kutscher, Artur. 1970. *Frank Wedekind. Sein Leben und seine Werke*. Vol. 2. New York: AMS Press. This is a reprint of the edition appearing in 1927.

Nef, Ernst. 1979. "Der betrogene Betrüger wider Willen." In *Viermal Wedekind*, edited by Karl Pestalozzi and Martin Stern. Stuttgart: Klett. 48–59.

Pissin, Raimund. 1905. *Frank Wedekind*. Berlin: Gose & Tetzlaff.

Rasch, Wolfdietrich. 1979. "Das Schicksal des Propheten." In *Viermal Wedekind*, edited by Karl Pestalozzi and Martin Stern. Stuttgart: Klett. 60–73.

Rothe, Friedrich. 1968. *Frank Wedekinds Dramen. Jugendstil und Lebensphilosophie*. Stuttgart: Metzler.

Schröder-Zebralla, Josephine. 1985. *Frank Wedekinds religiöser Sensualismus. "Die Vereinigung von Kirche und Freudenhaus?"* Frankfurt am Main, Bern, and New York: Lang.

Skrine, Peter. 1989. *Hauptmann, Wedekind, and Schnitzler*. New York: St. Martin's Press.

Spalter, Max. 1967. *Brecht's Tradition*. Baltimore: Johns Hopkins Press.

Stern, Martin. 1979. "Begleitwort." In *Viermal Wedekind,* edited by Karl Pestalozzi and Martin Stern. Stuttgart: Klett. 4–6.

Stewart, Corbet. 1985–86. "Comedy, Morality and Energy in the Work of Wedekind." *Publications of the English Goethe Society,* n.s., 56: 56–73.

Vinçon, Hartmut. 1987. *Frank Wedekind.* Stuttgart: Metzler.

Völker, Klaus. 1965. *Frank Wedekind.* Velber bei Hannover: Friedrich Verlag.

Wagener, Hans. 1979. *Frank Wedekind.* Berlin: Colloquim.

Wedekind, Frank. 1921. "Begegnung mit Josef Kainz." In *Gesammelte Werke.* Vol. 9. Munich: Georg Müller. 371–74.

———. 1921. "Was ich mir dabei dachte." In *Gesammelte Werke.* Vol. 9. Munich: Georg Müller. 431.

8: *Tod und Teufel* (1906)
The Celebration of Sensuality
Concludes in Disaster

The procurer Casti-Piani converses in a bordello with Elfriede von Malchus of The International League for the Prevention of Prostitution, who seeks to free Lisiska from his clutches. The advantage of women lies in their ability to sell their favors on the open market, Casti-Piani argues, promoting woman's rights by reinforcing prostitution with capitalism; the opponents of prostitution would deny women their only advantage in male-dominated society. Won over completely by his persuasion, Elfriede offers herself in marriage, an institution Casti-Piani denounces as a convention whereby the male exercises his dominance and strengthens his economic position; monogamy stands for the victory of private property rights; pure sensual joy is to be found only in the free market.

To prove his contention Casti-Piani invites Elfriede to observe with him from concealment the reception by Lisiska of her patron, the poet König. In her arms he seeks spiritual as well as physical satisfaction and will write poetry for the world about the sorrow of sold love. Lisiska reveals that she finds neither joy nor satisfaction in sexual intercourse and begs to be abused and tormented.

The two hidden spectators are astounded as they witness just the opposite of what they had expected. Elfriede is transported by the example of Lisiska's martyrdom and wants to be sacrificed on the altar of sensual love. Casti-Piani, aghast at such a revelation of human suffering and the absence of sensual pleasure, kills himself.

The early critic Kapp (1909) refuses to accept *Tod und Teufel* (Death and Devil, 1906) as the signal of a change in Wedekind's views regarding unrestrained indulgence in sensual pleasure; the work is a reflection of the author's momentary mood (84–85). And as if to confirm this opinion, Wedekind voices his plea for more liberal attitudes towards sexuality in a lecture the following year delivered as an introduction to the drama. This appeared as "Aufklärungen" (Clarifications) in 1910 and was later reprinted as "Über Erotik" (Concerning Eroticism). Here Wedekind expresses his contention that the flesh has its own spirit ("Das Fleisch hat seinen eigenen Geist." [IX, 384]).

But Fechter (1920) takes the drama as a very serious autobiographical confession of the dramatist's change of heart (63). Together with *Frühlings Erwachen* and the *Lulu* tragedy, the work contributes to Wedekind's general treatment of sexuality, lust, and compulsion (59). The audience is granted an insight into the horror of carnal desire that is satiable only in death (63), a conclusion so negative that by comparison that of the *Lulu* tragedy reflects rosy optimism (59).

The remarks of Wedekind himself published in 1921 as "What I Was Thinking about at the Time" do not suggest that the insights of Casti-Piani are those of the author (IV, 432), but Kutscher (1927) looks to Fechter and confirms the precedent which will prevail in the secondary literature: the drama marks a revision of the author's earlier vitalistic sexual attitudes, and in this regard the play may be considered a companion piece to *Hidalla* (II, 234). Disillusionment and revision, especially regarding Wedekind's attitudes towards the joys of prostitution, are noted by Faesi (1956, 225); Sokel (1966) describes the tragic demise of Wedekind's belief in the pleasures of erotic satisfaction and a growing recognition that sexual release must involve pain and ultimately death (202–3). The playwright recognizes as groundless his "dream of a world liberated by erotic radicalism," according to Spalter (1967, 181); the Marxist Kaufmann (1969) asserts that it is an illusion basic to (capitalist) society that one is able to achieve freedom from bourgeois conventions through sensuality (78).

A bold attempt is made to save Wedekind from the charge of revisionism by Rasch (1969), who singles out the site of the erotic transaction; the brothel emphasizes the commercial aspect which effectively reduces sensual pleasure to a commodity; the work is interpreted, therefore, not as a rejection of sensuality itself, but of commercial sex (422). That "nihilistic alienation" conveyed to Gittleman (1969, 100) sustains the majority view, and Kesting (1970) attempts to distinguish herself from Rasch by arguing that the play devalues eroticism itself as a refuge, whether commercial or not. Striking a parallel to *Hidalla* without referring to this work, Kesting interprets *Tod und Teufel* as the proclamation of a new morality which is recognized as false (192–93).

In attempting to get at the message of the play, the critics tend to single out language and behavior of one particular character, Casti-Piani, Lisiska, or even Elfriede. A more responsive feeling for the range of the work is conveyed by a view embracing all characters and the balance which is achieved as these figures change sides in opposition to one another and to the prevailing opinion of a single voice. Kalcher (1980) most closely assumes this approach. Agreeing with Sokel (203) that the play amounts to neither a thesis nor a drama of characters and rejecting the argument of Rasch that the work expresses social criticism, Kalcher emphasizes vitalism (307). Each character desires to understand Life or sexuality, and this is revealed as contradictory, paradoxical, dynamic, and diverse—so complex that it defies coherence (403).The work represents a battle between Life (sexuality) and Death (308), a generalization which Kalcher might have extended to *Frühlings Erwachen* and the *Lulu* tragedy.

Accepting the argument of Sokel (202–3) that eros in *Lulu* is cruel and unappeasable and in *Tod und Teufel* is painful, Willeke (1980) unaccountably conflates the dramas creating an identity between Lulu and Lisiska since both embody a female principle "revealed to be masochistic at its core" (29).

Influenced apparently by the words of Kalcher and employing a term usually associated with the drama of Bertolt Brecht, Vinçon (1987) characterizes the work as a didactic play, or *Lehrstück,* consisting of vitalistic social criticism, which had then become quite radical since society had become increasingly threatening towards *Lebensphilosophie*. Hibberd (1992), too, opposes the prevailing view, asserting that *Tod und Teufel* evidences no abandonment of Wedekind's earlier beliefs since one must focus upon Lisiska, who represents, as characters before her, the glorification of sexuality, albeit in an extreme and pathological example (102).

All aspects of Wedekind's dramatic technique are the objects of critical attention. Both Friedenthal (1914) and Fechter (1920) focus on the playwright's employment of irony, the former characterizing that final gesture with which the virgin Elfriede closes the eyes of the dead procurer as an example of romantic irony (90). Fechter considers the subject more generally, noting that Wedekind employs irony in order to preserve freedom and distance, thereby withholding a definite conclusion; the audience is provided a thesis and antithesis but no synthesis (64).

The central scene of interaction between Lisiska and König is of structural significance to both Diebold (1921) and Kutscher (1927). Here, the former submits, verse breaks through prose as the two observers experience the behavior of the lovers as a revelation, an epiphanic vision, shattering the moral faith of Casti-Piani and at the same time confirming Elfriede's conversion to the flesh (70). Musical verse is spoken by König with quiet rhythm and by Lisiska with passion, Kutscher (II, 236) observes, in a central scene about which all turns; in this sense, structure provides the generating force of the drama (233).

Faesi (1956) is more interested in literary history and emphasizes the expressionist style manifested in the work; expressionism is manifested in the author's projection of his inner voices into a dialectical dialogue, the rapid exchange of lines, and language that is polished, precise, and pointed (256).

The subject of irony considered by Friedenthal and Fechter attracts the attention of Sokel (1966). The motto of the play consists of a biblical quotation from Matthew promising harlots and publicans precedence before the righteous into the kingdom of heaven. Assuming that this is a reference to the Christian ideal of suffering, a double irony presents itself: the masochism of Lisiska is equated with this religious concept of suffering as is that mortification of the flesh and martyrdom that Elfriede seeks in sex (204).

Wedekind stages a debate between characters, the content of which is later contradicted by what occurs. In this reversal Kesting (1970) perceives an instance of that alienation technique later developed by Brecht (201). This argument might have been reinforced by emphasizing that the encounter of Lisiska and König amounts to a play within the play, a structure which reminds each member of the audience of his status as an observer.

Irmer (1970) returns to the aspect of structure, a subject which interested Diebold and Kutscher. Similarity to both *Kammersänger* and *Zensur* is suggested by the subtitle "three scenes," but Irmer perceives it differently. *Tod und Teufel* is described as a one-act play consisting of a large scene in which a smaller one is embedded so that there is a subdivision into three segments—the shorter, middle one serving as the object of observation and discussion (147).

Borrowing heavily from Fechter (64), Wagener (1979) considers the theoretical pattern of thesis and antithesis, which fails to resolve into a synthesis; the collapse of two personal value systems is represented, and no positive perspectives remain to the audience (77). A less rigorous view might have emphasized Wedekind's virtuosity, his demonstration of playing with theater, and showing the audience what he can do.

It is the white-slaver from *Die Büchse der Pandora* of the *Lulu* tragedy who appears as the central figure Casti-Piani. Kapp (1909, 82) describes the character's scorn as fascinating in its brutality, and in notes by Wedekind the author reveals that Mephistopheles served as the prototype for this character (IX, 431–32). In the course of the play the devil becomes his own victim; he dies of his own cynicism and brutality. The cold calculator is destroyed by his own logic; the confirmed pessimist falls victim to his own incurable pessimism.

On the basis of their mutual acquaintance, Kutscher (1927) purports to quote Wedekind regarding the close identity of Casti-Piani and the dramatist (II, 234–35). Kutscher points out that the figure develops from a state of raw cynicism and cold brutality to a condition devoid of feeling; he eventually comes to occupy a position in the row of Wedekind's egoists, adventurers, and confidence men (230).

Dosenheimer (1949) finds nobility in the tragic figure of the "moralist," who, upon recognizing the bankruptcy of his world view, is granted an inkling of his relationship to the cosmos; he commits suicide since the idea upon which he had based his life (however false this idea may have been) was more important to him than continued existence (198–99).

The arguments of Casti-Piani are of interest to Völker (1965), who remarks upon the fact that this figure attacks the women's emancipation movement for its blindness to the real interests of women (52). Further, Casti-Piani adopts the argument of Friedrich Engels that marriage is an institution by means of which the male increases his economic strength by the possession of a wife (38).

Rasch (1969) pursues the now familiar process of pinpointing aspects of similarity between the author and his central figure. Wedekind attributes to Casti-Piani the author's own repressed adolescence and the brutal domination the playwright experienced of father over mother; moreover, the two share critical attitudes towards society (417).

Appearing in *Tod und Teufel* as an "apostle of pleasure," Casti-Piani is described by Gittleman (1969, 98) as a totally new conception than that introduced under this name in *Lulu*. In distinction to Dosenheimer, who finds a heroic aspect to his death, Gittleman characterizes the suicide as "meaningless" (100). A metaphysical dimension is imputed to Casti-Piani when Kalcher (1980, 355) maintains that sensual pleasure assumes for him the proportions of an absolute, a religion that offers belief and illusion, and thereby supplants Christianity. And Wedekind's words regarding Mephistopheles evoke confusion, Diethe (1988, 70) laments, since the arguments of Casti-Piani lack the devil's wickedness and because Elfriede does not appear opposite him as Faust (70).

The attempt to link the author to his characters is renewed when Diethe asserts that Wedekind and Lisiska, as well as Lulu, harbor the desire for voluptuous death conceived as the most ecstatic sexual fulfillment; the repudiation of this belief drives Casti-Piani to suicide, Diethe continues (78), an assertion which is wrong since his death is the consequence of his insight into the absence of sexual pleasure. Hibberd (1992), on the other hand, rejects the idea that Casti-Piani serves as a mouthpiece for Wedekind's ideas since the playwright did not believe that prostitution was the source of true happiness nor that human existence was made meaningful only by sensual pleasure (104–5).

That turnabout in the views of Elfriede effected by the scorn of Casti-Piani is described by Kapp (1909, 82) as a grotesque somersault. But Friedenthal (1914, 89) explains this reversal by the fact that her opposition to prostitution is grounded merely in her repressed sensuality. Wedekind (1921) writes that although Elfriede was intended initially to be ridiculous, she emerges in her sincerity and passion as a much larger figure. And Kutscher (1927) agrees that she becomes increasingly sympathetic in the course of the work, even if in a comic light; she remains, however, a weak figure merely providing contrast to Casti-Piani. Moreover, Kutscher continues, Elfriede and Casti-Piani adopt each other's attitudes for different reasons: she desires execution on the altar of love as atonement for her earlier life, and he renounces his belief in sensual pleasure out of sympathy for Lisiska (II, 236–37). Elfriede's change of attitude with regard to Casti-Piani personally, that is, her recognition of him as a great man whom she passionately desires to marry, is characterized by Dosenheimer (1949, 197) as an impossible flip-flop.

In support of the Christian context of his interpretation, Sokel (1966, 204) points out that Elfriede's surname, Malchus, is borrowed from the servant of a high priest in the bible; this servant lost his ear to the sword of Peter (John 18:10). Expanding Sokel's association of sex with suffering and mortification of the flesh, Gittleman (1969) interprets Elfriede and Casti-Piani as individuals engaged in a struggle to save each other and therefore as "Christian moralists of sorts" (100).

In characterizing Elfriede's life prospects for the enjoyment of sensual pleasure as "masochistic" (100), Gittleman employs a term which would be more appropriate for Lisiska, since Elfriede's future experiences of sex will be heavily influenced by her past inhibitions and her moral views. Consistent with his interpretation in the light of vitalism, Kalcher (1980) submits that neither Elfriede nor Casti-Piani are equal to the phenomenon of sexuality or Life, which they witness (399); the critic contradicts himself, however, when he concludes that Elfriede will follow, and presumably will be capable of following, the example of Lisiska (408).

Kalcher borrows the terminology from Wedekind's "Thoughts about the Circus" to describe Elfriede as the practical idealist and tightrope walker; she is weak, indecisive, and easily influenced; Casti-Piani, on the other hand, is the abstract idealist and trapeze artist; he is superior, decisive, and immovable (323). When she assumes the viewpoint of Casti-Piani and declares her devotion to him, she transforms herself into a trapeze artist whose point of equilibrium is fixed safely above the trapeze (343–44). Not one to let such an argument go unchallenged, Hibberd (1992) borrows the terminology without the transformation from one type of circus performer to another and describes Elfriede's metaphoric gesture as "a ludicrously clumsy and desperate attempt at exchanging one trapeze for another in midair" (106).

Kapp (1909) does not know what to make of Lisiska's complexity, as is clear from his observation that the satisfaction of her lust is not to be found in sexuality but in beating and pain, as if all were not closely related (83). Lisiska appears within a historical perspective and as a sociological phenomenon to Friedenthal (1914), who points out that she bears a name of the Roman empress Messalina, noted for her profligacy and vices (90). Lisiska by her masochistic self-sacrifice reveals the extremes which the subjugation of the woman to the man has assumed in our culture (89).

Wedekind writes in 1921 that Lisiska demonstrates the absolute impossibility of raw, sensual pleasure (IX, 432), but Kutscher (1927) finds her inadequate as an illustration. Like Elfriede, Lisiska is a weak figure serving as a puppet to provide a contrast to Casti-Piani for formal reasons amounting to theatrical effect rather than because of internal dramatic necessity. Lisiska is not a large enough figure to effect the change of attitude that she does in a man of Casti-Piani's dimensions; she is too one-sided and pathological (II, 237).

Seeing beyond Kapp to the nature of Lisiska's lust that can be satisfied only by painful sexual pleasure, Sokel (1966, 203) strikes a parallel to another dramatic character of Wedekind: Lisiska consciously yearns for a sex murderer as did Lulu unconsciously (206); and irony lies in the fact that instead of receiving the beating she desires, she becomes the object of adulation by König (204). Continuing the comparison to Lulu and infusing the Wagnerian element, Rasch (1969) characterizes as *Liebestod* that end by which the two women desire to achieve the highest sensual pleasure in being beaten to death (419). Irmer (1970) submits that Lisiska can live from love as little as can Lulu; however, his assertion that the two bear a parallel to Jesus as the sacrificial lamb of God is preposterous (147).

Looking not to the *Lulu* tragedy but to *Frühlings Erwachen*, Hibberd (1992) points out that Lisiska's behavior illustrates the link between physical abuse, masochism, and sexual arousal most clearly represented in *Frühlings Erwachen* by Wendla Bergmann in the hayloft (111). Further, this critic provides a new and innovative spin in the contention that Lisiska sees a glimmer of happiness of which the other characters have scarcely an inkling (103); sexual intercourse provides "release from repressive respectability, duty, and discipline" (110) and represents "transcendence of earthly limitations and woes" (107).

The character of König contains something of the author; Wedekind (1921) writes that he put himself into this figure, through whom are expressed those impulses which led him to compose the work (IX, 432). Kutscher calls this character an abstraction without individuality (II, 236), but Irmer endows him with more stature when he identifies König as the Faust to Casti-Piani's Mephisto (202). Lisiska's customer illustrates the double morality, Kalcher (1980) contends, that allows to the man what it defames when practiced by the woman (386), but more important is his function in the play; with his poetry König transforms Lisiska's sexuality into something spiritual. Her misery is aestheticized in a manner characteristic of *Jugendstil* (394). And Hibberd addresses the same point: König perceives the spiritual aspect in Lisiska's lust and desire for pain (114). Of course, the critics might have noted that this is consistent with the introduction Wedekind provided to the work in 1910 when he emphasized that the flesh has its own spirit.

The negative reception of the drama by the critics is initiated by the words of Kapp (1909), who calls it tendentious. Preaching and sermonizing interrupt the sequence of events (81); and he concludes, therefore, that the work is a failure (87–88). Friedenthal (1914) faults the artistic weakness found in excessive theorizing; the play amounts to a treatise in dialogue since the work of art is lost in the discussion of problems (88). It is no doubt this which Kutscher (1927 II, 235) has in mind when he refers to the drama as a Dance of Death of ideas; moreover, the logic of the plot and the motivation of the characters are unconvincing (237). Crude, crass, and inadequate are the terms employed by Michelsen (1956), who finds the only value of *Tod und Teufel* in what it reveals of Wedekind's development as a dramatist (62).

Rasch (1969) is the first to free the play from the verdict of the literary critics that the work is dramatically unsuccessful and artistically inferior; he argues that the play contributes to understanding that sexuality, just as nature, has a negative as well as a positive side and is both destructive and creative (421).

Gittleman (1969) characterizes the treatment of sex as "tasteless" since Wedekind offers no solution (100). It may well be, as the Latin proverb tells us, that there is no disputing the nature of taste; but the failure to provide an answer constitutes a weak justification for a judgment of taste. Extending the observation which Kutscher (II, 237) limited to the two female figures, Gittleman describes all the dramatic characters as puppets (100). Irmer (1970) characterizes the conclusion as gruesome absurdity (150), and Wagener (1979) faults the characters for their lack of individuality (77). Kalcher (1980) indicates that the grotesque comedy reaches its peak in the reversal of positions by Elfriede and Casti-Piani (400); but the play amounts to neither tragedy nor comedy since it is from moment to moment first the one and then the other (335). Although Chick (1984, 38) is charitable in his evaluation of *Tod und Teufel* as "a satiric gem," the reasons provided by Hibberd (1992) accurately account for the fact that it has been critically ignored: the drama is embarrassing and shocking, breaks with Wedekind's emphasis upon the glorification of sensuality, seems to be of merely autobiographical significance, and, as Kutscher suggests, is unconvincing with regard to the motivation of characters and the logic of plot (101).

Works Cited

Chick, Edson M. 1984. "Frank Wedekind and his *Lulu* Tragedy." In his *Dances of Death. Wedekind, Brecht, Dürrenmatt, and the Satiric Tradition*. Columbia, South Carolina: Camden House. 11–45.

Diebold, Bernhard. 1972. "Wedekind der Narr." In his *Anarchie im Drama*. New York, London: Johnson Reprint Corporation. 43–76. The work first appeared in 1921.

Diethe, Carol. 1988. *Aspects of Distorted Sexual Attitudes in German Expressionist Drama*. New York, Bern, Frankfurt am Main, and Paris: Lang.

Dosenheimer, Elise. 1967. *Das deutsche soziale Drama von Lessing bis Sternheim*. Darmstadt: Wissenschaftliche Buchgesellschaft. This first appeared in 1949.

Faesi, Robert. 1956. "Ein Vorläufer: Frank Wedekind." In *Expressionismus. Gestalten einer literarischen Bewegung*, edited by Hermann Friedmann and Otto Mann. Heidelberg: Rothe. 241–63.

Fechter, Paul. 1920. *Frank Wedekind. Der Mensch und das Werk*. Jena: Lichtenstein.

Friedenthal, Joachim. 1914. "Einleitung." In *Das Wedekindbuch*, edited by Friedenthal. Munich and Leipzig: Georg Müller. 1–121.

Gittleman, Sol. 1969. *Frank Wedekind*. New York: Twayne.

Hibberd, John L. 1992. "'Sein frevler Mund / Tat das Bekenntnis schrecklich kund': Another Look at *Tod und Teufel*." In *Frank Wedekind Yearbook 1991*, edited by Rolf Kieser and Reinhold Grimm. Bern, Berlin, etc.: Lang. 101–25.

Irmer, Hans-Jochen. 1975. *Der Theaterdichter Frank Wedekind. Werk und Wirkung*. Berlin: Henschelverlag. This originally appeared in 1970.

Kalcher, Joachim. 1980. "Frank Wedekind: *Tod und Teufel*." In his *Perspektiven des Lebens in der Dramatik um 1900*. Cologne and Vienna: Böhlau. 292–410.

Kapp, Julius. 1909. *Frank Wedekind. Seine Eigenart und seine Werke*. Berlin: Hermann Barsdorf.

Kaufmann, Hans. 1969. "Zwei Dramatiker: Gerhart Hauptmann und Frank Wedekind." In his *Krisen und Wandlungen der deutschen Literatur von Wedekind bis Feuchtwanger*. Berlin and Weimar: Aufbau-Verlag. 47–84.

Kesting, Marianne. 1970. "Frank Wedekind." In her *Entdeckung und Destruktion*. Munich: Fink. 189–203.

Kutscher, Artur. 1970. *Frank Wedekind. Sein Leben und seine Werke*. Vol. 2. New York: AMS Press. This is a reprint of the edition appearing in 1927.

Michelsen, Peter. 1969. "Frank Wedekind." In *Deutsche Dichter der Moderne*, edited by Benno von Wiese. Berlin: Erich Schmidt. 51–69. The essay first appeared in 1965.

Rasch, Wolfdietrich. 1969. "Sozialkritische Aspekte in Wedekinds dramatischer Dichtung. Sexualität, Kunst und Gesellschaft." In *Gestaltungsgeschichte und Gesellschaftsgeschichte*, edited by Helmut Kreuzer. Stuttgart: Metzler. 409–26.

Sokel, Walter H. 1966. "The Changing Role of Eros in Wedekind's Drama." *The German Quarterly* 39.2: 201–7.

Spalter, Max. 1967. *Brecht's Tradition*. Baltimore: Johns Hopkins Press.

Vinçon, Hartmut. 1987. *Frank Wedekind*. Stuttgart: Metzler.

Völker, Klaus. 1965. *Frank Wedekind*. Velber bei Hannover: Friedrich Verlag.

Wagener, Hans. 1979. *Frank Wedekind*. Berlin: Colloquim.

Wedekind, Frank. 1921. "Aufklärungen." In *Gesammelte Werke*. Vol. 9. Munich: Georg

Müller. 384–90.

———. 1921. "Was ich mir dabei dachte." *Gesammelte Werke*. Vol. 9. Munich: Georg
Müller. 431–33.

———. 1921. "Zirkusgedanken." In *Gesammelte Werke*. Vol. 9. Munich: Georg Müller.
293–305.

Willeke, Audrone B. 1980. "Frank Wedekind and the 'Frauenfrage.'" *Monatshefte* 72.1:
26–38.

9: A Turning Point:
Musik (1908), *Die Zensur* (1908), and *Oaha* (1908)
The Advantages of Private Education, The Reunification of Church and Brothel, and the Langen Affair Revisited

Musik (Music, 1908), together with *Die Zensur* (The Censor, 1908) and *Oaha* (Oaha, 1908), comprises a group that marks a turning point in the direction of Wedekind's dramatic productivity. In these plays, all from the same year, he mounts a pulpit for the purpose of moralizing. Diebold (1921) first notes that the dramatist is philosophical and bitter here, cursing actors, the public, and police in defense of a morality which the world refuses to recognize (66). A turning point is also indicated in the content of *Zensur* and *Oaha*, which treat experiences and issues of an intensely personal nature; the plays provide an introduction to the late works, where the author once again assumes a stance which preserves more distance from his subject matter.

Musik. Sittengemälde in vier Bildern
(Music. A Portrait of Morals in Four Scenes, 1908)

Else Reißner rushes into the room of Klara Hühnerwadel with money for the young woman's ticket to Antwerp. While a private voice student of Josef Reißner, Klara became pregnant and received an abortion. When Klara's name became known at the trial of the abortionist, a warrant was issued for Klara's arrest. Should she should go to prison, Reißner would lose his students and position at the Music Conservatory.

Having returned from Antwerp at Reißner's behest, Klara is sentenced to prison, where Reißner visits her in order to demonstrate his concern. Else gains Klara a pardon, and she is congratulated by the prison director for having such loyal and devoted friends. Klara returns to her studies with Reißner, arousing the moral indignation of Franz Lindekuh at the threat she poses to the Reißner marriage once again. Lindekuh calls for public action, and Reißner accuses him of moralistic interference.

To Reißner's surprise Klara reveals that she is pregnant once again and has decided to keep the baby. The Reißners visit Klara and her sick infant at a simple house in the country, where Lindekuh accompanies Klara's mother. A doctor is unable to save the baby's life. Klara's mother assumes Lindekuh is the father and thanks Reißner for everything he has done for [to] her daughter during the last three years. Klara bemoans the curse of ridiculousness, about which Lindekuh exclaims that she has a song to sing.

Paragraph 218 of the penal code proscribed abortion, and Helene Stöcker, an ardent spokesperson for woman's rights, confronts Wedekind for having allegedly remarked that the women's movement fails to oppose this law. Writing in the journal *Morgen* in 1907, Stöcker states that Wedekind is misinformed and welcomes him heartily as a comrade in the struggle for woman's rights. She attempts further to refute the playwright's claim that the women's movement is making men out of women by arguing that the femininity in women is being emancipated (250).

Social criticism is also leveled by Leon Trotsky (1908), political thinker turned drama critic, in his consideration of *Musik*. He protests against a system which forbids a woman to free herself from the consequences of love but does not provide her the means to nurture the fruit of her union and concludes glumly that the capitalist audience is socially immune to his message (370).

Critics were uncertain as to whether they should take *Musik* seriously. The play is highly ambivalent. When played naturalistically, real people appear in a tragedy likely to be interpreted as tendentious; at the same time, however, the figures are caricatures in a ridiculous parody or comedy.

Although Friedenthal (1914) is quick to label the play tendentious (86), Fechter (1920) exercises more caution. Conceding that the drama is directed against the law, against sexually exploitative music instruction, and against the hypocrisy of feigned friendship, Fechter argues that *Musik* could be considered tendentious only if Wedekind were not a better dramatist than he is a moralist; the balladlike play presents human fate in a spooky reflection of reality reminiscent of Georg Büchner (98–99).

Characteristically, Wedekind's comments on his own work provide little help. In "What I was thinking about at the Time" the playwright denies that the drama is anything but fictitious; he calls it a character study amounting to cold-blooded caricature not to be taken seriously or sentimentally (IX, 434). But the words of the author are often overlooked. Adopting the views of Fechter entirely and even going so far as to give him partial credit therefor, Elster (1922) agrees that the work is not tendentious even though it is directed against the illegality of abortion and the sexual hanky-panky incident to music study (86). Distance creates objectivity in a poetic treatment that is sociological and psychological; moreover, the play possesses a lightly balladic quality, as Fechter points out (89).

Kutscher (1927) looks to Wedekind's words and interprets caricature as a reference to the comically grotesque style of a cabaret song adopted by the playwright to preserve superiority over the banality of the material. Situations that are comic, tragicomic, and tragic are combined to reflect a reality rendered unreal by the tempo of surprises, tearful breakdowns, small deceptions, and empty phrases (II, 246–47). Abortion is only a motif, and the work is not tendentious in intent (253).

Reality rendered unreal, as Kutscher phrases it, is the object of analysis by the playwright's daughter Kadidja Wedekind (1964–65) as she considers the grotesque nature of the play and the combination of comedy and tragedy. She suggests that her father appeals to the cruel sense of humor in his audience and then attacks this cruelty in the last scene as the comedy turns to tragedy (15). Such a tactic requires of the audience courage equal to self-criticism; one allows oneself to be led by laughter to a recognition of one's own cruelty (18).

Completely at odds with Kadidja Wedekind, who predicates her interpretation of dramatic technique on the bond of identification between Klara and the spectator, is Völker (1965), for whom Klara evokes no sympathy. *Musik* should not be played naturalistically since it is not pointed towards the abolition of the law prohibiting abortion; it should be played ironically since it consists of satire and is a parody of a trashy, tendentious work (56).

Implicitly supporting the view of *Musik* as tragedy, Spalter (1967) finds the drama illustrates a lesson; the audience observes a society where the mere appearance of propriety is sufficient, and behind the facade flourishes "amoral parasitism" (133).

Ignoring Wedekind's protestation that *Musik* is fictitious, Gittleman (1969) argues that the work is based upon materials gleaned from the newspapers and amounts to a "factually accurate documentary" that should be played as "semi-Naturalistic melodrama" (101). Emphasizing distance as does Elster, Gittleman points out that the playwright does not become involved with his figures. Noting as does Völker the absence of identification, Gittleman asserts that the audience reacts in the opposite manner as a character weeps or laughs. This technique is precursive to that employed by Bertolt Brecht, and the use of titles which reflect on the content of the acts is likewise a mark of epic theater (102).

Employing the terms *satire* and *parody* interchangeably, Völker sees behind *Musik* a tendentious work which is satirized. Kesting (1970, 200) perceives a story lending itself to satire that might have been based upon the popular illustrated weekly *Gartenlaube*, which appeared from the mid-nineteenth to the mid-twentieth centuries. Irmer (1970, 160), too, reads the work as parodic in form and content; the last line of the drama suggesting a parody of the final line of Gerhart Hauptmann's *Rose Bernd* (1903); moreover, the name Klara is borrowed from the central figure of Friedrich Hebbel's *Maria Magdalena* (1844).

Adorno (1974) and Wagener (1979) agree on one point. The play is to be presented naturalistically, according to Adorno, since it amounts to a tendentious cultural-political manifesto dealing with the right of free love, a subject decidedly inartistic (625). *Musik* is traditional in that it is naturalistic, asserts Wagener, and modern in anticipating the epic theater of Brecht and in offering a criticism of the bourgeois mentality (77–78).

While Kutscher argues that Wedekind borrows from the cabaret song its comically grotesque style, Harris (1981) looks to this song for the structure which it lends the play; comic, tragicomic, and pathetic elements reflecting the song are employed throughout to create "a highly stylized reality" (504–5).

The play illustrates what Skrine (1989) calls "a squalid everyday 'tragedy'" that we consider with detachment: when Klara accepts the double standard of society, she is forgiven; when she asserts her own moral values, society condemns her (109–110).

Recent scholarship explains Wedekind's comments on his play. In the notes to his two-volume edition of Wedekind's works from 1990, Weidl (II, 792) provides information which, when taken together with a reference from Kutscher (1927 II, 6), sheds light upon the reason the playwright insists that the work is fictitious and not to be taken seriously or sentimentally. Since the Reißners represent a couple with whom Wedekind was acquainted and the drama recasts actual, scandalous events, the author is evidently embarrassed at having treated the affair and tries to suggest that no confidences have been betrayed. Gittleman (1969) perceived the actual state of events when he observes that the drama amounts to a "factually accurate documentary" (101).

Considerable interest is generated by Wedekind's treatment of his characters. Franz Lindekuh is described by Fechter (1920) as a grotesquely exaggerated self-portrait of the author (99). Nevertheless, Lindekuh is represented more objectively and less ironically than other appearances of Wedekind in his confessional dramas, and the figure does not command central focus (102). When Lindekuh is identified as the father at the conclusion, the curse borne by Klara throughout passes to him in an act entitled "The Curse of Ridicule."

In Lindekuh, Elster (1922) sees a moral monomaniac in the grotesque self-portrait of the author (87). Wedekind reveals himself as a moralist and dramatist with a Weltanschauung (89). *Musik*, as does *Nicolo*, illustrates the saying "That's life!": the guilty party goes free, and the woman is sent to prison and condemned to the curse of ridiculousness shared with that man who sympathized with her (89).

Kutscher (1927) interprets Lindekuh on a number of levels: he is an impractical idealist, who acts naively with the best intentions; a skeptic, who misinterprets Klara and believes Else; and an egoist, who acts altruistically and causes disaster (II, 250). That a quality of comic grotesqueness is employed by Wedekind to treat himself ironically in Lindekuh is an observation by Kutscher (206) with which Kesting (1970, 200) agrees.

Despite Wedekind's description of Klara as a caricature to be played without sentimentality, Kutscher finds her excessively sentimental (II, 252). It never becomes clear as the playwright intended that Klara is eventually able to see herself as the victim, not of her passions, but of her stupidity, since her love affairs are ridiculous (248, note 2). Nevertheless, Klara has the ability to move some of the critics. Irmer (1970, 160) is stirred to indignation by the suffering she takes upon herself, and Haida (1973) suggests that the curse of being ridiculous is illustrated not just in the final act but throughout the entire work by Klara's shortsightedness and inability to learn (100, 105). Stewart (1985–86) thinks she is depicted in a "maliciously ironic" manner when humor lies in her failure to recognize her misfortunes (67, note 9). And Hibberd (1986) remarks that *Musik* opened Wedekind to the charge of cruelly and cynically exploiting human suffering (64).

Although some critics stood steadfastly by Wedekind, the earliest were not swept away by enthusiasm. The early critic Kapp (1909) is most devastating in his judgment. He describes *Musik* as the lowest point the dramatist has achieved in his creative production to date (88). The language is pompous and affected; aside from Klara, the characterization is poor; Lindekuh amounts to tasteless self-caricature; the motivation is faulty; and the irony of the author fails to break into his usual biting humor (94).

Heuß (1909) calls the work unclear and bad (268), and Friedenthal (1914) finds little artistic value (87), but Fechter (1920) and Kutscher (1927) support the playwright stalwartly. The former feels a tenderness seldom encountered in Wedekind (102), and Kutscher detects mastery in the construction of scenes and the drawing of characters. The work is engrossing as an experiment in style, even though aspects of the grotesque fail to run evenly throughout (II, 252).

There is "insufficient substance" in the characters for them to fulfill their intended role as caricatures, according to Gittleman (1969, 102). And Adorno (1974) objects both to the absence of a strong, central dramatic concept and to a conclusion with a flourish of melodramatic "Kitsch" (625–26). The critic, as an afterthought, assigns *Musik* a spot on the periphery of the author's creative writing (623). A most inelegant reference is that of Stewart towards the drama as "an off-loading of Wedekind's feelings of impatience with life's losers" (67, note 9).

Die Zensur. Theodizee in einem Akt
(The Censor. Theodicy in One Act, 1908)

The author Walter Buridan confesses to his lover, the actress Kadidja, the need for two weeks separation during which he may dedicate himself to isolated contemplation of problems such as the reconciliation of spirit and beauty. Since Kadidja has devoted herself to him for a year and a half, she interprets this as rejection.

Dr. Cajetan Prantl, secretary to the father confessor of His Majesty, reiterates the refusal of the church to sanction the performance of *Die Büchse der Pandora* since it constitutes a threat to public morality. Buridan protests that his deepest convictions are interpreted as blasphemy, and Prantl accuses him of misconstruing his role as a dramatist: his goal must consist of providing amusement to his audience rather than burdening it with the details of his most private concerns.

Buridan expresses his religiosity in the belief that every song which is sung reflects the immortality of the human soul, but Prantl rejects such a concession as ambiguous and faults the author's absence of Christian humility. Further, Prantl scores Buridan for representing in his work human debasement and the triumph of evil. The entrance of Kadidja in a new costume is perceived by Prantl as a ruse, and he denounces Buridan's overweening arrogance and admonishes him against tempting God.

Alone with Kadidja, Buridan subjects her to criticism as wrong and arbitrary as that which he suffers, but she refuses to be humiliated. Since she feels herself no longer loved and cannot live without him, she releases him to his world of reflection by flinging herself from the balcony. Broken, Buridan asks himself whether this is God's revenge for his mockery.

The second edition of the play includes a preface suggesting that the tendentious intent of the work may have been readily recognized in circles beyond that of the critics close to Wedekind. The senior government official and censor for Berlin was Kurt von Glasenapp, who is quoted as saying to stage director Victor Barnowsky that if Wedekind imagines that on account of *Die Zensur* the government is going to approve *Die Büchse der Pandora,* then the dramatist is greatly deluding himself (V, [105]).

One path in the criticism takes Wedekind to task for dramatizing his problems. This direction is initiated early by an implacable foe: Hofmiller (1909), who charges the author with "literary narcissism" and complains that it is boring to hear about Wedekind so often from his own mouth (118–19). Hofmiller compares the playwright to an old man with a barrel organ capable of playing only one tune (116) and a year later remarks further that Wedekind's appearance as Walter Buridan suggests that the dramatist's wealth of names for himself is as obvious as his poverty of ideas (1910, 117).

Wedekind himself provided fuel for the fire in remarks published in 1921, where he indicates that the title "Self-Portrait" or "Exhibitionism" would have been more appropriate (IX, 435). The author's opinion is sustained by Kutscher (1931) when he refers to the dramatist's penchant for self-flagellation (III, 44) since he expresses his torment in this work even more fully than in *Nicolo* (42). Personal experience is not successfully transformed into art (46), and Kutscher borrows the argument of the censor Prantl in the charge that the drama is excessively self-centered and treats matters better retained privately and left unsaid (44).

The charge of literary exhibitionism is sustained by Hill (1960, 87), who characterizes the play as "shamelessly autobiographical," and Spalter (1967) faults Wedekind for projecting his own egoism as moral doctrine (130, note 16). The drama serves "as a personal pamphlet," according to Gittleman (1969, 103), who echoes Kutscher in his conclusion that the work is so personal that it has serious limitations (105).

The position of Medicus (1982) is somewhat conciliatory when he argues that the name Buridan grants Wedekind ironic distance from himself (233); this is a degree of objectivity which critics such as Hofmiller are unwilling to concede. Nevertheless, Medicus observes, the playwright makes no secret of his enjoyment in being torn between the poles of spirit and sensuality (237).

Another path in the secondary literature indicates that not all critics, by any means, fault the dramatist for autobiographical elements in *Zensur.* Assuming that Wedekind and Buridan are one, Trotsky (1908) celebrates the experience of conversion; Buridan's fate is interpreted as a tragic protest against that cynical epicureanism for which Wedekind has hitherto stood (385). According to Kapp (1909, 96), Wedekind presents a partial accusation of himself and a measure of self defense in what constitutes a personal summation of accounts based on the history of the author's one-and-a-half-year-old marriage (99). The attempted self-justification with regard to religion and art is considered particularly painful and passionate by Frieden-thal (1914, 106).

Not defensiveness but skepticism is sensed by Fechter (1920, 110) in what amounts to Wedekind's most intensive attempt to justify his own work and life (103). This argument is extended by Dosenheimer (1949), who provides an important caveat. *Zensur* represents, she argues, a turning point in the author's production since the play constitutes an argument with himself, with the spirit of his work, and with the world (208). Consistent with the principles of New Criticism, Dosenheimer observes that a work is organic and self-contained, and when demands are made upon it externally, for example in a prologue or public utterance, the autonomous nature and artistic value of the piece is reduced. A statement extraneous to the work assumes a non-aesthetic direction and suggests that the author is not sufficiently confident of the effect of the work on its own merits (211–12).

Providing a refinement of Kapp's argument, Faesi (1956) contends that a direct reflection of the relationship of Wedekind to his young wife, actress Tilly Newes, is offered both in the inability of Buridan to satisfy Kadidja and in her vital energies that surpass his intellectuality (254).

What is the gist of *Die Zensur* and the meaning of the subtitle "Theodicy"? Kapp interprets the play consistent with the short prose piece "Rabbi Ezra" as an illustration that happiness between the sexes exists only when love unites the spirit and the flesh (98). While Kapp finds the subtitle "theodicy" misleading since the drama does not deal with the reason for the existence of evil (105), Hofmiller (1909) rejects the term as objectionable for its suggestion of religiosity (120).

Friedenthal (1914, 105) presents a unique interpretation of the play as a treatment of a peculiar problem associated with love, especially from the feminine viewpoint; the ability to evoke desire and provide satisfaction can be sustained only by occasional separation. Kadidja does not recognize this strategy and considers Buridan's desire for solitude as a threat to her love.

Jean Buridan was a fourteenth-century French philosopher who conceived of a hypothetical dog which was unable to choose between two equal amounts of the same food and therefore starved to death; this example is intended to illustrate the illusionary nature of noncausative decision making. Kutscher (1931) applies the example to Buridan, who is satisfied neither by the senses, woman, and the world on the one hand, nor by his work, the spirit, or God on the other. Buridan fails to choose and therefore loses both, in a drama which by no means can be justifiably characterized as a theodicy (III, 42, 46).

Striking a literary-historical parallel, Gundolf (1948) recalls the early romantics Ludwig Tieck, Wilhelm Wackenroder, and Friedrich Schlegel, who mistakenly needed to fashion a religion from art just as Wedekind does a religion from pleasure (202).

Zensur, from which Prantl emerges as the unconditional victor, is not a justification of God and his creation but an attempted justification of Wedekind, of course, says Dosenheimer (1949, 208). Buridan does not try to convince Prantl of the correctness of his views but lamely attempts conciliation. However, compatibility can only be apparent and sophistic since the two men employ different meanings for the same terms. The concessions Buridan makes have their source in the absence of a synthesis between the flesh and the spirit and reflect Wedekind's waning conviction in the validity of his worldview (210, 222–23).

In the political eyes of Irmer (1970) the drama exposes the manner in which censorship serves as a modern means for the proof of God (174). Prantl opposes not only Buridan and his work but also Kadidja, recognized as Lulu, the snake in paradise. Before Kadidja, Buridan, in turn, assumes the role of the censor vis-à-vis his creation, but he is not equal to the task, and she is able to assert herself. Buridan fails before both the spirituality of Prantl and the sensuality of Kadidja (176–77).

Although Best (1973) suggests a vindication of divine providence that is "perhaps" to be found in Buridan's realization of his "insignificance and impotence" (286–87), Medicus (1982, 233) dismisses the subtitle as pretentious. Further, Schröder-Zeballa (1985, 50–51) reads *Die Zensur* as a revelation of the repressive force of censorship as a means of finding sources for all evil in the world. Unwilling to avail himself of an answer that is too pat, Hibberd (1986) undertakes a dogged attempt to detect theodicy by interpreting the drama as a "justification of life despite its apparent evils" (51) and refers to Wedekind's vitalism as "a central part of his would-be theodicy" (64).

The form of *Zensur* consists of a tripartite construction shared with both *Kammersänger* and *Tod und Teufel;* the argument with Prantl is accompanied before and after by a discussion between Buridan and Kadidja. Friedenthal (1914), for one, thinks that the plot is twisted out of shape since Buridan's expression of artistic and moralistic self-justification before Prantl does not relate to the contents of the love theme (104). But Fechter (1920) relates the middle scene to those two framing it by suggesting that the debate with Prantl causes Buridan to regard Kadidja differently in two distinct, but related, aspects: as if Buridan were a god unifying flesh and spirit, he subjects Kadidja as an object to his censorship; and failing to see in her anything but her physical qualities, he forgets that she is a person and drives her to take her life (109). This final scene does not fit together artistically with the foregoing and accounts for the lack of unity in the work, according to Kutscher (1931 III, 45), and Faesi (1956) describes a superficial union of the themes of sexuality and the desire for artistic recognition (253). But Irmer (1970) finds sufficient justification for the structure in its resemblance to that of *Kammersänger* and *Tod und Teufel; Zensur* is similarly a one-act play, consisting of three dialogues, the central one of which is the most significant (174).

Criticism since the sixties has tended to unify autobiography with aesthetics and the subject of the artist, at the same time reducing the problem of structural unity. Shaw (1964) initiated this new direction. Conceding that Wedekind calculated with the sensation-seeking public interest in the marriage of famous stage personalities such as Tilly Newes and himself (21), Shaw argues that the dramatist has taken autobiographical detail and abstracted it to form a universal statement. This is a metaphysical representation of the relationship, not between Frank and Tilly, but of the sexes, the forces of procreation and conception. The drama illustrates the formative artistic spirit and that which is given shape (25–26).

In 1973 Best argues that the drama constitutes social criticism. The milieu of the artist is a reflection of society. The object of Buridan's criticism is a society which exploits, censors, and rejects those weaker than itself (287). Two years later Best modifies his position somewhat by placing additional emphasis on Buridan; this figure is unable to distinguish between art and life since art is for him both a reflection of society and a statement of his view of the world (48). The defeat of Buridan illustrates the arbitrary nature of social standards (52).

Developing the idea of Shaw that beauty and holiness, eros and religion, are one, Wagener (1979) unifies the drama more completely. He argues that Prantl, who represents public fame, denies to the artist Buridan, representative of the spirit, that sensual beauty incorporated by Kadidja that is necessary to realize his art (81–82).

With nary a nod of acknowledgment to her predecessors, Schröder-Zebralla (1985) appropriates the perception that Buridan attempts in his discussion with Prantl to unify religion with eros and, in his argument with Kadidja, spirit with eros, or the flesh (32). In Buridan's words to Prantl lie a classic example of Wedekind's use of dialectical irony to illustrate, in the negative, the point he wishes to make; when the author denies having alluded to the reunification of church and brothel in the socialist state of the future, he draws public attention to the existence of this view (37–38). A work of art and a product of Buridan, Kadidja is characterized by self-honesty and straightforwardness that are unknown to him (186, 190–91). Unable to condone the sensuality of Kadidja, Buridan resorts to social convention and Christian moralism (199–200).

Finding that dramatic unity which eluded Kutscher, Hibberd (1986) notes the religious language used by Buridan throughout *Die Zensur;* the tone of his speech grants the work the universal import expected of art (48). With acknowledgment to Best, Hibberd underscores Prantl's role as a representative of organized society, possessing a spiritual dimension which Buridan seeks and respects (50, 54). Buridan presents a problematic image of the artist; suffering from "a terrible clash of needs and values" (61), he harbors a religion which amounts to "his conviction of his own artistic mission as a search for truth" (55).

As did Schröder-Zebralla, Hibberd compares Kadidja with Lulu as a representative of the flesh. Poised on the rolling drum, she conveys her innocence, faith, inner equilibrium, and adaptability; but Buridan lacks the strength of character to take pleasure from her (53, 59).

Pankau (1989) implicitly draws a parallel between Prantl and the critic Josef Hofmiller, whom Pankau characterizes as a notorious censor of Wedekind (289). Best's argument of 1973 that Wedekind is engaged in an ironic game with his critics is dismissed by Pankau as facile (309, note 42). Generalizing, without acknowledgment, upon the remarks by Hibberd regarding Buridan's problematic existence,

Pankau perceives those conflicts basic to the modern author. This artist is isolated from his external world and withheld from experience by an ego which is fragmented; fragmentation has been caused by contradictory feelings towards society, attitudes of protest and accommodation, repulsion and attraction. Moreover, the author is subject to a distorted perception of himself and surrounding reality; he experiences by turns feelings of inferiority and superiority; the artist is insecure, indecisive, ambivalent, narcissistic, and pathological (302–7).

How do the critics evaluate *Die Zensur*? Consistent with his regard for religion, or the absence of such regard, Trotzky (1908) attributes spiritual poverty and cowardice to what he interprets as Wedekind's turning to God in a conclusion which is pitiful, wretched, and humiliating (385). Kapp (1909), on the other hand, finds the conclusion dramatic and effective; moreover, the language is lively and witty throughout and the work quite unique (105–6).

Predictably, Hofmiller (1909) is unenthusiastic, calling Wedekind's earlier works better (119). And Friedenthal (1914) looks to the future for which *Zensur* prepares its audience; with brilliant dialogue and well-formulated thoughts it furnishes a prologue to consideration of the subject of marriage and the family as this will be treated in *Schloß Wetterstein* (104). And Fechter (1920), too, considers the work relative to its position in the corpus of Wedekind's dramas; as *Tod und Teufel* comprises a negative summary of the development of the playwright's attitudes in the course of the dramas dealing with sex, so *Die Zensur* concludes the series of confessional dramas expressing skepticism regarding the dramatist's morals and the merit of his writing; the works following *Zensur* will tend to look back to the beginning and complete the circle (110).

Finding the dialogue excellent and the scenes well constructed, with the second scene being particularly dramatic, Kutscher (1931), nevertheless, reaches agreement with Hofmiller when the critic describes *Die Zensur* as a nadir in Wedekind's work descending from *Hidalla*. Kutscher finds *Die Zensur* to be marked by tendentious rigidity, stagnation, and the repetition of motifs (III, 46).

Postwar critics are more charitable. Dosenheimer (1949, 208) calls the drama unique not only in the corpus of Wedekind's works but in world literature, and Hibberd (1986) seems remotely absorbed as he reflects that *Die Zensur* is the representation of "a struggle potentially amusing in its pitiful clumsiness, but amply grave in its consequences" (66).

Suggesting a parallel in structure to *Kammersänger* as did Irmer, Pankau (1989) extends the comparison also to theme, characterizing *Die Zensur* as both an aesthetic treatment of Wedekind's personal experience, that is, modern in a fascinating way, and a radical illustration of the problems of the contemporary artist (290–91).

Oaha, die Satire der Satire
(Oaha, the Satire of Satire, 1908)

The author Max Bouterweck is dissatisfied with the pay received from his employer Georg Sterner, editor of the satirical journal *Till Eulenspiegel*. Since Sterner believes that the office of the state's attorney exists to create publicity for such journals by suppressing them and thereby arousing public attention and increasing circulation, the editor ensures that a poem by Bouterweck appears. "Palästinafahrt" provokes the charge of lèse-majesté, and the issue of *Till Eulenspiegel* is confiscated.

To escape imprisonment, Sterner flees to Switzerland, where he becomes an international celebrity. Pardoned by the government through the influence of his father-in-law, Sterner returns to the editorship, shared with Dr. Kilian. Since Bouterweck has developed too much self-respect, he is no longer a ready source of wit for the journal. Fortunately, Sterner had discovered in Switzerland an imbecile named Oaha, who will meet their needs; Oaha is deaf and dumb and when assigned a theme he laughs uncontrollably and then writes his joke with chalk on a blackboard.

Wanda Washington, insatiable in her hunger for love, attempts unsuccessfully to kill herself after rejection by Sterner; she promises to guide Oaha through the labyrinth of lust.

The three illustrators, together with Kilian, assume editorial control, relegating Sterner to a fifth fractional position, where Oaha suggests that Sterner be employed as the nominal editor in charge of provoking legal suppression of the journal to ensure its growth and prosperity.

This is a work in which real people appear behind fictitious names, and the author intends his audience to recognize the personalities and events depicted ("ein Schlüsselstück"). Wedekind reworks the circumstances which drove him into exile and earned him a prison term for lèse-majesté. Georg Sterner, publisher of *Till Eulenspiegel,* represents Albert Langen, and the journal stands for *Simplicissimus*, with which Wedekind, here Max Bouterweck, was associated.

Oaha provoked a retort as Wedekind's former colleagues answered in kind. Two scenes by Ludwig Thoma, alias Dr. Kilian, appeared in *Simplicissimus* on 26 October 1908 under the title "Der Satanist" (The Satanist). The devil's advocate is Franz Wendelgrind, who stands as a defendant before the Leipzig court facing the charge of lèse-majesté. Shaking with fear and begging for mercy, he is denounced as an adherent of heinous doctrine summarized in a parody of the concluding line of *Keith:* "Die Poesie ist eine Rutschbahn" ("Poetry is a slide").

Of primary literary critical concern are the style of *Oaha,* its literary value, and its reflection upon Wedekind's abilities. Convulsing comedy in the opinion of Pollatschak (1908), *Oaha* is satire directed at the production of humor in humorless Germany; it is as modern as the dirigible (254). With more restraint Hofmiller (1909) calls *Oaha* caricature and literary burlesque that demonstrates Wedekind's talent for comedy. Comparing it as literary satire to Ludwig Tieck's romantic comedy based on the fairy tale *Der gestiefelte Kater* (Puss and Boots, 1797), Hofmiller finds the latter much superior and *Oaha* only moderately successful (121, 125).

The prestigious drama critic Alfred Kerr (1909, 140) describes *Oaha* as the expression in comedy of Wedekind's hate and desire for revenge, and a work which is much more than literary satire and far superior to that of Arno Holz. Although the drama by Holz goes unnamed, Kerr probably means *Sozialaristokraten* (Social Aristocrats, 1896), a satire which also deals with the founding of a literary journal and extends in a heavy-handed way to politics.

The reputation of Heuß (1909, 268) was not that of Kerr; and it is a good thing for Wedekind that that was so. Heuß calls *Oaha* a miserable undertaking poorly disguised by a few witty notions. *Musik, Zensur,* and now *Oaha* demonstrate a diminishing of the author's creative abilities and his lively assurance in depicting the interaction of people and events; the plays are all loquacious and boring.

A year later Hofmiller (1910, 118) speaks again, noting how the Albert Langen affair has been reworked since *Hidalla*. Now the critic seems to revise his opinion upwards, however slightly, by qualifying his observation: to the extent that *Oaha* is caricature, it is successful (124).

The ready support usually forthcoming from Friedenthal (1914) and Fechter (1920) is notable in its absence. The former calls *Oaha* embarrassing and weak with some touches of wit (87). Fechter contends that the play is not satire of satire, as the subtitle suggests, but satire of a satirical journal. It is comedy directed at literature in the tradition of Christian Dietrich Grabbe, August Graf von Platen, Ernst Wolzogen, and Holz. *Oaha* is, however, decidedly second rate; Wedekind's hate, bitterness, and desire for revenge cause the work to become so personal that is grotesque rather than comical (78–79). And in lines published in 1921 Wedekind concedes as much; he admits a lack of objectivity that prevents him from recalling the events quite accurately (IX, 436).

What Fechter characterizes as excessively personal and Wedekind himself as insufficiently objective is described by Elster (1922) as humor insufficient to allow the author to triumph over his characters; they are too colored with his hate. As in all the literary comedies from Grabbe and Platen to Holz and Josef Ruederer, the figure of the author amounts to a miserable role in a poor work because he is too involved in the events represented. The drama has some value as a picture of the times, but it is absolutely second rate as a work of Wedekind (96).

Unabashedly borrowing the observation of Pollatschak that *Oaha* emphasizes the humorlessness of the times and especially of Germany, Kutscher (1927) distinguishes the play from the literary comedies of Tieck, Platen, and Grabbe by its effectiveness on stage. The comedy contains some entertaining scenes, very funny situations, and a number of good jokes; and the technique employed in both the monologue and dialogue is dramatically effective. The play borders on parody, and romantic irony is illustrated in Sterner's request that Bouterweck write him a *Till Eulenspiegel* comedy. However, the figure of Oaha has by no means the desired comic effect, and this work belongs among the weakest of the author's dramas (II,

261–62).

Hill (1960, 87) refers to *Oaha* as "shamelessly autobiographical," and Gittleman (1969) faults Wedekind for using the stage "as a personal pamphlet" (103). The play is an indication of the difficulty the author has in developing new ideas (106), and Gittleman, while pretending to agree with Kutscher, actually outdoes him by calling this Wedekind's single weakest work (108). Nevertheless, good words are reserved for two characters in particular. Sterner is described as "a composite of Keith-Launhart, a brutal and brilliant exploiter" (107). And while Kutscher perceives in Wanda Washington the incorporation of misfortune and a vampire who finds happiness by sucking the strength from others (II, 258), Gittleman characterizes her as "a delightful parody" of Lulu (108).

Although assigning value to *Oaha* as a cultural-historical document, Irmer (1970) states that it has little literary merit and amounts to a failure as a comedy (103); and Wagener (1979) joins Gittleman in calling it Wedekind's weakest work (82).

Works Cited

Adorno, Theodor W. 1974. "Frank Wedekind und sein Sittengemälde *Musik*." In *Noten zur Literatur*, edited by Rolf Tiedemann. *Gesammelte Schriften*. Vol. 2. Frankfurt am Main: Suhrkamp. 619–26.

Best, Alan. 1973. "The Censor Censored: An Approach to Frank Wedekind's *Die Zensur*." *German Life and Letters* 26.4 (July): 278–87.

———. 1975. *Frank Wedekind*. London: Oswald Wolf.

Diebold, Bernhard. 1972. "Wedekind der Narr." In his *Anarchie im Drama*. New York and London: Johnson Reprint Corporation. 43–76. The work first appeared in 1921.

Dosenheimer, Elise. 1967. *Das deutsche soziale Drama von Lessing bis Sternheim*. Darmstadt: Wissenschaftliche Buchgesellschaft. This first appeared in 1949.

Elster, Hanns Martin. 1922. *Wedekind und seine besten Bühnenwerke*. Berlin and Leipzig: Franz Schneider.

Faesi, Robert. 1956. "Ein Vorläufer: Frank Wedekind." In *Expressionismus. Gestalten einer literarischen Bewegung*, edited by Hermann Friedmann and Otto Mann. Heidelberg: Rothe. 241–63.

Fechter, Paul. 1920. *Frank Wedekind. Der Mensch und das Werk*. Jena: Lichtenstein.

Friedenthal, Joachim. 1914. "Einleitung." In *Das Wedekindbuch*, edited by Friedenthal. Munich and Leipzig: Georg Müller. 1–121.

Gittleman, Sol. 1969. *Frank Wedekind*. New York: Twayne.

Gundolf, Friedrich. 1948. "Frank Wedekind." *Trivium* 6: 187–217. This appeared posthumously.

Haida, Peter. 1973. *Komödie um 1900. Wandlungen des Gattungsschemas von Hauptmann bis Sternheim*. Munich: Fink. 92–107.

Harris, Edward P. 1981. "Freedom and Degradation. Frank Wedekind's Career as a Kabarettist." In *The Turn of the Century. German Literature and Art, 1890–1915*, edited by Gerald Chapple and Hans H. Schulte. Bonn: Bouvier. 493–525.

Heuß, Theodor. 1909. "Frank Wedekind." *Der Kunstwart* 22.17 (June): 262–69.

Hibberd, John L. 1986. "'Die Wiedervereinigung von Kirche und Freudenhaus.' Wedekind's

Wedekind's *Die Zensur* and his ideas on religion." *Colloquia Germanica* 19.1: 47–67.

Hill, Claude. 1960. "Wedekind in Retrospect." *Modern Drama* 3.1 (May): 82–92.

Hofmiller, Josef. 1909. "Wedekinds autobiographische Dramen." *Süddeutsche Monatshefte* 6.1: 116–25.

———. 1910. "Wedekind." In *Zeitgenossen*. Munich: Süddeutsche Monatshefte. 88–131.

Irmer, Hans-Jochen. 1975. *Der Theaterdichter Frank Wedekind. Werk und Wirkung.* Berlin: Henschelverlag. This originally appeared in 1970.

Kapp, Julius. 1909. *Frank Wedekind. Seine Eigenart und seine Werke.* Berlin: Hermann Barsdorf.

Kerr, Alfred. 1909. "Thoma-Wedekind-Shaw." *Die Neue Rundschau* 20: 137–42.

Kesting, Marianne. 1970. "Frank Wedekind." In her *Entdeckung und Destruktion*. Munich: Fink. 189–203.

Kutscher, Artur. 1970. *Frank Wedekind. Sein Leben und seine Werke.* Vols. 1, 2, 3. New York: AMS Press. This is a reprint of the editions appearing successively in 1922, 1927, and 1931.

Medicus, Thomas. 1982. *Die große Liebe. Ökonomie und Konstruktion der Körper im Werk von Frank Wedekind.* Marburg an der Lahn: Guttandin & Hoppe.

Mennemeier, Franz Norbert. 1980. "Frank Wedekind." In *Handbuch des deutschen Dramas,* edited by Walter Hinck. Düsseldorf: Bagel. 360–73, 568–69.

Pankau, Johannes G. 1989. "Exhibitionismus und Scham. Zur Problematik der Ich-Konstitution in Wedekinds *Die Zensur*." In *Kein Funke mehr, kein Stern aus früh'rer Welt,* edited by Elke Austermühl, Alfred Kessler, and Hartmut Vinçon. Darmstadt: Georg Büchner Buchhandlung. 289–310.

Pollatschak, Stefan. 1908. "Wedekinds *Oaha*." *Die Gegenwart* 74.42: 253–54.

Schröder-Zebralla, Josephine. 1985. *Frank Wedekinds religiöser Sensualismus. "Die Vereinigung von Kirche und Freudenhaus?"* Frankfurt am Main, Bern, and New York: Lang.

Shaw, Leroy R. [1964]. "Bekenntnis und Erkenntnis in Wedekinds *Die Zensur*." In *Frank Wedekind zum 100. Geburtstag,* edited by Richard Lemp. Munich: Stadtbibliothek. 20–36.

Skrine, Peter. 1989. *Hauptmann, Wedekind, and Schnitzler.* New York: St. Martin's Press.

Spalter, Max. 1967. *Brecht's Tradition.* Baltimore: Johns Hopkins Press.

Stewart, Corbet. 1985–86. "Comedy, Morality and Energy in the Work of Wedekind." *Publications of the English Goethe Society,* n.s., 56: 56–73.

Stöcker, Helene. 1907. "Wedekind und die Frauenbewegung." *Morgen* 1: 250–51.

Trotsky, Leon. 1968. "Frank Wedekind." In his *Literatur und Revolution.* Translated by Eugen Schaefer and Hans von Riesen. Berlin: Gerhardt. 366–87. The article appeared in German in *Die neue Zeit* April 1908.

Völker, Klaus. 1965. *Frank Wedekind.* Velber bei Hannover: Friedrich Verlag.

Wagener, Hans. 1979. *Frank Wedekind.* Berlin: Colloquim.

Wedekind, Frank. 1921. "Was ich mir dabei dachte." In *Gesammelte Werke.* Vol. 9. Munich: Georg Müller. 434–51.

Wedekind, Kadidja. 1989. "Mutmassungen über *Musik*." In *Kein Funke mehr, kein Stern aus früh'rer Welt,* edited by Elke Austermühl, Alfred Kessler, and Hartmut Vinçon. Darmstadt: Georg Büchner Buchhandlung. 15–18. This first appeared in 1964–65.

Weidl, Erhard, ed. 1990. *Werke.* Vol. 2. Munich: Winkler.

10: The Late Works:
Schloß Wetterstein (1912), the Scene of Depravity;
Franziska (1912), the Female Faust;
Simson (1914), or Modesty and Jealousy;
Herakles (1917), Bastard of the Gods

Following a caesura defined by *Musik, Zensur,* and *Oaha, Schloß Wetterstein* (Castle Wetterstein, 1912) initiates a last phase in the body of Wedekind's drama that includes *Franziska* (Franziska, 1912), *Simson* (Samson, 1914), and *Herakles* (Hercules, 1917). This periodization is first established by Fechter (1920), who notes that in the late works Wedekind increases the distance which he maintains between himself and his figures (111). Kutscher (1931) observes further that Wedekind demonstrates more coldness, intellect, and objectivity; the playwright is less involved in self-analysis and self-flagellation (III, 108). Variations and analogies appear now to themes employed earlier, Dosenheimer (1949, 213) submits. Faesi (1956) suggests that in order to avoid subjectivity, Wedekind turns to myth and heroics, remaining nevertheless quite attached to his central figures (258).

Schloß Wetterstein marks for Rothe (1968) not the commencement of Wedekind's final period, but a new beginning in neoclassicism. Among the features of this style is argumentative dramatic language rather than unresponsive monologue. Uncertainty generated by marriage and family or biblical and mythical conflicts brings forth strong individuals who fashion their own fate; gone are the marionettes that react to natural instincts and social drives (118–19). Recognizing that the drama leaves behind the treatment of social struggle to concentrate upon the fate of the individual who is heroic and monumental, Hahn (1969), nevertheless, sees a continuity in the effort of the dramatist to reunify sensuality and morality, thereby achieving a higher degree of humanity (I, 89).

Both Wagener (1979, 83) and Schröder-Zebralla (1985, 200) speak of the works of this period by reference to Wedekind's supposed state of mind, the sources for his writing, and the styles he adopts. Convinced that the playwright has relinquished the ideals of his earlier days, the critics see him reconsider with resignation the lifestyle of the bourgeoisie; he turns, and there is no causal connection suggested, to verse drama and to subjects from classical and biblical mythology.

Schloß Wetterstein
(Castle Wetterstein, 1912)

The father of fifteen-year-old Effie, Major von Gystrow, was killed in a duel a year and a half earlier by Rüdiger von Wetterstein. The Major, his wife Leonore, and Rüdiger's own wife doubted the fidelity of their marriage partners because of letters received or discovered. Revealing that he wrote these letters in order to make this moment possible, Rüdiger asks for Leonore's hand in marriage. Proclaiming his belief in her and the institution of marriage, he promises that Leonore shall belong to herself and live freely together with him and beside him.

Having discovered that Rüdiger has embezzled millions from him and exploiting Rüdiger's fear of the police, the brutish Meinhard Luckner demands possession of Leonore. Effie advises her mother to repel this human animal by throwing herself upon him with all the appearances of lust. Effie confesses her regard for those exceptional people to whom the impossible is possible. Heeding the advice of her daughter, Leonore challenges Luckner and defies him to seize her, causing him to kill himself. Leonore goes to prison knowing Effie and Rüdiger will become lovers.

Castle Wetterstein is the scene of a brothel, where Effie plies her trade and supports Leonore and Rüdiger. Dr. Scharlach tells Effie that her lifestyle and perception of the world are an illness, her hunger for men attributable to the disfunction of liver and gallbladder. This destroys her belief in the holiness of her sexuality.

The Argentine Chagnaral Tschamper offers one hundred thousand dollars for the opportunity to commit suicide by poison in Effie's presence. What she does not understand is Tschamper's refusal of her repeated offers to disrobe. His nerves are taut; the flesh has its own spirit. At considerable anguish to Effie, he forces her to tell of the most tragic events of her life: her first act of adultery and the death of her father. Becoming increasingly aroused, she kisses Tschamper, avows her love, and insists that he must live; with a master such as Tschamper to subdue her, Effie would have never become a whore. Declaring that she needs a man for whom to sacrifice herself as Tschamper does a woman who sacrifices all for him, Effie drinks the poison. Tschamper finds the death lovely and so much sweeter than that of his other victims. Upon departure he observes that Effie and he chatted harmlessly about her home life, a subject which no prostitute is able to bear.

In his preface to the play, Wedekind notes that it contains his views concerning the inner needs upon which marriage and the family rest, the plot development being of minor significance (XI, 5). But the words of the playwright carry little weight for the author and critic Erich Mühsam (1910), writing in the prestigious journal *Die Schaubühne*. Unlike most of the critics to follow, he encounters little difficulty with the work. It consists of a trilogy representing the relation of the sexes to each other in different ways: a comedy illustrating that depravity committed for a woman's sake evokes her love; a drama showing that nothing is more embarrassing to a rapist than a woman's eager surrender; and a tragedy of sacrificial celebration (1269–70).

Veiling the work in the thought of Nietzsche and borrowing Effie's comment regarding the individual able to perform the impossible, Kempner (1911) derives a unifying concept for all three acts and then forces this idea upon them like the bed of Procrustes. The critic sees an allusion to the superman in males living according to their natures and heedless of others; he links this idea to the conception of the human ability to perform the impossible and perceives both demonstrated with increasing intensity from act to act. In each case the impossible amounts to a male forcing himself upon a woman (49–50).

Kempner's interpretation of the unifying structure of the male ability to do the impossible is deconstructed by Friedenthal (1914) with the observation that Rüdiger is the only male able to achieve this goal. Leonore voluntarily sacrifices herself to Luckner in order that her husband be spared, and the aroused Effie gives herself to Tschamper in suicide as a response to his impotent lust (95–96).

Taking issue with Wedekind's assertion that content and plot are of secondary importance, Fechter (1920) emphasizes the dramatist's interest in aspects of cohabitation as well as human needs and compulsive behavior. Fechter observes that the theme of the trilogy is the same as that of the *Lulu* tragedy, namely the conflict and struggle of male and female for pleasure during various stages of social and moral decline (112).

In 1921 Wedekind explains that the trilogy was originally conceived as individual works associated with a man, woman, and child; with Rüdiger, the comedy *In allen Sätteln gerecht* (Ready for Anything); with Leonore, the drama *Mit allen Hunden gehetzt* (Wily as a Fox); and with Effie, the tragedy *In allen Wassern gewaschen* (Too Clever by Half). Wedekind submits that the spiritual and moral theme of the dialogues is marriage and its opposite, prostitution (IX, 452–53). His words are widely understood by critics as an attempt to mislead censors, and Elster (1922) perceives the theme of the work in the conflict between feeling and will devoid of feeling, between desire and the mind. Increasingly from act to act, mind triumphs over life and death; the male can rise to a state of intellect without feeling, but the woman remains subordinate to emotion (102).

With a variation on Kempner and Friedenthal that shifts the focus from the male figures in the attempt to find a common thread in the three plays, Kutscher (1931) suggests that the characters united by their ability to achieve the impossible are Rüdiger, Leonore, and Effie: Rüdiger for marrying the wife of a man he has slain; Leonore for throwing herself on Luckner with such shamelessness that he is rendered impotent and commits suicide (III, 96); and Effie for offering in death the richness of her fertility to the impotent Tschamper (103).

As does Kempner, Kutscher sees a reflection of Nietzsche in figures living according to their lights and regardless of others. But Nietzsche's big figures are not erotic. Here, on the other hand, human beings larger than life play in a drama of the sexes, the action of which unfolds by means of increasingly horrible deeds (III, 100–101, 107).

Just as on other occasions where Wedekind remarks on his works, Dosenheimer

(1949) reminds the reader how literary criticism operates. A piece of literature is a self-contained entity and has nothing to prove but itself, she observes. The author's comments constitute non-aesthetic, external standards which he is imposing on the literature. The critic concludes that if Wedekind had wanted to mount an argument, he should have written a theoretical tract; at least it would have been less ambiguous (214–15).

Rothe (1968, 124) attempts to formulate another pattern to unify the drama. He argues that the first marriage of Leonore was patriarchal in nature, and this gives way to a new conception of marriage represented by Rüdiger. In act 2 this marriage is destroyed by prostitution. And finally family order is reestablished by patriarchal domination reflected in the nature of Effie. It is the last observation in this interpretation by Rothe that is most dubious.

Harking back to Fechter (1920, 112) without acknowledging him, Irmer (1970, 161) perceives a principle of composition similar to that employed in the *Lulu* tragedy, namely that of theme and variation; each act represents the life and death struggle of man and woman. The dynamics are so intense, however, that every act becomes independent and assumes its place in a collection of one-act plays. Such literary theorizing, however, does not cause Irmer to neglect his Marxist politics; he maintains that the play illustrates the psychological power of men over women in male-dominated bourgeois society (162).

Sharing with Rothe an interest in the patriarchal nature of Leonore's relationship to her deceased husband, Lorenz (1976) concerns herself almost exclusively with the first act. She singles out the themes of marriage to Rüdiger as a union of equals, repression of women, and patriarchy; these suggest the debt of Wedekind to the socialist thinking of Friedrich Engels and August Bebel (54–55).

Although Audrone Willeke (1980) does not refute Dagmar Lorenz, the two could not disagree more strongly. Willeke asserts that masochism and sadism here provide a warning that patriarchal relationships in marriage are preferable to the destruction that ensues when the sexes are emancipated (31–32).

The two central figures of the final act attract the most attention among all the characters. Although Effie is widely compared to Lulu, some distinctions are made. Mühsam (1910), for example, contends that Effie is an enlightened Lulu (1269) and Friedenthal (1914) that Effie is another kind of woman with other feelings and a pale counterpart to Lulu (96). Describing Effie as an incorporation of the joys of love, Kutscher (1931) is the first to detect irony since the spirit of her sexuality is grounded in a physiological dysfunction, namely that of liver and gallbladder (III, 102–3).

A decade and a half before Sokel (1966), Dosenheimer (1949) alludes to the parallel between Effie and Lulu since both meet their demise by sex murder. Dosenheimer draws a closer comparison between Effie and Lisiska in *Tod und Teufel* since both characters recognize the infernal nature of sex and are ready for orgiastic self-destruction (214). Sokel puts it only somewhat differently when he observes that Effie combines the fate of Lulu with the nymphomaniac desire of Lisiska (207).

Compared with Lulu, Effie is self-conscious and disturbed by uncertainty, features which according to Rothe (123) make her characteristic of Wedekind's neoclassic period. Gittleman (1969, 112) both compares and contrasts, describing Effie as "the ultimate reincarnation of Lulu" while at the same time pointing out that Effie lacks that mythic context in which Lulu operates. The fact that Effie's appetite for men originates in a physical disorder causes Wagener (1979, 85–86) to perceive the destruction of hetaerism; the glorification of female sexuality is revealed as self-delusion.

Medicus (1982) distinguishes Lulu, a being without origins, from Effie, a concrete person with family. But the critic does not pause here, he extends to Effie the full Freudian treatment: since her clitoris is inferior, she desires a penis, for which a child serves as substitute. Her sensuality thus stems from the repressed wish for a child (253). Confirming the myth of prostitution born from the Oedipus complex, Effie finds in Tschamper the father as love object (255–56).

The figure of Tschamper, writes Mühsam (1910), entails the reworking of a motif from *Tod und Teufel;* that is, the association of erotic satisfaction with physical torment. Tschamper attempts to evoke the deepest suffering in order to satisfy his lust with the sensual pleasure lent by the sight of pain (1270–71). Probably since this character is addressed as "Mister" and pays in dollars for services rendered, Kempner (1911) comes to the conclusion that he is an American. And based on this interpretation the critic contends that Tschamper has that opportunity and inclination known only to an American, namely to employ his money to strip all fantasy from existence (49). Tschamper's American nationality is reaffirmed by Scheller (1912, 581), Friedenthal (1914, 96), and Fechter (1920, 112), for whom this character represents mind without feeling; like Jack the Ripper, Tschamper commits sex murder, with the difference that he achieves it mentally by eliciting suicide (116).

The solicitation of Tschamper is linked morally with nationality in the words of Dosenheimer (1949, 213), who characterizes his offer as a model case of American dollar decadence ("ein Schulbeispiel amerikanischer Dollar-Dekadenz"). Both Gittleman (111) and Irmer (1970, 166) agree that he is an American, the latter remarking that he plays upon Effie's imagined daughter-father relationship to him. Rothe's observation regarding patriarchy (1968, 124) is reworked by Irmer in the context of socialism: in male-dominated bourgeois society women are conditioned to make inhumane self-sacrifices, and Tschamper knows how to use this female pre-disposition.

Borrowing the idea of Kutscher (1931 III, 99) that Tschamper is the incorpora-tion of death, Wagener at the same time develops an alternate concept of primal male strength; Tschamper's dominance overrides and dispels sexual pretension, and Effie drinks poison since she recognizes in him a man whose strength is equal to her beauty (85–86). Willeke (1980, 32) assumes Rothe's interpretation of Tschamper as a patriarch and Medicus (252) that of Irmer that he is an American father figure. It is not until Chick (1984) that Tschamper is identified as what the text clearly describes him as being: an Argentine millionaire (38).

The critics tend to center their attention upon three individual one-act dramas, becoming increasingly negative, indeed downright condemnatory in their evaluation of the work throughout the years as they approach the present day. Defending Wedekind against the censors, Mühsam (1910) calls him the truest depicter of people and the most capable dramatist in Germany. The second work of the trilogy is the most dramatically effective and the last the deepest and most poetic (1270–71). Scheller (1912) unabashedly describes Wedekind's dramatic abilities as the most powerful since Shakespeare; the first work is a comedy with brilliant dialogue and the final a tragedy with electric tension and the most extreme intensity (581–82).

The absence of coherent form for the drama as a whole is faulted by Friedenthal (1914), who singles out the first one-act drama as the best; a small, self-contained art work that is convincing, lean in structure, and, as Scheller notes, furnished with brilliant dialogue (93–94).

In Shakespeare's *Richard III,* the central figure, the Duke of Gloucester, marries Lady Anne, widow of Edward, Prince of Wales, whom Richard has murdered. Fechter (1920) is the first to point out the parallel to these events in the first act where the murderous Rüdiger asks the widow Leonore for her hand (113); the critic describes this as the strongest act, remarking however that the work as a whole is not conceptually clear (116). On the other hand, Diebold (1921, 71) finds this act fashioned after Shakespeare improbable because of the rapidity with which the successful suit unfolds.

Both Diebold and Elster (1922) take Wedekind at his word when in the preface he purports to treat the subjects of marriage and family. Diebold asserts that when such matters provide the purpose of the drama and the plot is not the organic nucleus, but of secondary importance as Wedekind insists, the result is theatricality and the bankruptcy of drama (71). Elster, on the other hand, credits Wedekind with insight into personalities; the work constitutes an intuitive psychological treatment of those drives which account for the cohabitation of the sexes in marriage (103).

Reiterating the opinion of Fechter and ignoring the thematic explanation offered by the author, Kutscher (1931) faults the three one-act plays for the absence of a central concept (III, 99); the first act can stand alone but the succeeding ones cannot. Moreover, the behavior of the figures Luckner and Tschamper is not convincing; they are not very deep and therefore not readily understandable (106–7).

Although Faesi (1956, 257) considers the thought content of the work unclear, it conveys a distinct impression, namely that the behavior represented is so monstrously criminal and pathological that it is incredible (256). Sokel (1966) speaks of Wedekind's "tragic" failure to maintain his artistic quality (207), and Spalter (1967) uses the adjectives "morbid" and "nightmarish" (133), referring to "the smell of neurosis" and "a ghastly vision" (133–34, note 21).

Assuming Wedekind's original intent to deal with sex and society, Gittleman (1969) contends that the drama reflects "incredible distortion" and the dramatist's "inability to deal meaningfully with his ideas" (110). The work is "prurient" (113), constitutes "provocative exhibitionism" (110), and offers "a display of sadism and hard-core voyeurism almost unparalleled in serious dramatic literature" (112).

Reading the first act as parody of *Richard III* and the final one as parody of the death of Lulu, Irmer (1970) rejects the suggestion that *Schloß Wetterstein* marks a fading in Wedekind's creative powers as a dramatist (162). However, that is exactly the opinion of Friedmann (1975, 174) and Stewart (1985–86, 73).

Franziska. Ein modernes Mysterium in fünf Akten
(Franziska. A Modern Mystery Play in Five Acts, 1912)

Based on what she has witnessed of her parents' domestic relations, the eighteen-year-old Franziska Eberhardt concludes that there is no such thing as marital happiness. Determined to rid herself of her innocence and provided with insurance against pregnancy by her elderly patron Baron von Hohenkemnath, Franziska seduces Dr. Hofmiller, rejecting his marriage proposal, however, since she is determined to learn to know herself.

Entering her chamber through a window, Veit Kunz confesses having admired her body at the insurance office. As an impresario Kunz offers to develop her entertainment skills; the two strike an agreement whereby she will experience the freedom and pleasure granted a male for a period of two years, after which time she will belong to Kunz. Franziska appears as Franz among merrymakers in a wine cellar.

Franz endures a grotesquely unhappy marriage to Sophie, during the course of which Franz has been Kunz's lover and become pregnant. When Sophie's brother learns from Dr. Hofmiller that his sister has married a woman, the brother tells Sophie, and she kills herself. Kunz seeks roles for Franz which provide opportunities for developing her talents, including an appearance as a supernatural being to the Duke of Rothenburg.

Franziska and Kunz find happiness, which is very short-lived as she slips away into the arms of the actor Ralf Breitenbach. Kunz curses himself for having believed Franziska capable of self-sacrifice equal to becoming his property. Von Hohenkemnath prevents the suicide of Kunz and asks him if he has ever known a man who understands a woman.

In rustic surroundings Franziska devotes herself to her four-year-old son Veitralf with the financial support of von Hohenkemnath. Her doctor advises her to marry Karl Almer, who loves her and the child. Kunz and Breitenbach deny paternity but wish to assume roles in her life. She will have nothing of either and enjoys tranquil, domestic bliss as Almer paints her portrait.

Although the resemblances to Goethe's *Faust* are readily apparent, Hardekopf (1911) is little impressed and writes that the very idea of a female Faust is itself banal (440); the comparison to *Faust* is rejected by Elsner as well (1912) since Franziska is not a personality but a one-sided erotic being, for whom the thirst for knowledge is trivial.

Elsner finds it more meaningful to consider *Franziska* in the light of *Frühlings Erwachen:* the relationship of Franziska to her mother reflects that of Wendla to Frau Bergmann since in both instances there is no communication regarding the subject of sex (6–7). Moreover, the Masked Gentleman reappears as Veit Kunz, alias Frank Wedekind (9–10). Taking this as a shortcoming of the playwright, Elsner becomes judgmental; Wedekind, by once again injecting his personal attitudes and experiences, has created characters that are simply marionettes speaking his words. Moreover, the dramatist repeats himself, an indication that his creativity is exhausted (13). The term *banal* applied by Hardekopf to the idea of a female Faust is employed by Elsner with reference to the conclusion of the work depicting Franziska as she relishes maternal bliss (25).

A review by Erich Mühsam (1912) addresses the views of Elsner, without deigning to recognize him by name. Mühsam characterizes *Franziska* as a symphony of tones, grotesque and lyrical, romantic, tragic, amusing, and racy (667). It is Wedekind's richest, deepest, and most brilliant work, his boldest in its conception (664). The marriage of Franz and Sophie, an idea which Elsner terms perverse (11), represents a master accomplishment of Wedekind's dramatic art; it is a ghastly, grotesque joke (665). The conclusion of the work presents redemption for Franziska from a life of confusion and contention in the happiness of maternity. *Franziska* is a statement of love, affirmation of life, and reverence for women (667).

As does Mühsam, Schwarz (1912) perceives the fulfillment of Franziska's destiny in maternity. *Franziska* outlines the developmental history of the emancipated woman, who ultimately experiences conversion; having seen the boundaries of her world and having accomplished a full life without being subject to a husband and master, she now finds rest and equanimity (236–37).

Friedenthal (1914) focuses upon the two main characters, Franziska and Veit Kunz. She in her desire to be more than a woman incorporates Faustian longing and attains unlimited freedom in the union of the male and female sexes, a feature distinctive of romanticism. Without explicitly saying so, Friedenthal perceives an analogous unity in the central figure of the work; this is Veit Kunz, the new Mephistopheles, who unites God and the devil in one breast (110–11).

The critic places particular emphasis on two scenes for their contributions to the work. That set in the Berlin restaurant and wine cellar is one of the most effective on stage (112), and the first scene of act 4 reflects the fleeting happiness of Franziska and Veit Kunz in the pure poetry of *Frühlings Erwachen* (113). Despite these strengths, Friedenthal (114) agrees with Hecht (1914, 674), who in the same year characterized the work as shallow and banal.

The employment of the Faust materials suggests to Fechter (1920, 117) Wedekind's literary wit. Mephistopheles is not a devil, but an insurance agent; the modern world has replaced belief in God with faith in an insurance company. Whereas Friedenthal (110) mentions merely in passing that Veit Kunz incorporates Wedekind's personal struggle, Fechter elaborates upon this idea; he asserts that Wedekind is present at the outset in Franziska but then passes over to Veit Kunz. This character, asserts Fechter, is perhaps the most important figure for understanding the late Wedekind; the playwright is now more interested in his own relationship to women, and the woman Franziska is seen therefore from the male perspective (118).

As does Friedenthal, Fechter characterizes the scene depicting the brief happiness found by Franziska and Veit Kunz as one of the most beautiful love scenes Wedekind ever wrote (121), and the conversation between Kunz and Hohenkemnath after the attempted suicide as one of the most marvelously human (123). While Elsner finds the conclusion banal and Mühsam and Schwarz interpret it as a positive statement regarding the role of women, Fechter has a marked difference of opinion. The conclusion amounts to a song of scorn; it is an expression of Wedekind's most bitter derision regarding the ability of women to develop themselves; here he takes revenge on women and on himself because of his longing for love (124).

Wedekind remarks on his own work with reference to those scenes which have attracted the most attention (IX, 453). The marriage of Franz and Sophie, characterized by Mühsam (1912, 665) as ghastly and grotesque, is described by the playwright as his attempt to construct a marriage that was impossibly unhappy; he suggests no reason for this. Wedekind's comment upon the love scene of Franziska and Kunz reveals something of his attitude towards woman's rights; this scene turns, he writes, about the question of whether a human being may be considered a piece of property in someone's possession.

Diebold (1921) is little satisfied with the work; he asserts that the subtitle "Mystery" is employed since the author mystified himself, and the designation provides an excuse for a poorly constructed drama that is scattered into nine sections. Elsner emphasizes Franziska's erotic nature, suggesting by implication that she shares little of the intellectual curiosity or spiritual quality of Faust; and Diebold develops this idea. What for Faust amounts to the constraints imposed upon the human facilities regarding knowledge and experience amounts in Franziska's case to the limitation inherent in being a single sex, a purely physiological problem; Franziska serves as a hermaphrodite in a Faustian phantasmagoria (72–73).

Diebold has never been very supportive of Wedekind's attempt to reconcile the flesh with the spirit; now his patience wears thin. He asserts, baldly, that nature is a matter of morality determined by the will and not the flesh (73); in human beings the flesh fails when it conflicts with the soul formed by the spirit (75–76), whatever that means.

No raging feminist, Elster (1922) levels a charge at Wedekind widely supported by advocates of woman's rights and probably accurate at that, notwithstanding the dramatist's comment about owning a person as a piece of property. Elster contends that for Wedekind the woman has no other meaning than that assumed in the sphere of love (109–10). The critic then moves into Wedekind's biography when he submits that in the dramatist's advanced age he had concluded that the woman, however daring and adventurous in affairs of love, ultimately finds solace in the idyll of the arbor ("Gartenlaubenidylle"). Kunz, as Wedekind, thought he possessed the most perfect union of love and desire, but it slipped away; both the dramatic character and the author learn that there exists only a longing for love, not a reality which may be achieved (109–10).

Elster submits that the value of the work as a parallel to *Faust* is enhanced by Wedekind's originality. The scene in the wine cellar is a combination of two from Goethe's work; these are the Witch's Kitchen and Auerbach's Cellar. Wedekind's scene is populated by writers and whores, proletarians and barons, physical and spiritual prostitutes; the critic refers to an atmosphere rich in cynicism, dialogues about art, spiritual brutality, coarse jokes, and ingenious conceits (105–6).

Kutscher (1931) suggests a contradictory quality in the drama. Wedekind's development of the woman to her greatest potential concludes in resignation and pessimism (III, 121–22); the playwright's activism and tendentiousness are overcome. At the same time Kutscher finds this Wedekind's most exuberant work (130–31) and describes the conclusion in quite uplifting terms. Here Franziska comes to realize as a mother her full value as a woman (120); she finds her way back to her true nature in love and reconciliation (130–31). The figure of Karl Almer poses a new type of masculine love that is founded in mutual well-being (122).

Kutscher notes (III, 122–23) that Franziska has her literary forbears in independent women such as Nora in the drama *A Doll's House* (1879) by Henrik Ibsen and Hedda Gabler in Ibsen's play by that name (1890). Franziska distinguishes herself from Wedekind's own Lulu by her more highly developed self-consciousness and sense of responsibility for herself (121).

In an expression of feminist ire unexpected of Elise Dosenheimer (1949) and almost unheard generally during the forties, Dosenheimer scrutinizes Wedekind's intent and places her finger squarely on the source of critical ambiguity. Either the conclusion is meant positively with Franziska appearing not as Faust but as Gretchen, an outcome which Dosenheimer characterizes as banal in any case, or the work is intended as satire reflecting negatively on the woman's movement (216, 219). Of one mind with Elsner (1912) regarding the marriage of the two women Franz and Sophie, Dosenheimer describes this arrangement as tasteless, embarrassing, repulsive, and immoral. She seems to be looking to her own experience when she avers that this caricature of a marriage does not address the true nature of the union (217).

Rothe (1968) is as little troubled by the ambiguity of the work as are Schwarz (1912), Fechter (1920), Elster (1922), and Kutscher before him. Franziska's desire to be a man is exposed as contrary to the natural order; her striving for emancipation is revealed, therefore, as illusory (127). Rothe supports the observation of Fechter (124) that Wedekind's bitterest song of scorn is reserved for the belief in the ability of women to develop themselves. Regarding the merits of the drama, Rothe calls it hollow (131–32).

Assuming a position diametrically opposed to Fechter and Rothe and every bit as single-minded although wrong in one respect, Gittleman (1969, 114) interprets what he calls "an airy mixture of prose and verse" as an affirmative statement in behalf of conventional marriage and motherhood. Of course, there is no marriage, but the point is that Gittleman detects not a trace of satire in Franziska's contentment; her feelings are genuine, and "Lulu has finally been domesticated" (115–16).

Borrowing from Fechter the idea that the central figure is now Franziska, now Veit Kunz, Irmer (1970) interprets the transformations of Franziska as lightly parodistic and similar to an operetta (206–7). Irmer's interpretation is sustained by his analysis of the work as a parody of a bourgeois family drama: recognizing the limits drawn by nature and society, Franziska acknowledges herself as a woman, while at the same time rejecting bourgeois marriage. In a family without husband and father, Franziska achieves a private matriarchy. Karl Almer, seen as representative of a new kind of masculine love by Kutscher, appears here as a parody figure (208–9).

Totally ignoring the accurate distinction which Kutscher draws between Wedekind's two feminine characters, Kesting (1970) indulges in a crass oversimplification of the nature of Franziska when describing her as an extension of Lulu, who finds in the idyll of the arbor a refuge and the only alternative to the catastrophe which befell Lulu (194–95).

Recalling society dominated by males as it existed at the turn of the century, Jelavich (1979) and Willeke (1980) interpret the work similarly. Jelavich reads the outcome as "a justification of conventional patriarchal values," the drama illustrating that it is "unnatural" for a woman to attempt to undertake masculine activities (235). Drawing a comparison with the behavior of Princess Russalka in the tale by that name, Willeke sees yet another example of the woman who demonstrates "complacent acceptance of the status quo." The conclusion is "conciliatory" since the female recognizes her assigned role; the "promised emancipation" of Franziska, which is never realized, is the Mystery of the subtitle (32–33).

Vinçon (1987) divulges what he touts as a perception hitherto unshared by literary critics: Franziska is not an individual seen from the male perspective as she attempts to realize her femininity; she is an allegory of Life in a work which constitutes Wedekinds critique of vitalism. The strength of the play is, however, vitiated by the conclusion—a humorous portrait of the Madonna and holy family that amounts to "Kitsch" or sentimental rubbish (232–33).

Totally at odds with Best (1975, 59), Diethe (1988) considers the work a failure to the extent that it is intended as a serious attempt to emulate Goethe's *Faust*. She is, however, less clear regarding the conclusion, where she, as many critics, finds it difficult to see into the playwright's head. Diethe faces with uncertainty, therefore, the question whether it is intended satirically or seriously (112).

Simson oder Scham und Eifersucht
(Samson or Modesty and Jealousy, 1913)

Delilah calls together the princes of the Philistines, to whom she will deliver Samson, the champion of the downtrodden. On previous occasions he has overcome all attempts to subdue him, but this time he has betrayed in Delilah's arms the secret of his strength, his untrimmed hair. While asleep, he is shorn and thereby captured and blinded. Delilah promises herself to Prince Og if Samson's life be spared.

Reduced to menial work, Samson turns a mill with music and poetry on his lips, sustained by the love of Delilah, who protects him for his lyrical gifts. She is reproached by Og for that shamelessness which reflects unfavorably upon the prince's male dignity. He refuses to touch her body until Samson dies; and as the captive provides musical accompaniment, Delilah seduces Og.

Their marriage is celebrated at the Temple of Dagon, where Samson is subject to public humiliation for the entertainment of the guests. His hair having partially regrown, Samson is led to a position between two columns of the temple at the length of each arm. An unsuccessful attempt is made by two princes to assassinate Og, and he cuts the throat of the faithless Delilah. Pushing the columns from beneath the temple, Samson brings it down to wreak his revenge.

Samson is portrayed as the instrument of Delilah's lust (115–16) and stands as the central figure of scenes bristling with hate and scorn directed at the Philistines, in the view of Friedenthal (1914, 119–20), who hails the drama as one of the most prominent literary works of the time.

But the opinion of Fechter (1920) is less favorable. Although the struggle between the sexes, a recurring motif in Wedekind's work, is treated here within the context of modesty and jealousy, nevertheless, the work lacks a central concept. The inevitable autobiographical connection is made with the observation that Wedekind is blind and lonely like Samson; the playwright portrays his aging self in the strong man who is broken by his trust of a woman and emerges from subjugation greater than all his enemies (125, 129). Of special interest is the seduction scene suggesting the discrepancy between poetry and life: the blind Samson sings of the love of a warrior for his maid as Og acts out the words of the lyrics on the person of Delilah (127).

While Fechter interprets the work as representation of the struggle between the sexes, Diebold (1921) reads it as an illustration of female superiority. The hero suffers a pompous downfall in a work the banality of which is unlikely to inspire imitation (74–75).

The antithetical construction of the play interests Kutscher (1931), who notes the themes of modesty and shamelessness as well as blindness and sight; antitheses are sustained in the configurations Delilah and Samson, Delilah and Og, and Samson and Og. Kutscher describes this construction as logical and external but unrelated to the nature of the drama. The artistic nucleus of the work is the association of pain with creativity; blindness and torment assume symbolic meaning as creative powers. The scene in which Samson sings the warrior's song unaware of the lovemaking before his blind eyes demonstrates the exclusion of the creative spirit from the real world. The central concept of the work associating suffering and creativity lacks, however, sufficient dramatic motivation (III, 142–43).

Even as Friedenthal terms Wedekind's representation of the Philistines grotesque, Kutscher sees satire and caricature reminiscent of that found in the early drama *Frühlings Erwachen* (III, 143). He finds further that *Simson* is uneven in quality as illustrated by language which is at times rhythmic and beautiful and at others banal and stilted; the play is abstract, artificial, and sometimes unconvincing (144–45).

Likewise emphasizing the grotesque features of the work, Faesi (1956) pays slight regard to this tragicomedy and looks to Fechter when describing it as a paraphrase of the author's fate (258). It is this interpretation of the play which causes Natan (1963) to characterize *Simson* as "a return to the sado-masochistic tendency to which Wedekind remained prone all his life" (118).

Samson's creative lyrical abilities emerge after his blinding and capture, and Rothe (1968, 134) is the first to indicate an exchange of sexual roles with the suggestion that music may have feminine origins engendered by subordination or subjugation. When act 2 opens with Samson as a slave, the central figure has been recast in a different mold, a transformation leading Rothe to remark that Wedekind anticipates the manner in which Bertolt Brecht disassembles the character Galy Gay and refashions him in the drama *Mann ist Mann* (A Man's a Man, 1926).

Gittleman (1969) echoes Diebold (1921) when he characterizes the work as "wooden, at times pompous" (116), but Irmer (1970) exercises more independence and originality. He argues that shame and jealousy cannot coexist harmoniously because these feelings predicate inequality and the dominance of one person over another (183). The theme of *Simson* is the struggle for human dignity, and without providing any explanation Irmer asserts that theme dictates style, which is not neo-classicistic but nearly expressionistic in its abstract representation of human beings (178–79).

According to Vinçon (1987), Wedekind has modernized myth by injecting this lore with issues of contemporary concern, among them the origins of modesty and jealousy as well as feminine emancipation. Vinçon ignores Mennemeier's (1980, 373) characterization of the work as classicistic and cites Irmer for the contention that the style is not neoclassicism but a parody thereof. Rejected is Fechter's assertion that Samson is Wedekind's self-portrait and that the loneliness of the character is that of the author; the loneliness is that of society on the eve of World War I, depicted in a parable predicting the destruction this catastrophe will bring (234–35).

Herakles
(Hercules, 1917)

The introductory words of Hermes, the messenger of the gods, prepare the audience for the dramatic representation of a human fate; it is that of Hercules, a bastard between men and gods, a mortal with divine gifts who struggles for human happiness but fails to gain the love of mankind.

Hercules bests King Eurytus in archery competition and frees himself from slavery by overcoming his desirous mistress, Queen Ophale. Having rescued Deianeira from the river god, Hercules marries her. He kills the centaur Nessus as it falls upon Deianeira but not before it gives her its poisoned blood falsely represented as a magic potion to ensure her lover's fidelity.

Her father and brothers having been slain by Hercules, Iole joins his retinue, and Deianeira prepares for him a garment soaked in the centaur's blood to defeat her rival. Racked by pain from the poison, Hercules mounts a funeral pyre, and Deianeira throws herself from a tower.

In the afterlife upon Olympus, Hercules meets Hera, the wife of Zeus, who reveals that she has always opposed him since he is a bastard by her husband. Nevertheless, Hera grants him Hebe, the goddess of youthful beauty.

A companion piece to *Simson* and likewise an adaptation of myth in verse, *Herakles* constitutes an equally unsuccessful illustration of the female as the stronger sex, in the opinion of Diebold (1921, 74–75). While Heinrich Mann (1929, 548) recasts the author Wedekind as the heroic Hercules wrestling with fate, Kutscher (1931) interprets the struggle of Hercules in very different terms by focusing on his opponent: it is himself with whom Hercules is contending (III, 216). Hercules is Wedekind as well as the tragic symbol of the creatively artistic, struggling human being (224). The hero is greatly influenced by the power of eros, and Kutscher makes the startling observation that eros is more closely associated with Hercules than with any other male character of Wedekind (217–18). More satisfied with the language of *Herakles* than he is with that of *Simson*, Kutscher describes the verbal pattern as spare, rhythmic, and stylized; the quality of the characters as well as the structure of the work are highly dramatic (222–21).

Faesi (1956) regards the drama as unimpressive autobiography (258), and Rothe (1968) calls it a failure (143). The latter submits that the only unity is provided by the central character. In the absence of dramatic development, the structure consists of a series of individual scenes or "Stationen" (139). Referring to *Herakles* as both "neoclassical" (118) and "classicistic," Rothe characterizes its message as a call for the emancipation of the flesh, that theme Wedekind pursued throughout his life (142).

Unlike Kutscher, who is satisfied, Gittleman (1969) calls the language "hollow"; moreover, the latter critic detects a different theme, one widely perceived in *Keith.* That work deals with the outsider, here represented by a creature, half-human and half-god, searching for a way to exist in an alien world; peace is to be found ultimately only in death (119).

As in the case of *Simson*, Irmer (1970) detects an abstract quality in the characters that suggests expressionism (178–79). Borrowing from Kutscher without acknowledgment, Irmer interprets Hercules as struggling with himself to ascertain his human identity and understand existence in this world as an artist. Moreover, Hercules strives to achieve the dignity of man (186), and the politics of the former East German Republic emerge when Irmer argues that Hercules serves on the vanguard of socialism that maintains a front against capitalism (192).

Friedmann (1975) reads *Herakles* as a glorification of the hero and of the use of force that constitutes a justification for World War I (168–69), and Willeke (1980) calls it a eulogy of the Wilhelmine order (35). But Vinçon (1987) pointedly rejects

Friedmann's interpretation, arguing that *Herakles* is a modernization of myth. Wedekind implies that what the earth needs is human beings not heroes; the playwright deplores the fact that those returning from the front are received by a world that is planning destruction (238–39). Disagreeing with Fechter (1920, 132), who suggests the dramatist confused Greece with Germany during these years, and with Rothe (142) and Mennemeier (1980, 373), who call the style classicistic, Vinçon describes it as a parody of the attempts of classicism to combine or harmonize Greek elements with those of modern times. As a parody, however, it borders on trash, or "Kitsch" (238–39).

Works Cited

Best, Alan. 1975. *Frank Wedekind.* London: Oswald Wolf.

Chick, Edson M. 1984. "Frank Wedekind and his *Lulu* Tragedy." In his *Dances of Death. Wedekind, Brecht, Dürrenmatt, and the Satiric Tradition.* Columbia, South Carolina: Camden House. 11–45.

Diebold, Bernhard. 1972. "Wedekind der Narr." In his *Anarchie im Drama.* New York and London: Johnson Reprint Corporation. 43–76. The work first appeared in 1921.

Diethe, Carol. 1988. *Aspects of Distorted Sexual Attitudes in German Expressionist Drama.* New York, Bern, Frankfurt am Main, and Paris: Lang.

Dosenheimer, Elise. 1967. *Das deutsche soziale Drama von Lessing bis Sternheim.* Darmstadt: Wissenschaftliche Buchgesellschaft. This first appeared in 1949.

Elsner, Richard. [1912]. "Frank Wedekind. *Franziska.*" In *Moderne Dramatik in kritischer Beleuchtung,* edited by Elsner. Heft 15. Berlin-Pankow: Sozialpädagogischer Verlag. 3–26.

Elster, Hanns Martin. 1922. *Wedekind und seine besten Bühnenwerke.* Berlin and Leipzig: Franz Schneider.

Faesi, Robert. 1956. "Ein Vorläufer: Frank Wedekind." In *Expressionismus. Gestalten einer literarischen Bewegung,* edited by Hermann Friedmann and Otto Mann. Heidelberg: Rothe. 241–63.

Fechter, Paul. 1920. *Frank Wedekind. Der Mensch und das Werk.* Jena: Lichtenstein.

Friedenthal, Joachim. 1914. "Einleitung." In *Das Wedekindbuch,* edited by Friedenthal. Munich and Leipzig: Georg Müller. 1–121.

Friedmann, Jürgen. 1975. *Frank Wedekinds Dramen nach 1900.* Stuttgart: Hans-Dieter Heinz.

Gittleman, Sol. 1969. *Frank Wedekind.* New York: Twayne.

Hahn, Manfred. 1969. "Frank Wedekind. Leben und Werk." In *Frank Wedekind. Dramen I.* Berlin and Weimar: Aufbau-Verlag. 7–93.

Hardekopf, Ferdinand. 1911. "Wedekinds Maske." *Die Schaubühne* 7.2: 440–41.

Hecht, Georg. 1914. "Ein Wort gegen Wedekind." *Die Aktion* 4: cols. 673–74.

Irmer, Hans-Jochen. 1975. *Der Theaterdichter Frank Wedekind. Werk und Wirkung.* Berlin: Henschelverlag. This originally appeared in 1970.

Jelavich, Peter. 1979. "Art and Mammon in Wilhelmine Germany: The Case of Frank Wedekind." *Central European History* 12: 203–36.

Kempner, Hans. 1911. *Frank Wedekind als Mensch und Künstler.* Berlin-Pankow: Oskar

Linser.

Kesting, Marianne. 1970. "Frank Wedekind." In her *Entdeckung und Destruktion*. Munich: Fink. 189–203.

Kutscher, Artur. 1970. *Frank Wedekind. Sein Leben und seine Werke*. Vol. 3. New York: AMS Press. This is a reprint of the edition appearing in 1931.

Lorenz, D. C. G. 1976. "Wedekind und die emanzipierte Frau. Eine Studie über Frau und Sozialismus im Werke Frank Wedekinds." *Seminar* 12.1 (February): 38–56.

Mann, Heinrich. 1929. "Damit der *Herakles* gespielt wird." In his *Sieben Jahre. Chronik der Gedanken und Vorgänge*. Berlin, Vienna, and Leipzig: Paul Zsolnay. 548–52.

Medicus, Thomas. 1982. *Die große Liebe. Ökonomie und Konstruktion der Körper im Werk von Frank Wedekind*. Marburg an der Lahn: Guttandin & Hoppe.

Mennemeier, Franz Norbert. 1980. "Frank Wedekind." In *Handbuch des deutschen Dramas*, edited by Walter Hinck. Düsseldorf: Bagel. 360–73, 568–69.

Mühsam, Erich. 1912. "*Franziska.*" *Die Schaubühne* 8.2: 664–68.

———. 1910. "*Schloß Wetterstein.*" *Die Schaubühne* 6.2 :1269–71.

Natan, Alex. 1963. "Frank Wedekind." In *German Men of Letters*, edited by Natan. Vol. 2. London: Oswald Wolf. 101–29.

Rothe, Friedrich. 1968. *Frank Wedekinds Dramen. Jugendstil und Lebensphilosophie*. Stuttgart: Metzler.

Scheller, Will. 1912. "*Schloß Wetterstein.*" *Die Neue Rundschau* 23.1: 580–84.

Schröder-Zebralla, Josephine. 1985. *Frank Wedekinds religiöser Sensualismus. "Die Vereinigung von Kirche und Freudenhaus?"* Frankfurt am Main, Bern, and New York: Lang.

Schwarz, Karl Johannes. 1912. "Wedekind-Woche." *Merker* 3.1: 236–37.

Sokel, Walter H. 1966. "The Changing Role of Eros in Wedekind's Drama." *The German Quarterly* 39.2: 201–7.

Spalter, Max. 1967. *Brecht's Tradition*. Baltimore: Johns Hopkins Press.

Stewart, Corbet. 1985–86. "Comedy, Morality and Energy in the Work of Wedekind." *Publications of the English Goethe Society*, n.s., 56: 56–73.

Vinçon, Hartmut. 1987. *Frank Wedekind*. Stuttgart: Metzler.

Wagener, Hans. 1979. *Frank Wedekind*. Berlin: Colloquim.

Wedekind, Frank. 1921. "Was ich mir dabei dachte." In *Gesammelte Werke*. Vol. 9. Munich: Georg Müller. 452–53.

Willeke, Audrone B. 1980. "Frank Wedekind and the 'Frauenfrage.'" *Monatshefte* 72.1: 26–38.

11: Other Genres
The Poetry and Prose

Poetry

Wedekind's verse is important in its influence but receives scant treatment in the secondary literature. The early poetry appeared in the collection *Die Fürstin Russalka* (Princess Russalka) in 1897 gathered under the rubric "Die Jahreszeiten" (The Seasons) and subdivided into four groups corresponding to seasons; this amounted to eighty-four poems revealing great diversity. Most of these poems appeared again in 1905 in the collection *Die vier Jahreszeiten*.

Wedekind wrote poetry throughout his lifetime and included it in his dramas. Moreover, the author composed songs and ballads for presentation at the cabaret *Die Elf Scharfrichter* (The Eleven Executioners) in Munich beginning in spring of 1901.

The critics tend to consider the verse in terms of categories which are not mutually exclusive and may overlap; the groups are defined by atmosphere or tone, subject matter, and the context in which the poem appeared. Among the lyric poetry the most highly regarded poems are "Heimweh" (Homesickness), "Abschied" (Leave Taking), "Einkehr" (A Stop for Rest), and "Alte Liebe" (Old Love). Verse written for, and included in, dramas is best represented by "Bajazzo" (Clown) from *König Nicolo* and "Die Schriftstellerhymne" (The Author's Hymn) from *Franziska*. Some poems deal with the central figures of the dramas and bear the titles "Ilse," "Lulu," "Erdgeist," and "Franziska." Wedekind's contributions to the cabaret earn him recognition for revival of the street ballad ("Bänkelsang," "Moritat"); his best compositions in this vein are taken to include "Brigitte B.," "Die Keuschheit" (Chastity), "Das arme Mädchen" (The Poor Girl), "Die Hunde" (The Dogs), and "Der Tantenmörder" (The Aunt Murderer).

Political poems were written for *Simplicissimus;* these consist of thirty-three poems appearing between 1897 and 1902 that range in length from five to forty stanzas. The first seven are each entitled "Ein politisch Lied" (A Political Ballad). This collection includes "Meerfahrt" (Ocean Voyage) and "Im Heiligen Land" (In the Holy Land), which provoked the charge of lèse-majesté and earned the author a prison term. In these poems, Wedekind hides behind a number of pseudonyms, including that of Hieronymus Jobs.

The influence of the style of Heinrich Heine upon the poetry of Wedekind is noted widely throughout the criticism and for the first time in 1908 by Leon Trotsky, who emphasizes the characteristic combination of realism, romanticism, and self-irony common to both poets (371). But peculiar to Wedekind is that skepticism or pessimism which is the lot of the contemporary artist (373).

Kapp and Heuß, both writing in 1909, are more judgmental. Making an aesthetic distinction, Kapp divides the poetry into serious, artistic verse and that of lesser quality, which is high-spirited and cynically sarcastic. The former is personal and confessional and manifested particularly in the early poems (22). Although Heuß is satisfied with the parody in the ballads "Ilse" and "Brigitte B." and the poet's sure style in the grotesque social and political protests, this critic finds little artistic merit in most of what is included in *Die vier Jahreszeiten*. The poetry is nihilistic and bawdy and represents erotic sensationalism beyond the bounds of good taste. Some poems have the tone the author assumes in his dramas when he seems to say, 'It is my duty and my curse that make me say the most ugly things; it is the helpless nature of my condition as a human being!' (263–64).

Bachmair (1912) in the journal *Die Aktion* places Wedekind's poetry in a tradition to which his drama is often assigned; the verse is seen to flow in the vein that begins with J. M. R. Lenz and runs to Heinrich von Kleist, Christian Dietrich Grabbe, and Christian Friedrich Hebbel. The poetry is not "modern" but what Bachmair prefers to call "gothic," or German through and through. The best examples of Wedekind's poems from *Die vier Jahreszeiten* are "Ilse," "Der Taler" (The Taler), "Brigitte B.," "Die Keuschheit," "Das arme Mädchen," and "Das Lied vom armen Kind" (The Song of the Poor Child). Those features that are particularly gothic are, in the first place, the authenticity of the material and the harmony of content and form; secondarily gothic is the obvious cruelty united with the deepest innocence and painful wit, which amount to blunt, crude fun (855–56).

Friedenthal (1914, 20) demonstrates his ability at discernment when he illustrates the considerable variety assumed by Wedekind's verse; the critic distinguishes elements which are lyrical, romantic, scornful, cynical, satiric, grotesque, and tragic. Noting features of the ballad, Friedenthal emphasizes aspects of the modern "Moritat" as well. To those poems mentioned by Bachmair, he adds the fragment "Felix und Galathea" (Felix and Galathea), "Einkehr," "Heimweh," "Konfession" (Confession of Faith), "Die Hunde," and "Unterm Apfelbaum" (Under the Apple Tree).

Common to all the poetry is the sexual or erotic motif, maintains Fechter (1920, 142), who stresses the uniqueness of the verse while coincidentally showing its similarity to that of other poets. Fechter argues that the poetry is not to be subsumed under the normal concept of lyric verse (136). Besides resemblances to Heinrich Heine reflected in Wedekind's coolness, skepticism, parody, and romantic irony, the verse shows possible influences of another poet; Christian Morgenstern is similarly the author of gruesome, spooky ballads with coarse humor (138–41).

Supportive of Wedekind from an early date, Kutscher (1927) distinguishes himself by his interpretations of the drama and prose; in view of this, it is startling to encounter his bald assertion that the poetry proves that Wedekind is primarily a dramatist (II, 38).

Speaking from what was then still the German Democratic Republic, Krohn

(1958) assesses Wedekind's political poetry and attributes to him a revolutionary fervor to which other critics will make reference some two decades later. Krohn argues that Wedekind was characterized by an anticapitalistic streak that was unfounded in any ideology (85); he stood in isolation as a radically opposed bourgeois intellectual unsupported by the practice and ideology of the revolutionary working movement (94). Wedekind struggled not for a new social order but against the old, dying social system (84). His verse from *Simplicissimus* illustrates his social-critical attitude towards a German-American trade agreement, German imperialism in China, nationalism, militarism, and political parties. Even his eroticism is an expression of protest against bourgeois morality and its decline (92).

Ignoring the political verse altogether and allowing the historical fact that Wedekind was a performer to reflect upon the quality of his verse, Hill (1960) observes, curiously, that Wedekind was "no genuine lyrical poet, but rather a chansoneur of songs and ballads" (87).

Both Natan (1963) and Hahn (1969) address themselves to the ambivalent nature of Wedekind's writing. The Englishman writes "one is never sure whether it is mocking laughter or veiled weeping which echoes from this poetry" (121). The lyrics, notes Hahn, have a tragicomic tone from which the grotesque erupts (I, 82).

Both Wagener in his essay of 1979 and Schumann in the same year take Krohn to task for his assertion that Wedekind opposed a dying social order. Wagener argues both that the poet confronts an outdated social morality (244) and that the verse is more sarcastic and mocking than political (248). Schumann, too, concludes that Wedekind's attitudes were not political but moral. Wedekind was a critic not of the regime but of society. He objected to the climate of Wilhelmine Germany; its conformity, lack of tolerance, hypocrisy, and materialism (242–43).

Wedekind the cabaret performer is of interest to Harris (1981) as he is to Hill. Characterizing his songs as skeptical, ironic, urbane, macabre, and bizarre, Harris emphasizes the fact that the verse conveyed a great deal more than that which strikes the reader from the printed page; much was added by Wedekind's style in performance, by his sense of timing and emphasis (495).

Paying Wedekind his rightful historical due, Vinçon (1987) observes that his poetry has little to do with expressionism and a lot to do with the verse of Bert Brecht, Erich Mühsam, and Kurt Tucholsky (159).

Prose

The first collection of Wedekind's tales appeared in June 1897 from Albert Langen under the title *Die Fürstin Russalka* (Princess Russalka); this included, besides the title piece, the stories "Rabbi Esra," "Das Opferlamm" (The Sacrificial Lamb), "Der greise Freier" (The Hoary Suitor), and "Der Brand von Egliswyl" (The Fire at Egliswyl). Wedekind's single novel fragment first appeared in 1901 and exists in several versions; this is "Mine-Haha oder Über die körperliche Erziehung der jungen

Mädchen" (Mine-Haha or Concerning the Physical Education of Young Girls).

Gundolf (1948) characterizes Wedekind's tales as novelle in the tradition of Georg Büchner and Heinrich von Kleist and deems them superior to those of the latter (187). The critic finds Wedekind's literary figures motivated by a monomaniacal desire for life (204); his tales glorify pleasure and are told with the passion of medieval legends of the saints, evoking in their eroticism exactly the opposite effect of such piety (202). The prose style is described as "lucid and sophisticated" by Hill (1960, 87), but Gittleman (1969) will have nothing of it. Distinguishing himself from Gundolf, Gittleman contends that the stories have received "hardly any critical attention," presumably since they constitute "no appreciable contribution to German or European letters" (120).

If the observation of Gittleman is accurate, Vinçon (1987) provides a partial explanation, albeit without acknowledging him. Wedekind's poetry and prose received scant critical attention, Vinçon asserts, because the author wanted to be known primarily as a dramatist. Moreover, the prose tales do not fit very well into the framework "early writing, middle period, late work," so they were long seen as secondary to the drama (164–65). That the prose is regarded by the critics as related to the stage works, however, will be observed below.

Vinçon considers the doctoral research of Audrone Barunas Willeke demonstrating that Wedekind employs the structure of the nineteenth-century novella. An introductory framework presents the characters and the situation, and a dialogue is initiated, which becomes a monologue as the speaker in the first person recalls a prior event. At the conclusion of this narrative there is a reversion to the initial framework, and the reaction of the listener is suggested by another dialogue or a conclusion. The effect of this technique, Vinçon observes, is that a single voice dominates the narration with idiosyncratic speech (170–71).

"Die Fürstin Russalka"

> Princess Russalka explains to the Baroness Hohenwart that her youth and childless first marriage account for her identity as a Social Democrat married to a leader of that party.
>
> "Self-absorbed, self-righteous, and pious as a teenager, I knew there was no such thing as illegitimacy since children were not born outside of marriage. I proved this to my satisfaction by an affair with the Duke of Galliera, which led to marriage, continued childlessness, and divorce. Converting to atheism, I devoted myself to women's issues and turned aside the marriage offer of the distinguished Social Democrat Dr. Rappart since I considered myself infertile. He persisted and persuaded me of the woman's calling to make the male happy. We married and you see before you the small, blue-eyed Social Democrat in the cradle."
>
> The baroness laughed, "I'd rather have a small baron or even a baroness."

The social issue of unmarried pregnancy, a theme treated predominantly in

Frühlings Erwachen, is considered here too superficially, in the opinion of Kapp (1909, 33). And Kutscher (1927), too, takes objection that socialism and societal problems are just touched upon and the subjects of education and religion, usually so important to Wedekind, are ignored. The critic describes the Princess as a child with the touch of an intellectual, playing the central role in a tale of conversion from woman's rights to true womanhood; it is a story that amounts to the weakest in the collection (II, 27–28).

Gundolf (1948) illuminates the novella with the light of irony by suggesting that the tale of a woman who marries a socialist agitator and becomes a dutiful mother could, in the pages of *Simplicissimus*, have been intended as a horror story (203).

As does Kapp, Gittleman (1969, 121–22) interprets the story as a companion piece to *Frühlings Erwachen* since Princess Russalka, like Wendla Bergmann, is ignorant of the biological origins of life outside of matrimony. Intended as satire of the central figure—pious adolescent and wife, feminist, and self-satisfied member of the bourgeoisie—Wedekind's irony is unequal to his task. Moreover, since the Princess is unconvincing and the narrative lacks sufficient tension, Gittleman calls the story insignificant (122), and Wagener (1979) agrees with Kutscher that this is the weakest tale of the group (51).

"Rabbi Esra"

At age twenty, Moses confides to his father Rabbi Esra the desire to become engaged to Rebekka, whom he loves with all his heart. The old man suggests that Moses knows neither women nor himself and relates of his own experience. In order to curb base desires and withstand the temptations of the flesh, Esra marries Lea, whom he loves but who provides little companionship. When she is snatched from him by death during childbirth, Esra curses Jehovah and forgets his misery and love for Lea in the arms of prostitutes. He gains the realization that the more he indulges his senses, the more he feels free of sin and close to the Almighty. For this reason he seeks a beauteous woman as his second wife and finds in Sarah a woman who stands the test and a heart which is a brother to his own. The night of their marriage is consummated by the conception of Moses.

Consistent with the tendency of the critics to draw a relationship between these tales and various dramas, Pissin (1905) compares "Rabbi Esra" to *Frühlings Erwachen* in the treatment of that transitional period of puberty when adolescents, such as Moses, find their bodies are undergoing peculiar changes (9). Kapp (1909), on the other hand, distinguishes the two works since the enlightenment of youth is represented in this tale in a positive light absent in the drama (32). Moreover, Kapp states his high regard for the story, in part, because of its message that love unites flesh and spirit, expressed here without the author's customary skepticism or cynicism (31). Friedenthal (1914, 33) describes the tale as a masterpiece, and Fechter (1920, 145) rates it among Wedekind's most mature and best works.

Underscoring Kapp's perception of adolescent education presented here in a positive light, Kutscher (1927 II, 33–34) emphasizes the dramatic character of the relationship of Esra to Moses. This is an idea subsequently developed by Gittleman (1969), who suggests that Moses as listener plays such a diminutive role that the tale amounts to a play with one character or a dramatic monologue. The old man's expression of his recovery conveys an "honest freshness about Esra's reconciliation with himself"(127). Gittleman calls it "one of the most moving of Wedekind's prose pieces" (125–26).

The critics might have noted that the story distinguishes itself from the other tales in that the interpretation to the narrative given by the listener Moses is indeterminate. Following Lea's death, Esra turns to the harlots seeking self-degradation through sex after the manner of Lisiska in *Tod und Teufel*.

"Das Opferlamm"

It was not enough for the gourmet to enjoy the favors of the young girl in the brothel; he wanted to revel in her misery and insisted upon being told of the circumstances which had brought her to this place. Martha, in her own mind the sacrificial lamb, relates her story.

"I worked in a shop at fourteen and fell in love with a fellow who demanded that I prove my love. Not knowing what this meant, I turned to a reader of cards who advised that I should deny him nothing. I became his lover, left my family, and took a room. It was to my horror that I learned a child may be born out of wedlock. When he abandoned me, I felt betrayed and wanted to complete my degradation, so I asked to be directed to a brothel, where I service the most loathsome of men and never refuse."

Thereafter, when the gourmet thought of the young girl, he despised himself. Now, he had learned to believe in innocence, so he felt he was not completely lost. This conviction remained with him for the rest of his life.

It is in relation to the drama *Tod und Teufel* that this tale is considered most widely. Fechter (1920) calls it a study for the play: a young man, at first cynically superior, engages in conversation in a brothel and departs with an insight; this is a suggestion of what leads to the demise of Casti-Piani in *Tod und Teufel* (149). In that play the young man and the sacrificial lamb also appear, Kutscher (1927) remarks, emphasizing the delicacy and tact with which the characters are drawn in "Das Opferlamm." The effectiveness of this artistically significant work lies both in the cruelty and sadism with which the patron forces Martha to torture herself and then in the self-contempt he feels later when he thinks back upon his behavior. The male bears characteristics of Wedekind himself (II, 28–29).

"Das Opferlamm" is juxtaposed to *Tod und Teufel* as a companion piece by Gittleman (1969, 122), since in both a prostitute confesses her unhappiness. Martha's need for self-degradation is described as "pathological" as is that of Lisiska; it is the same force that drives Lulu into the arms of Jack the Ripper (123) and, Gittleman might have added, Rabbi Esra to the harlots.

A parallel is also struck to *Schloß Wetterstein*. The young man listening to Martha's story is aroused only when he hears of the sordid circumstances which brought her to prostitution; this young man suggests Tschamper, who wrings from Effie her story and relishes her death agony (122).

With the conclusion of the work there is a shift of focus from the girl back to her patron, whose jaded cynicism has turned to compassion. This ending is described by Gittleman as "trite" as is the story of the "good-hearted and much abused whore who saves a youth on the road to perdition"(123).

The contribution of Wagener (1979) is significant; he reads the story as the sharpest social criticism and is alone in emphasizing the understanding which is revealed for the motives of the young girl (53).

A point might have been made that Martha is related to Princess Russalka and Wendla Bergmann in her oblivious disregard for the possibility of conception outside the bounds of marriage.

"Der greise Freier"

While lying in bed on their honeymoon, Leonie Fischer relates to her new husband what she experienced as a fifteen-year-old schoolgirl.

"My sister Klara had a foreboding that something would prevent her from marrying. Although Klara experienced a nightmare in which she was forced to marry an old man and indeed received a proposal from such a person, this marriage never took place. Young, handsome Rudolf Elsner found his way into her life as if sent by heaven. They became engaged and spent hours together, but always in my presence for the sake of propriety. They longed for each other, and such a contrived arrangement ultimately took its toll when Klara suffered a collapse and had to be confined to bed. In her dreams she was tormented by an old man, appearing as her fiancé and attempting to force himself upon her. Since the doctor described Klara's condition as hopeless and because I recognized the old man as death and Rudolf as life, I allowed him admission to her room so that they might make love before Klara died. After Rudolf had departed, she spoke joyfully of marriage; and on the next morning she was dead."

The new husband congratulates himself on his choice of the wife at his side.

Although Kapp (1909) denies that the story is dramatic or even credible, he remarks on the effective contrast achieved: a tale of young lovers consumed with passion is narrated by coolly, self-contained newlyweds lying in bed (32–33). And Fechter (1920) focuses upon the same aspect of the story, adopting the terminology often associated with the genre of the novella in the description of its structure: the newlyweds provide a frame to the narrative concerning the courtship and intercourse of another couple; and the young groom closes the frame with a self-congratulatory remark reflecting upon the selflessness and devotion of his wife (148–49).

Absolutely unique among the interpretations, although not substantiated by Wedekind's description, is the observation of Gundolf (1948) that the old man in Klara's dream is her first suitor (203).

This "frighteningly sinister story," as Gittleman (1969, 123) calls it, accompanies *Frühlings Erwachen* as a statement of protest against a repressive society determined to preserve the propriety and formality of "the pre-marital ritual of courtship." Leonie is one of Wedekind's most enlightened figures, conforming to the moral conventions of her parents' generation and at the same time allowing others to follow pursuits more conducive to their own happiness (124–25).

Wedekind in the words of Leonie identifies the dream figure as death, whom Leonie deprives of its virgin prey, according to Diethe (1988, 90). But this critic does some violence to the concept of *Liebestod* since Klara dies well after intercourse.

"Der Brand von Egliswyl"

The narrator recalls the story he had heard as a twelve-year-old from the lips of a convicted arsonist. Hans had grown up as a farmhand in a neighboring Swiss village, where he learned from the girls the practices of love. He made the acquaintance of the chambermaid Marie from Swabia, who was not as smitten by him as were the others of her sex. Marie toyed with his emotions, finally granting him a nocturnal visit to her room, which concluded with disaster. He departed leaving Marie just as he had found her; she had neither laughed nor cried and was as if frozen in ice.

Alone and humiliated, Hans blamed the other women for his failure; he felt as if flames engulfed him and saw fire everywhere he looked. In a rage he set fires within the village and returned to show them delightedly to Marie from her window as evidence of his manliness; she responded by summoning help to capture him.

The critics are unanimous in their praise of this story. Heuß (1909), who has practically nothing good to say about Wedekind's bawdy and erotically sensational poetry, speaks of the extraordinary power of the work, mocking anyone who would call the author decadent. No word is superfluous; each has its own place, lending greatness and impact to the style (264–65).

Friedenthal (1914, 33) calls the tale a masterpiece, and Fechter (1920) detects here the hectic tempo of Heinrich von Kleist (147) in what belongs to Wedekind's best and most mature works (145). In a unique manner the author creates from the young man's love a combination of shame and compulsion that dissipates his strength. The teenage boy who heard the story will finally come to understand it in the light of his advanced age and increased experience (147).

In the eyes of Kutscher (1927), "Der Brand von Egliswyl" is Wedekind's most significant prose work and belongs to the best tales of our time (II, 31). The language in direct quotation is dialect, natural, highly individual, rich in images, characteristically naive, and terse, allowing much to be read between the lines. Wedekind has found such language in the drama of J. M. R. Lenz and Georg

Büchner and applied the technique of the theater to his prose (32–33).

Hill (1960, 87) reaffirms Fechter's comparison with Kleist, contending that this piece "ranks with the best, most concise and powerful prose in German literature." Wedekind is credited with psychological insight in advance of modern psychoanalysis, which has established a relationship between sexual anxiety and arson only relatively recently (88).

Ude (1966) echoes Kutscher in calling the story an example of Wedekind's finest prose (56), the narrative skill of which is demonstrated more in that which is left unsaid or omitted, rather than fully expressed (57–58). It is this aspect of the story to which Gittleman (1969, 128) alludes when he speaks of a "dark power" associated with the sexual drive and impotency. Maria is "diabolical"; by means of "destructive teasing" and repression "she controls and contains Hans's instincts until he is driven wild" (129). Characterizing the story as Wedekind's most significant and most mature prose piece, Gittleman (127) notes the language style; the speech of Hans's narration is simple and naive, that of the frame "elevated and stylized," the author preserving thereby distance and detachment. That the boy listening to the story is the young Wedekind is a view Gittleman (129) shares with Kutscher (II, 31).

In this tale, which Wagener (1979) calls the best of the group, the critic praises the quality of dramatic compression; a unified image of the peasant boy's character is conveyed in his language by his distinctive vocabulary and diction (51–52).

"Mine-Haha oder Über die körperliche Erziehung der jungen Mädchen"

The narrative voice of Hidalla relates how she as a young girl learned from her mentor Gertrud together with other children how to walk, run and jump, and bathe. Older children took care of the younger ones, and at the appropriate time Hidalla was segregated from the boys and grew up with others of her sex in a house in a large park. Here for seven years she learned music, dance, and acting in the theater. The park was financed by theater productions, such as that of "Der Mückenprinz" (The Mosquito Prince) before an enthusiastic crowd. The Prince took various girls to bed, and the girls did not understand why, except that it was wrong. Members of the audience made lewd comments.

Before the girls were admitted to the world, they had to disrobe for physical inspection before women to whom they showed how they carried themselves. Then from the theater the girls were transported to the train station and to a great hall where amid flowers and music they were turned over to the boys.

This, Wedekind's longest prose work, takes its title from Henry Wadsworth Longfellow's *Song of Hiawatha* (1855), where it serves as the name of an Indian maiden meaning "laughing waters." Wedekind purports to provide the introduction to an autobiographical fragment written by the eighty-four-year-old retired teacher named Helene Engel, who has recently committed suicide.

Alone in his political interpretation, Trotzky (1908) hails Wedekind's vision of a system for the socialized education of children. Moral cynic and aesthete that Wedekind is, the author, nevertheless, provides a solution to the problem of the modern family in which two generations are forcibly bound by the common knot of economic dependency and stand in each other's way (378–79). The harmonious world of children educating one another is, however, not set within a social framework and amounts to merely a glimpse of the future (380–81).

The early critics emphasize the graceful style of a work childlike in its perspective and manner of expression. Further, Heuß (1909, 267) justifies "Mine-Haha" as a statement of Wedekind's sexual morality defining the purpose of a woman in her beauty and strength. Kapp (1909), however, has moral objections founded in the allusions to sadism, masochism, and lesbian love; the dance pantomime manifests terrible cynicism by exposing innocent girls to variations on the sexual act (40–41). Friedenthal (1914) would explain these objections by the perceived intention of Wedekind to diminish the spiritual aspect of the human being by exaggerated concern with the physical (43). The author visualizes a utopia, and Friedenthal implies that it need not be taken too seriously (39, 41).

A strange mixture of utopia and satire, fantasy and pedagogic propaganda, half diary and half formless novella, "Mine-Haha" is, in the view of Fechter (1920), one of Wedekind's most fascinating prose pieces, a union of moral fantasy and reality with concealed tenderness (151, 149). The allegedly pornographic aspects of the theatrical performance comprises satire of the normal education of young girls; the work moves from the idealistic education in physical beauty in the park to exposure in the theater of innocent children to sexuality (154–55).

Siding by implication with Friedenthal, Kutscher (1927 II, 130) characterizes the work as whimsical, wishful thinking unconcerned with practical realization, and therefore not to be taken seriously. The two critics part company, however, when Kutscher deplores the representation of an upbringing which is strictly physical and excludes the spiritual. This poetically exaggerated education is, nonetheless, something hygienically, morally, and aesthetically valuable.

Having had the advantage of access to the author's literary effects, Kutscher explicitly corrects Fechter's view of the work as a satire of the customary education of girls; the novel fragment is part of a larger project known as "Die große Liebe" (The Grand Passion), which represents a cult of eroticism (133). The theater event is intended as an orgy and as such amounts to that intolerable cynicism first sensed by Kapp (1909, 131).

Both Gundolf (1948, 204) and, nearly two decades later, Ude (1966, 72) develop the idea of Kutscher that the work amounts to wishful thinking by suggesting that the adult Wedekind is giving form to his pubescent dreams and erotic fantasies.

The utopian aspects of "Mine-Haha" are considered from various perspectives. Utopia is perceived by Hahn (1969 I, 87) in a social sense and by Gittleman (1969) in a utopian children's world that is "blissfully wholesome" (132). What the latter critic characterizes as "this strange paean to physical fitness"(131) is the author's personal statement regarding the education of women (130). It is an asexual utopia, according to Glaser (1974), where drives are temporarily repressed only to erupt in the form of corporal punishment for infractions incurred in improper walking and stage performance (173). Lorenz (1976) harks back to Trotsky, without paying him his due, when she describes a utopia, where, consistent with the socialist thinking of August Bebel and Friedrich Engels, full sexual equality is practiced between male and female and where education is no longer determined by parents (48). And utopia is divorced from any social, political, or sexual context by Wagener (1979, 55), who uses the term to mean whimsical and unrealistic; physical education is revealed as natural eroticism, and the behavior of the theater public at the performance is intended as social criticism (55).

Mennemeier (1980) puts his finger on the problem which besets interpretation: Wedekind's ambivalence. "Mine-Haha" provides a positive vision of sexuality as a vital force and contains a masculine voyeur's view of sexuality. The work is ambivalent even in its construction; it takes place in an idyllic, self-enclosed world which is at the same time the scene of rituals of subjugation and punishment that are common to pornography. As in all of Wedekind's work the physical and sensuous are associated with suffering as well as elevated passion (364). The dance pantomime of young girls involves bizarre and shocking gestures, erotic in a fascinating way (373).

No one goes further to defend Wedekind than Muschg (1980), who argues that the lines emanating from the author's fantasy are ornamental and tender; Wedekind's ideas are far from being obscene, since he is puritanical. The theatrical productions are lascivious and underscore the fact that the girls are destined as articles of consumption for a paying public. The ultimate conveyance of the girls to the world beyond the park demonstrates that the sterile sensuality of their existence cannot be transplanted to society (44–45).

Asserting that sexuality as a subject is taboo to the Marxists, Vinçon (1987, 165) seeks support for his generalization. He argues that Trotzky (1908) refers to Wedekind's aesthetic cult as a cross between education for maidens and muscular exercise (307); Trotzky does indeed say this, but it is not the thrust of his argument, as indicated above. Vinçon seeks further grounds in support of his assertion when the Marxist Hahn (1969) describes "Mine-Haha," without any mention of sex, as merely a social utopia (I, 87).

Considering the disclosure of Kutscher that the novel fragment belongs to a larger project known as "Die große Liebe" dealing with a cult of eroticism, Vinçon comes to the peculiar conclusion that since the sketches have not been published it is premature to pass literary historical judgment (169). By quoting Muschg out of context, Vinçon suggests that his interpretation of the disciplinary school for girls is negative (168).

Vinçon's own contribution to the body of interpretation lies in his emphasis upon the bourgeois world and its repressive sexuality, which exists as a counterpart to the idyllic utopia. The rupture between the two is manifested in the theater performance (167).

Boa (1987) weighs the possibilities: "Mine-Haha" is either a utopia, "an alternative childhood" similar to some of the ideas expressed by Moritz in *Frühlings Erwachen* (191); a dystopia, a "nightmare world of rigid control" (192); or a grotesque satire of the way young women are actually brought up (194).

Works Cited

Bachmair, Heinrich Franz. 1912. "Zu einem Band Gedichte." *Die Aktion* 2: cols. 855–57.

Boa, Elizabeth. 1987. *The Sexual Circus. Wedekind's Theatre of Subversion*. Oxford: Blackwell.

Diethe, Carol. 1988. *Aspects of Distorted Sexual Attitudes in German Expressionist Drama*. New York, Bern, Frankfurt am Main, and Paris: Lang.

Fechter, Paul. 1920. *Frank Wedekind. Der Mensch und das Werk*. Jena: Lichtenstein.

Friedenthal, Joachim. 1914. "Einleitung." In *Das Wedekindbuch*, edited by Friedenthal. Munich and Leipzig: Georg Müller. 1–121.

Gittleman, Sol. 1969. *Frank Wedekind*. New York: Twayne.

Glaser, Horst Albert. 1974. "Arthur Schnitzler und Frank Wedekind. Der doppelköpfige Sexus." In *Wollüstige Phantasie. Sexual Ästhetik der Literatur*, edited by Glaser. Munich: Hanser. 148–84.

Gundolf, Friedrich. 1948. "Frank Wedekind." *Trivium* 6: 187–217. This appeared posthumously.

Hahn, Manfred. 1969. "Frank Wedekind. Leben und Werk." In *Frank Wedekind. Dramen I*. Berlin and Weimar: Aufbau-Verlag. 7–93.

Harris, Edward P. 1981. "Freedom and Degradation. Frank Wedekind's Career as a Kabarettist." In *The Turn of the Century. German Literature and Art, 1890–1915*, edited by Gerald Chapple and Hans H. Schulte. Bonn: Bouvier. 493–525.

Heuß, Theodor. 1909. "Frank Wedekind." *Der Kunstwart* 22.17 (June): 262–69.

Hill, Claude. 1960. "Wedekind in Retrospect." *Modern Drama* 3.1 (May): 82–92.

Kapp, Julius. 1909. *Frank Wedekind. Seine Eigenart und seine Werke*. Berlin: Hermann Barsdorf.

Krohn, Paul. 1958. "Frank Wedekind's Politische Gedichte." *Neue Deutsche Literatur* 6.5 (May): 84–95.

Kutscher, Artur. 1970. *Frank Wedekind. Sein Leben und seine Werke*. Vol. 2. New York: AMS Press. This is a reprint of the edition appearing in 1927.

Lorenz, D. C. G. 1976. "Wedekind und die emanzipierte Frau. Eine Studie über Frau und Sozialismus im Werke Frank Wedekinds." *Seminar* 12.1 (February): 38–56.

Mennemeier, Franz Norbert. 1980. "Frank Wedekind." In *Handbuch des deutschen Dramas*, edited by Walter Hinck. Düsseldorf: Bagel. 360–73, 568–69.

Muschg, Adolf. 1980. "Frank Wedekind: *Mine-Haha*." In his *Besprechungen 1961–1979*. Basel, Boston, and Stuttgart: Birkhäuser. 43–45.

Natan, Alex. 1963. "Frank Wedekind." In *German Men of Letters*, edited by Natan. Vol. 2. London: Oswald Wolf. 101–29.

Pissin, Raimund. 1905. *Frank Wedekind*. Berlin: Gose & Tetzlaff.

Schumann, Willy. 1979. "Frank Wedekind—Regimekritiker? Einige Überlegungen zur 'Majestätsbeleidigung' in den 'Simplicissimusgedichten.'" *Seminar* 15.4 (November): 235–243.

Trotsky, Leon. 1968. "Frank Wedekind." In his *Literatur und Revolution*. Translated by Eugen Schaefer and Hans von Riesen. Berlin: Gerhardt. 366–87. The article appeared in German in *Die neue Zeit* April 1908.

Ude, Karl. 1966. *Frank Wedekind*. Mühlacker: Stieglitz.

Vinçon, Hartmut. 1987. *Frank Wedekind*. Stuttgart: Metzler.

Wagener, Hans. 1979. *Frank Wedekind*. Berlin: Colloquim.

12: The Development of Wedekind Criticism

The early criticism to appear during Wedekind's productive lifetime was necessarily incomplete since the author continued to write until his death. Following the precedent established by the sciences, literary criticism was positivistic; it clung to empirical facts and made a link between the author's life and his works, demonstrating how experience had become literature.

The first monograph is that of Raimund Pissin, an essay which appeared in 1905 intended to popularize Wedekind. And three years later Paul Goldmann (1908) turns his attention to the dramatist with very different intentions evidenced by his conclusions. Goldmann decides that Wedekind is unable to construct a scene or act, write dramatic dialogue, or create an effective dramatic figure other than Lulu and the court singer Gerardo (115).

The first significant recognition of Wedekind in international criticism is an essay by Leon Trotsky that appeared in 1908 in *Die neue Zeit*, a journal edited by Karl Kautsky that was most prestigious during the Second International. Trotsky notes the cosmopolitan tastes of the time and attributes to Wedekind a popularity among Russian intellectuals exceeding that which the dramatist enjoys in Germany. The critic finds this popularity unfortunate since Wedekind dispels the memory of the unsuccessful revolution of 1905, which should be kept foremost in the consciousness. The dramatist is seen to offer Trotsky's countrymen what they want: a combination of social nihilism, skepticism regarding the fate of collective man, and erotic aestheticism (386–87). In order to diminish the influence of Wedekind and at the same time to reaffirm the cause of Marxism, Trotzky argues that Wedekind himself has come to recognize the errors of his ways; he has experienced both an internal revolution marked by the collapse of his vitalist philosophy of eroticism and a turn from cynical epicureanism (381, 385).

Ignoring the writing of Goldmann the year before and describing the work of Pissin as confused and poorly arranged for the popular audience, Julius Kapp (1909) sets himself a goal, namely that of attempting to defend Wedekind against detractors who charge him with excessive social criticism and pornography. The defense to both charges is art: the author is attempting to achieve an artistic ideal that necessarily includes aspects of human baseness and misery (12–13). The single theme of Wedekind's work is physical love, a subject treated with artistic intentions which preclude him from being characterized as immoral (13–14).

Kapp emphasizes Wedekind's uniquely strong artistic personality; he is without predecessors and will have no successors; he opens new paths which no one can further explore upon his demise (9). If his figures appear as improbable caricatures, that is because one sees human beings for the first time as they really are. Kapp notes that Wedekind's refusal to adhere to convention causes his audience to open their eyes and look at things in a new light, and here Kapp unwittingly anticipates the alienation effect of Bertolt Brecht (139–40).

Writing in 1909, Theodor Heuß concentrates upon Wedekind's contemporary reputation and belittles him as the literary sensation of yesterday (262). Opposed to the social norm since the world has become too ugly, intellectual, and Christian, Wedekind resorts, it is charged, by turning to tendentious drama. His thesis that the confrontation and struggle of male and female are the foundations of society and life amounts to sexual radicalism that has earned him the reputation of an immoral revolutionary; but he does not deserve this label, for he fails to do justice to the family, to popular organizations, and to the economy. He is, therefore, not a reformer or a radical revolutionary but a philistine reactionary. From the impertinent cynic and fanatical moralist has developed the sentimental, bankrupt romantic (267–68).

Following the same method as Kapp, Hans Kempner (1911) emphasizes the artistic personality of Wedekind. Nephew of the prestigious drama critic and Wedekind proponent Alfred Kerr, Kempner uses a positivistic approach consisting of descriptions and quotations illustrating an interaction between the author and his dramas as these are shown to be engendered by his attitudes and ideas. Kempner relates that Wedekind characterized the work of Pissin as stupid twaddle ("blödes Gefasel"), and Kempner describes Kapp's contribution as philologically sound in its precision and style (94).

Preserving the emphasis on the personality of the dramatist, *Das Wedekindbuch*, edited by Joachim Friedenthal (1914), appeared on the occasion of the author's fiftieth birthday; it includes more than forty contributions by contemporary literary figures and people associated with the theater, such as Hermann Bahr, Franz Blei, Max Halbe, Alfred Kerr, and Heinrich and Thomas Mann. An extensive introduction by Friedenthal written just four years before Wedekind's demise in 1918 includes most of his writing and emphasizes his role as a pessimist and moralist.

Friedenthal was the first to periodize the corpus of Wedekind's writing, grouping it in the following manner: the work of his youth, including poems and prose, which finds its summit in *Frühlings Erwachen;* a second period marked by the magnificent *Lulu* tragedy and including *Der Marquis von Keith* and *König Nicolo;* a period of crisis represented by confession and moralizing, theory, and polemics, expressed most clearly in *Die Zensur* and including *Tod und Teufel, Musik,* and *Schloß Wetterstein;* and his late work evidencing increased objectivity regarding the world and himself, found in *Franziska* and *Simson.* In his contribution to this volume of Friedenthal, Franz Blei (1914) arranges the works of Wedekind in a very similar fashion based on style, and this periodization developed by the two of them has been widely accepted.

During the postwar period of the Weimar Republic in the absence of a censor, Wedekind's works became popular upon the stage to a degree he had never known during his lifetime. The broad censorship to which his plays had been subjected during the Wilhelmine period contributed to the perception of him as a dissident and to his discovery by the generation of the expressionists.

Paul Fechter wrote in 1920 the first important book-length treatment of Wedekind's works. Although Fechter considers the prose and poetry, he reduces the importance of the author to his dramas. These are ordered as follows: the Tragedies of Sex, with which he was occupied mostly during the nineties; Grotesque Comedy and Drama; and Tragic Comedies representing the playwright himself during the sentimental period of his writing from 1901 to 1908. Fechter asserts that Wedekind had a compulsion to confess and that the content of his drama touches on his existence and the world about him (170, 167).

Wedekind's drama deals not with the conflict of ethical absolutes, continues Fechter, but with the struggle to satisfy hungry desires. Since hunger can never be permanently eliminated and will ultimately begin to gnaw once more, satisfaction provides a respite, which is in turn followed by renewed striving so that the dramatic line of development forms a zigzag (169). Involvement in the internal life of a character identifies Wedekind's position in literary history. He stands at the division between receding impressionism with its emphasis upon the artistic and approaching expressionism with its increased subjectivity; the latter movement finds its first voice in this dramatist (167–68).

Confronting the charge of Wedekind's immorality, Bernhard Diebold (1921) presents a neat solution, more comprehensible to himself than to his readers. Characterizing the author as amoral, Diebold describes him as an ethical spokesman against his will since his hatred for conventional morality serves a higher truth (43).

The most influential promoters of Wedekind research were the circle about him comprised of Joachim Friedenthal, Paul Fechter, Fritz Strich, and Artur Kutscher. Friedenthal and Kutscher edited the collected works, and Strich put out another edition as well as two volumes of Wedekind's letters.

In 1922 Kutscher began the three-volume work on Wedekind's life and writing, which was concluded in 1931. This includes biography, contemporary reflections on his person and writing, textual history based on his literary estate, and theater reception. Kutscher's presentation is positivistic through and through, comprising a massive collection of empirical data in a scientific fashion. The study is assembled under the premise that literature is to be understood as the result of the author's experience, and the material presented here has dominated Wedekind biographical scholarship. Unfortunately, there is considerable unreliability regarding the citation of sources and quotations.

Hanns Martin Elster (1922) emphasizes Wedekind's individuality and the manner in which this reflects upon his dramatic figures. As a young man, Wedekind discovered that in the flux of Life the only permanence was represented by the central force of sensuality and instinct; this insight became paramount and accounted for his singularity, and everything spiritual, ethical, or artistic became subordinate. Subjected to his own drives, Wedekind was threatened by self-destruction, Elster argues further, and the only protection against this was cynicism. He turned the cynicism upon himself with romantic irony when he represented the conflict of spirit and instinct, or flesh, in himself. He was never able to rise above this conflict, which he proclaimed and to which he was victim (10–11).

All of his dramatic figures are to be understood in this light. Elster describes them as marionettes, not beings free to decide and act, but slaves to their instincts. The critic concludes that Wedekind's work is neither tragedy nor comedy but both at the same time (12–13). The dramatist is the first conscious expressionist; he attempts to convey his experience and the relationship of himself to his external world (15), and in that sense his writing is confessional (17).

During the Third Reich, Wedekind's writing was accorded both the silent treatment and official discouragement. The influence of Georg Lukács, the theoretician of critical realism, extended from the thirties to the German Democratic Republic, where Wedekind was classified as hopelessly decadent. In the Federal Republic the criticism, rather than reverting to the earlier positivism, turned to interpretation and exegesis.

Formerly a disciple in the circle about Stefan George, Friedrich Gundolf died in exile in England, and writing from his literary effects was published posthumously in 1948. In an essay he describes Wedekind in strange terms, characterizing him as an author obsessed with the furor of a seer devoid of judgment. Gundolf seems to allude to those events which drove him into exile when he calls the dramatist a herald of those historical forces which cannot be dismissed as fable if humanity shall continue as humanity (217).

The critic places Wedekind in a literary historical matrix. The explosive energy of his dramatic scenes, which are unrelated to what precedes them or follows, recalls the tradition of Shakespeare and the movement of Sturm und Drang. The playwright is an heir of Georg Büchner and a forerunner of expressionism (206). Among his contemporaries, he is closely related to August Strindberg (189) and from Friedrich Nietzsche he borrows neither philosophy nor poetry but animal spirits and the predominance of the self (195).

Elise Dosenheimer (1949) defined the subgenre of social drama during the early postwar years. Wedekind's works are included since they deal with the question of whether the human being with his or her undeniable demands is congruent to society (188). Sex is Wedekind's central concern as he demonstrates how an excessive sexual drive may be an individual's fate; his dramatic figures and the works in which they appear thus serve as a deterrence to unbridled sensuality. The mistaken notion that Wedekind glorifies immorality arises both from accepting his examples as something he endorses and from interpreting his utterances as the expression of his own views, which they may not be (221–22).

The playwright contributes to cultural development, Dosenheimer argues, by exposing the manner in which the sensuality of the human being has been devastated for thousands of years. Wedekind celebrates the human creature as a total entity and seeks a renewal of bourgeois society, which would then lead to a new sexual morality and relation between the sexes (219–20). However, he exaggerates sensuality and fails to do justice to the spiritual nature of man. The concept of spirit contains that of morality within it; if spirit declines, or is reduced, morality likewise declines or is reduced; if the one is impinged upon, so is the other (220–21).

Wedekind served as a pioneer, continues Dosenheimer, in the creation of drama that is new in content and form, unique, and enriching in its influence on the theater which follows (223). He is not a naturalist, but neither is he an expressionist since he denies the spirit; he might be more properly called an ancestor of this latter movement (187).

According to Lion Feuchtwanger (1952), in Wedekind's dramas the highest goal of the healthy individual is recognized as "unfeigned sensual pleasure"; this is attainable only by someone who lives beyond the range of society and its conventions (13). Society is represented by the world the playwright creates on stage. This social world is riddled with contradiction and antithesis; its tragic and ridiculous aspects are exposed in a sequence of rapid alternation causing them to collide against each other while the dramatist stands outside this world observing with detached irony (14).

Feuchtwanger writes that Wedekind "wages war against bourgeois society with bourgeois manners, speech, and mode of dress." Crude plots with little motivation serve to drive home the doctrines with which he attempts to educate the public. Suffering and enjoying the ambiguity of life, the playwright himself appears as the subject of a "modern morality play." The audience hears "one long confession" as he shouts to be understood with exaggerated articulation, often directly to the audience (15–16); regardless of the character part he played on the stage, the actor remained Wedekind (17).

Feuchtwanger observes that Wedekind's language, brief, abrupt, and aphoristic, anticipated expressionism; his stylistic heirs are Heinrich Mann, Carl Sternheim, Georg Kaiser, and Bertolt Brecht (21). And Robert Faesi (1956), too, singles out these authors as successors for whom Wedekind provided the model. Faesi undauntedly classifies the playwright as an expressionist best typified by *Tod und Teufel*, where the dialogue consists of a dialectical discussion conducted by the inner voices of the author projected upon the characters. Expressionist technique is manifested in polished, cold, pointed dialogue, the lines of which follow in rapid succession (256).

Without any pussyfooting regarding expressionism or the anticipation thereof, Wilhelm Emrich (1958) describes Wedekind as uniquely exceptional ("[einen] Sonderfall"), the *Lulu* tragedy mirroring the crisis of modern tragedy and also its new formulation (209). Religion and the world of classical values dissolved during the nineteenth century; absolute, overarching values no longer exist, only individual ones do as these stand in opposition to society. Now the unconditional, absolute value of the individual can only appear to society as negative, as inversion, paradox, and grotesque distortion of all so-called positive values. Consistent with this, all representatives of unconditional individual values in Wedekind's drama run to madness or crime (Lulu, Keith, Nicolo, Hetmann, and so on). This is paradigmatically true for all tragedy since Wedekind (228).

Borrowing from Dosenheimer without acknowledgment, Claude Hill (1960) rejects Wedekind's role as an expressionist since the dramatist lacked the requisite social consciousness; Hill designates him, however, as a forerunner of the movement, who influenced it more than any other dramatist of his generation (92). Of particular interest is the emphasis which Hill places upon the value of psychoanalysis in understanding Wedekind and his works. Hill faults Kutscher, who "in his rather inadequately naive way" reflects nothing regarding the playwright's familiarity with the thought of Freud (89). Wedekind's dramatic dialogue is unique and calculated to reveal the subconscious (90–91).

Hill is quick to point out the faults in Wedekind's writing but concludes upbeat. Among the weaknesses are the prevalence of coincidence and improbability, poorly developed plot lines, caricature, and fluctuation between verse and prose (90). Observing that Wedekind has fallen on hard times, Hill is unable to resist a Wall Street spin and predicts that his "undervalued stock is bound to rise again" (92).

Just as Kutscher represents the standard biography with his massive array of data, Günter Seehaus (1964) provides the seminal treatment of Wedekind in the theater with a staggering collection of facts, figures, and statistics. A chapter deals with the transformation of Wedekind's image in the light of critical support provided by Alfred Kerr, Maximilian Harden, and Karl Kraus while simultaneously under the fire of the censors. Chapter 2 focuses upon the theaters in regions of Germany and neighboring German-speaking countries as well as Milwaukee and Baltimore, with an indication of what works were played when. The following chapter constitutes theatrical history of the various works in chronological order, including the critical reception, productions, scenery, and casts. The appendix provides statistics and magnificent photos of scene design and moments of performance.

Contemporaries of Wedekind pointed to the similarities in his open dramatic form to plays by such predecessors as J. M. R. Lenz, Christian Grabbe and Georg Büchner, but it was not until 1967 when Max Spalter brought forth an excellent and extensive analysis that there was an in-depth comparison. Employing Bertolt Brecht as his focal point and investigating the works of the dramatists mentioned as well as Karl Kraus, Spalter treats theatrical techniques and form as well as commonalities of temperament and outlook shared by the authors, namely "incongruous mixtures of moral outrage and cynical perception" (xii).

An influential work of interpretation is that by Friedrich Rothe (1968), which places Wedekind's work in the thematic context of vitalism as it manifested itself at the turn of the century, especially in *Jugendstil*. Wedekind's writing demonstrates a tension between social criticism on the one hand, and hope for nature or an apparent redemption on the other. Rothe is concerned with how the natural relates to the social and the interchangeability of art and reality; *Frühlings Erwachen* and *Lulu* are singled out as exemplary instances of literary *Jugendstil*.

From what was the German Democratic Republic, Hans Kaufmann (1969) analyzes Wedekind's conception of human personality in a sociopolitical light. The playwright is seen to visualize a person who is self-contained and free of the formative influences of society; this individual leads an isolated physical and sensual existence devoted to unrestrained egocentricity and sexuality. Wedekind's doctrine of individualistic sensualism is a protest against the constraint of the human being by modern capitalistic society as well as a spontaneous consequence of this restraint. Theoretically, the idea of an individual unformed by society is absurd (69).

Wedekind is defended against the charge of being an amoral advocate of sexuality by Wolfdietrich Rasch (1969), who argues that the author recognizes that unrestrained sexuality is socially destructive. Wedekind does not criticize society for trying to restrain it, but for the manner in which it is restrained, hypocritically and compulsively (410–11).

The difficulty of Wedekind's dramas is the focus of Paul Böckmann (1969), who perceives borderline situations of human consciousness that are presented and explored in paradoxes and antinomies. The playwright opened up new possibilities for drama by questioning the self-certainty of individual existence and reflecting upon existential paradox (87).

Sol Gittleman (1969) in the *Twayne World Authors* series provides the first book length English language treatment of Wedekind's works, including the poetry and prose. Here one reads that "Wedekind was the first German dramatist to reject Aristotelianism in the theater." The spectator is fully alienated and witnesses a demonstration of the stupidity of life, that is, how it should not be (140).

Hans-Jochen Irmer (1970) criticizes Emrich's theory of tragedy based on the *Lulu* dramas. Emrich is understood to argue that tragedy is the conflict between the unqualified and uncertain value of the individual and the qualified and certain values of society. As the old, idealistic fate of classical drama is left behind, a new relationship emerges between the individual and society. They are alienated from each other; a subject-object dialectic is established, a reciprocal antimony. It is the conflict between the unqualified value of the individual, nature, autonomous morals, on the one hand, and the qualified values of society, convention, dependent morality, on the other. Irmer argues that Emrich fails to understand, however, that Wedekind fashions the individual, and especially Lulu, as a creation of society and as a counter-creation to society (55).

To the extent that Wedekind can be interpreted as an advocate of sexual equality, argues the Marxist Irmer, the playwright's vision is utopian since the opposition between male and female constitutes the oldest class distinction (143). Horst Albert Glaser (1974), however, argues that Wedekind is not concerned with the problems of the struggle of the sexes; the dramatist demonstrates the attitudes of contemporary patriarchal bourgeois society and its repressive and unjust ways.

From 1969 Sol Gittleman's work dominated the field of English language scholarship. This changed with the appearance of a modest, excellently written monograph by the English Germanist Alan Best (1975) that presents a thesis in the light of which the dramas may be considered. Best argues that Wedekind selects artists and socially marginal types as dramatic characters to the end of social criticism. Such figures have been made to feel inferior, insecure, and inadequate by society (24). Unable to nurture mutual, reciprocal relationships, they stand in confrontation to each other (28). Happiness for such individuals constitutes a demonstration of superiority to other people or the ability to manipulate them. The figures follow the practices of bourgeois society in a context which reveals its insensitive and inhuman aspects. Wedekind chooses this half-world since his audience sees it as distinct from itself and does not feel threatened when he criticizes it. Gradually the dramatist reveals that there is no difference between this community and the audience, and his criticism emerges. Just as the selection of these dramatic characters is the means to a socially critical end so is the employment of the subject of sex. In regard to sex, society is ambivalent and hypocritical; the human being is degraded and deprived of a sense of worth and self-respect (25–26).

Disregarding the fact that Wedekind was no socialist, D. C. G. Lorenz (1976) considers the extensive degree to which his works reflect the views of August Bebel and Friedrich Engels regarding women's liberation in a patriarchal society. Satire and tragicomic situations illustrate the confusion of sex, money, and power under male domination. Historically, the more conservative branch of the women's movement strove primarily for political advancement while the socialists demanded that the sexes should have equal power and rights. Lorenz argues that with Wedekind the emancipation of women and social reform go hand in hand, that is, the free enjoyment of sexuality provides the foundation for equal rights between the sexes (38–39).

Distinguishing himself from Lorenz without noting her, Franz Norbert Mennemeier (1980) suggests that Wedekind may have been opposed to socialism and the women's movement as bourgeois illusions (363). His drama is social by virtue of the author's fine scent for the fundamental process of decay which bourgeois society is undergoing, a process which he recorded with contradictory feelings of anxiety and pleasure (367). At a time when the market economy commercialized the desire for the emancipation of the senses and their satisfaction, Wedekind represented a society striving to satisfy these needs but restricted by economic and political conditions (363). Borrowing without acknowledgment an idea from Rothe and extending it, Mennemeier notes that the playwright anticipated the theories of Wilhelm Reich that account for individual and social disorders as a consequence of repressed sexuality (363).

While Best argues that the dramatist employs socially marginal creatures to criticize his audience without causing it to feel threatened, at least initially, Mennemeier places a different emphasis on Wedekind's dramatic characters emanating from the lower strata. Schön, Keith, Casti-Piani, and others are twilight figures with a middle-class veneer that gradually wears away; they move in a chaotic society which has no boundaries between the middle class and the portion of the proletariat which lacks class consciousness ("Lumpenproletariat"). Dangerously dynamic types from a background that is not bourgeois or is petty bourgeois ascend a steeply rising political career as do individuals later under National Socialism (367).

Mennemeier considers the factors for the divided critical opinion regarding Wedekind's work: the dramatist was provocative and intentionally shocking; he injected his personality into his work by public statements about his dramas and by his appearance on stage; and he adopted from the circus and cabaret theatrical effects unknown to the canon (361–62).

Wedekind's intention to be provocative with regard to sexuality receives the attention of Alfons Höger (1981), who asserts that the playwright identified the sexual drive with the will to live. Wedekind saw a danger posed to rigid, bourgeois society by the irresistibility of sexuality. Although a member of the middle class himself, the dramatist was preoccupied with destroying its illusions. But with the reception accorded *Die Büchse der Pandora,* Wedekind learned a lesson; he discovered that the theme of sexuality could not be treated in an open manner. Therefore during his middle period, the dramatist turned to the figure of the outsider, who as a genius or a fool pursues a career opposed to the competitive world (26–27).

Anna Kuhn (1981) attempts to classify Wedekind with regard to a particular school or movement. Although his social criticism is naturalistic, he shares little of the style of that school, and his work is distinguished by vitalism and formal innovations. Wedekind is not a forerunner of the expressionists since he did not set abstract theories upon the stage, but Kuhn agrees specifically with Irmer that Wedekind's influence on the expressionists lay in the manner with which he extended and projected the problematics of his theme into a metaphysical dimension (230–31).

The influence on expressionism is further developed by Peter Jelavich (1983, 142) with regard to theme, sexuality, generational conflict, and the limits of language; as well as style, episodic structure, monologues, and fantastic imagery. Satire and features of the grotesque foreshadow the alienation effect of Brecht (145), and Wedekind's anticapitalism is reflected in Sternheim, Kaiser, Brecht, and Dürrenmatt (149).

The playwright's use of dialogue in which characters talk right by one another is extended by John L. Hibberd (1984) to the theater of the absurd as exemplified by Eugène Ionesco and Samuel Beckett, where people are revealed as incapable of communicating in a world "without one objective meaning" (351).

Edson Chick (1984) summarizes Feuchtwanger, Faesi, and Jelavich when he writes that the "best writers for the German theater in this century, Sternheim, Kaiser, Brecht, Dürrenmatt," all acknowledged their debt to Wedekind (11).

The relationship of commerce and art as well as the position of the artist in bourgeois society is the subject of Gerhart Pickerodt (1984), who argues that the artist has two alternatives: either he surrenders himself to the commercialized business of culture, relinquishing his freedom and the possibility of realizing himself, or he is condemned to uselessness as a misunderstood genius. Pickerodt concludes that the claim of the artist to aesthetic autonomy and social effectiveness is worthless (6).

An excessively broad generalization of M. Helena Gonçalves da Silva (1985) interprets Wedekind's work as the expression of his "total rebellion" against bourgeois conventions, social structures, and Christian values since society is "intrinsically sick" (1).

Wedekind's work demonstrates "basic moral infantilism," which, according to Corbet Stewart (1985–86), should be borne in mind when a claim is made for the playwright's ability to diagnose the ills of society. In the dramas the protagonist opposes a counterforce and demonstrates "unreflecting absorption in the realizing of his or her own will," the effect of which is "authoritarian." This authoritarianism evidences a lack of moral complexity upon the author's part since there is no recognition of anything beyond this counterforce. Protagonists show "a curious imperviousness to anything not directly related to the satisfaction of their needs" (72–73).

Distinguishing herself from Stewart, who thinks that Wedekind's protagonists are authoritarian, Elizabeth Boa (1987) cites the playwright for his attacks upon authoritarianism and upon institutions of bourgeois society, but her thesis is that the dramatist is "subversive"; he is contradictory and ambiguous. While making such attacks, for example, he illustrates the limitations of individual values and those of the middle class (1).

Providing an exhaustive treatment of Wedekind, Boa characterizes the unique quality of his writing. Unlike the drama of symbolism or neoromanticism, Wedekind's work is not non-naturalist; "it is anti-Naturalist. It calls for acting against the Naturalist grain, and mixes details of contemporary life and social themes with myth and symbol, subversive humor and melodrama" (16). His drama manifests techniques of anti-illusionism, an aspect of modern literature which emphasizes that it is unreal, that it is fiction. The most characteristic feature of modern theater finds its antecedents in him. This trait is the fusion of dramatic genre or what Boa terms the "tragi-comic travesty of the modes" (212).

Accepting the argument of Jelavich without crediting him, Carol Diethe (1988) justifies the description of Wedekind as an expressionist because of his treatment of sexuality, his method of constructing dialogue from a series of monologues, and the "submerged" theme of generational conflicts (54). Diethe's thesis is that the author conveys sexual attitudes which are "distorted," however current these may have been during his time. Among the distorted sexual attitudes the playwright presents are masculine aggressiveness and female passivity, a combination culminating in sexual violence towards women, brutality which Wedekind "condones." The dramatist accounts for prostitution by nymphomania, and the misogamy of Friedrich Nietzsche and Arthur Schopenhauer explain his opposition to woman's rights (3–4).

Lorenz attributes to Wedekind a social message, an assertion Diethe finds unsupported and "exaggerated" (249). Moreover, Diethe rejects the argument that the dramatist embraces the egalitarian socialism of Engels and Bebel. Recognizing that feature which Boa identified as subversive, Diethe qualifies her observations by noting that Wedekind's stand on any issue is ambivalent and ambiguous because of his indiscriminate mocking and ridicule (57).

Considering Wedekind in the company of Gerhart Hauptmann and Arthur

Schnitzler, Peter Skrine (1989) contends that Wedekind's language suggests that he lacks the ear for "idiomatic subtleties" with which the other two authors were endowed. This fact may have served to Wedekind's advantage because his works lose less in translation than do those of the others; it may also account for the "relatively greater" success he has enjoyed abroad (94).

Kwangsun Kim's work from 1993 does not readily lend itself to a consideration of trends and currents in the development of Wedekind criticism since it breaks ground in a hitherto untouched area, namely music. Providing an important contribution toward understanding the role which Wedekind's songs play in his dramas, this valuable study extends to the figure of the musician, to contemporary musical influences, and to the dramatist's parody of Wagner and his operas.

Bibliography

Primary

Gesammelte Werke. 1920–21. Edited by Artur Kutscher and Joachim Friedenthal. 9 vols. Munich: Georg Müller.

Ausgewählte Werke. 1924. Edited by Fritz Strich. 5 vols. Munich: Georg Müller.

Gesammelte Briefe. 1924. Edited by Fritz Strich. 2 vols. Munich: Georg Müller.

Prosa, Dramen, Verse. 1960, 1964. Edited by Hansgeorg Maier. 2 vols. Munich: Albert Langen-Georg Müller.

Ich habe meine Tante geschlachtet. Lautenlieder und "Simplicissimus"-Gedichte. 1967. Edited by Manfred Hahn. Munich: Albert Langen-Georg Müller.

Der vermummte Herr: Briefe Frank Wedekinds aus den Jahren 1881–1917. 1967. Edited by Wolfdietrich Rasch. Munich: Deutscher Taschenbuch-Verlag.

Werke. 1969. Edited by Manfred Hahn. 3 vols. Berlin and Weimar: Aufbau.

Die Tagebücher. Ein erotisches Leben. 1986. Edited by Gerhard Hay. Frankfurt am Main: Athenäum.

Werke. 1990. Edited by Erhard Weidl. 2 vols. Munich: Winkler.

Secondary

Kraus, Karl. 1958. *"Die Büchse der Pandora."* In his *Literatur und Lüge. Werke*, edited by Heinrich Fischer. Munich: Kösel. 9–21. These are remarks made at the first performance in Vienna on 29 May 1905.

Pissin, Raimund. 1905. *Frank Wedekind*. Berlin: Gose & Tetzlaff.

Andreas-Salomé, Lou. 1907. *"Frühlings Erwachen."* *Die Zukunft* 58 (19 January): 97–100.

Stöcker, Helene. 1907. "Wedekind und die Frauenbewegung." *Morgen* 1: 250–51.

Goldmann, Paul. 1908. *"Frühlings Erwachen."* In his *Vom Rückgang der deutschen Bühne*. Frankfurt am Main: Rütten & Loening. 111–23.

———. 1908. *"Hidalla."* In his *Vom Rückgang der deutschen Bühne*. Frankfurt am Main: Rütten & Loening. 97–110.

Pollatschak, Stefan. 1908. "Wedekinds *Oaha*." *Die Gegenwart* 74.42: 253–54.

Trotsky, Leon. 1968. "Frank Wedekind." In his *Literatur und Revolution*. Translated by Eugen Schaefer and Hans von Riesen. Berlin: Gerhardt. 366–87. The article appeared in German in *Die neue Zeit* April 1908.

Heuß, Theodor. 1909. "Frank Wedekind." *Der Kunstwart* 22.17 (June): 262–69.

Hofmiller, Josef. 1909. "Wedekinds autobiographische Dramen." *Süddeutsche Monatshefte* 6.1: 116–25.

Kapp, Julius. 1909. *Frank Wedekind. Seine Eigenart und seine Werke*. Berlin: Hermann Barsdorf.

Kerr, Alfred. 1909. "Thoma-Wedekind-Shaw." *Die Neue Rundschau* 20: 137–42.

Goldmann, Paul. 1910. "Der Marquis von Keith." In his *Literatenstücke und Ausstattungs-*

regie. Frankfurt am Main: Rütten & Loening. 103–14.

Hofmiller, Josef. 1910. "Wedekind." In *Zeitgenossen*. Munich: Süddeutsche Monatshefte. 88–131.

Mühsam, Erich. 1910. "*Schloß Wetterstein*." *Die Schaubühne* 6.2: 1269–71.

Hardekopf, Ferdinand. 1911. "Wedekinds Maske." *Die Schaubühne* 7.2: 440–41.

Kempner, Hans. 1911. *Frank Wedekind als Mensch und Künstler*. Berlin-Pankow: Oskar Linser.

Bachmair, Heinrich Franz. 1912. "Zu einem Band Gedichte." *Die Aktion* 2: cols. 855–57.

Elsner, Richard. [1912]. "Frank Wedekind. *Franziska*." In *Moderne Dramatik in kritischer Beleuchtung,* edited by Elsner. Heft 15. Berlin-Pankow: Sozialpädagogischer Verlag. 3–26.

———. [1912]. "Frank Wedekind. *Frühlings Erwachen*." In *Moderne Dramatik in kritischer Beleuchtung,* edited by Elsner. Heft 1. Berlin-Pankow: Sozialpädagogischer Verlag. 10–23.

Mühsam, Erich. 1912. "*Franziska*." *Die Schaubühne* 8.2: 664–68.

Scheller, Will. 1912. "*Schloß Wetterstein*." *Die Neue Rundschau* 23.1: 580–84.

Schwarz, Karl Johannes. 1912. "Wedekind-Woche." *Merker* 3.1: 236–37.

Blei, Franz. 1914. "Marginalien zu Wedekind." In *Das Wedekindbuch*, edited by Joachim Friedenthal. Munich and Leipzig: Georg Müller. 128–50.

Friedenthal, Joachim. 1914. "Einleitung." In *Das Wedekindbuch*, edited by Friedenthal. Munich and Leipzig: Georg Müller. 1–121.

Hecht, Georg. 1914. "Ein Wort gegen Wedekind." *Die Aktion* 4: cols. 673–74.

Mann, Thomas. 1953. "Eine Szene von Wedekind." In his *Altes und Neues. Kleine Prosa aus fünf Jahrzehnten*. Frankfurt am Main: Fischer. 31–38. This essay first appeared in 1914.

Brecht, Bertolt. 1967. "Frank Wedekind." In *Gesammelte Werke*. Vol. 15. Frankfurt am Main: Suhrkamp. 3–4. This first appeared 12 March 1918 as an obituary.

Fechter, Paul. 1920. *Frank Wedekind. Der Mensch und das Werk*. Jena: Lichtenstein.

Diebold, Bernhard. 1972. "Wedekind der Narr." In his *Anarchie im Drama*. New York and London: Johnson Reprint Corporation. 43–76. The work first appeared in 1921.

Elster, Hanns Martin. 1922. *Wedekind und seine besten Bühnenwerke*. Berlin and Leipzig: Franz Schneider.

Kutscher, Artur. 1970. *Frank Wedekind. Sein Leben und seine Werke*. 3 vols. New York: AMS Press. This is the reprint of the edition of three volumes appearing successively in 1922, 1927, and 1931.

Weiß, Ernst. 1982. "Ein Wort zu Wedekinds *Schloß Wetterstein*." In *Gesammelte Werke*. Vol. 16, *Die Kunst des Erzählens,* edited by Peter Engel and Volker Michels. Frankfurt am Main: Suhrkamp. 187–90. This essay first appeared in 1924.

Benjamin, Walter. 1972. "Frank Wedekind: *Frühlings Erwachen*." In *Gesammelte Schriften*, edited by Rolf Tiedemann and Hermann Schweppenhäuser. Vol. 4, Part 1, edited by Tilman Rexroth. Frankfurt am Main: Suhrkamp. 551–52. This essay first appeared in 1929.

Mann, Heinrich. 1929. "Damit der *Herakles* gespielt wird." In his *Sieben Jahre. Chronik der Gedanken und Vorgänge*. Berlin, Vienna, and Leipzig: Paul Zsolnay. 548–52.

Gundolf, Friedrich. 1948. "Frank Wedekind." *Trivium* 6: 187–217. This appeared posthumously.

Dosenheimer, Elise. 1967. *Das deutsche soziale Drama von Lessing bis Sternheim*. Darmstadt:

Wissenschaftliche Buchgesellschaft. This first appeared in 1949.

Feuchtwanger, Lion. 1952. Introduction to *Five Tragedies of Sex,* by Frank Wedekind. Translated by Frances Fawcett and Stephen Spender. London: Vision. 7–21.

Faesi, Robert. 1956. "Ein Vorläufer: Frank Wedekind." In *Expressionismus. Gestalten einer literarischen Bewegung,* edited by Hermann Friedmann and Otto Mann. Heidelberg: Rothe. 241–63.

Emrich, Wilhelm. 1968. "Wedekind—Die *Lulu*-Tragödie." In *Das Deutsche Drama,* edited by Benno von Wiese. Vol. 2. Düsseldorf: Bagel. 209–30. This first appeared in 1958.

Krohn, Paul. 1958. "Frank Wedekinds Politische Gedichte." *Neue Deutsche Literatur* 6.5 (May): 84–95.

Wedekind, Pamela. 1959. "Mein Vater Frank Wedekind." In *Der Kammersänger,* by Frank Wedekind. Stuttgart: Reclam. 57–66.

Hill, Claude. 1960. "Wedekind in Retrospect." *Modern Drama* 3.1 (May): 82–92.

Natan, Alex. 1963. "Frank Wedekind." In *German Men of Letters,* edited by Natan. Vol. 2. London: Oswald Wolf. 101–29.

Seehaus, Günter. 1964. *Frank Wedekind und das Theater.* Munich: Laokoon.

Shaw, Leroy R. [1964]. "Bekenntnis und Erkenntnis in Wedekinds *Die Zensur.*" In *Frank Wedekind zum 100. Geburtstag,* edited by Richard Lemp. Munich: Stadtbibliotek. 20–36.

Wedekind, Kadidja. 1989. "Mutmassungen über *Musik.*" In *Kein Funke mehr, kein Stern aus früh'rer Welt,* edited by Elke Austermühl, Alfred Kessler, and Hartmut Vinçon. Darmstadt: Georg Büchner Buchhandlung. 15–18. This first appeared in 1964–65.

Hartwig, Wolfgang. 1965. "Materialien zum Verständnis des Textes." In *Der Marquis von Keith,* by Wedekind. Komedia 8. Berlin: de Gruyter. 92–120.

Michelsen, Peter. 1969. "Frank Wedekind." In *Deutsche Dichter der Moderne,* edited by Benno von Wiese. Berlin: Erich Schmidt. 51–69. The essay first appeared in 1965.

Völker, Klaus. 1965. *Frank Wedekind.* Velber bei Hannover: Friedrich Verlag.

Hamann, Richard, and Jost Hermand. 1966. *Impressionismus.* Berlin: Akademie-Verlag.

Sokel, Walter H. 1966. "The Changing Role of Eros in Wedekind's Drama." *The German Quarterly* 39.2: 201–7.

Ude, Karl. 1966. *Frank Wedekind.* Mühlacker: Stieglitz.

Spalter, Max. 1967. *Brecht's Tradition.* Baltimore: Johns Hopkins Press.

Maclean, Hector. 1968. "Wedekind's *Der Marquis von Keith*: An Interpretation Based on the Faust and Circus Motifs." *Germanic Review* 43.3 (May): 163–87.

Rothe, Friedrich. 1968. *Frank Wedekinds Dramen. Jugendstil und Lebensphilosophie.* Stuttgart: Metzler.

Böckmann, Paul. 1969. "Die komödiantischen Grotesken Frank Wedekinds." In *Das deutsche Lustspiel.* Vol. 2, edited by Hans Steffen. Göttingen: Vandenhoeck & Ruprecht. 79–102.

Gittleman, Sol. 1969. *Frank Wedekind.* New York: Twayne.

Hahn, Manfred. 1969. "Frank Wedekind. Leben und Werk." In *Frank Wedekind. Dramen I.* Berlin and Weimar: Aufbau-Verlag. 7–93.

———. 1969. *Frank Wedekind. Prosa III.* Berlin and Weimar: Aufbau-Verlag. "An einen Kritiker," 452–54. "An Fritz Basil," 580–81.

Kaufmann, Hans. 1969. "Zwei Dramatiker: Gerhart Hauptmann und Frank Wedekind." In his *Krisen und Wandlungen der deutschen Literatur von Wedekind bis Feuchtwanger.* Berlin and Weimar: Aufbau-Verlag. 47–84.

Maclean, Hector. 1969. "The King and the Fool in Wedekind's *König Nicolo.*" *Seminar* 5.1

(Spring): 21–35.

Rasch, Wolfdietrich. 1969. "Sozialkritische Aspekte in Wedekinds dramatischer Dichtung. Sexualität, Kunst und Gesellschaft." In *Gestaltungsgeschichte und Gesellschaftsgeschichte,* edited by Helmut Kreuzer. Stuttgart: Metzler. 409–26.

Rothe, Friedrich. 1969. "*Frühlings Erwachen.* Zum Verhältnis von sexueller und sozialer Emanzipation bei Frank Wedekind." *Studi Germanici* 7: 30–41.

Irmer, Hans-Jochen. 1975. *Der Theaterdichter Frank Wedekind. Werk und Wirkung.* Berlin: Henschelverlag. This originally appeared in 1970.

Kesting, Marianne. 1970. "Frank Wedekind." In her *Entdeckung und Destruktion.* Munich: Fink. 189–203.

Shaw, Leroy R. 1970. "The Strategy of Reformulation. Frank Wedekind's *Frühlingserwachen.*" In his *The Playwright and Historical Change.* Madison: University of Wisconsin Press. 49–65.

Arntzen, Helmut. 1979. "Der Ideologe als Angestellter." In *Viermal Wedekind,* edited by Karl Pestalozzi and Martin Stern. Stuttgart: Klett. 7–21. This first appeared in 1971.

Neumann, Editha S. 1971. "Musik in Frank Wedekinds Bühnenwerken." *German Quarterly* 44.1 (January): 35–47.

Thomas, Klaus Wolfram. 1971. "Gerardo-Dühring: Ein Selbstgespräch Wedekinds." *German Quarterly* 44.2 (March): 185–90.

Bayerdörfer, Hans-Peter. 1973. "Non olet – altes Thema und neues Sujet. Zur Entwicklung der Konversationskomödie zwischen Restauration und Jahrhundertwende." *Euphorion* 67: 323–58.

Best, Alan. 1973. "The Censor Censored: An Approach to Frank Wedekind's *Die Zensur.*" *German Life and Letters* 26.4 (July): 278–87.

Bullivant, Keith. 1973. "The Notion of Morality in Wedekind's *Frühlings Erwachen.*" *New German Studies* 1: 40–47.

Haida, Peter. 1973. *Komödie um 1900. Wandlungen des Gattungsschemas von Hauptmann bis Sternheim.* Munich: Fink. 92–107.

White, Alfred. 1973. "The Notion of Morality in Wedekind's *Frühlings Erwachen*: A Comment." *New German Studies* 1: 116–18.

Wysling, Hans. 1973. "Zum Abenteurer-Motiv bei Wedekind, Heinrich und Thomas Mann." In *Heinrich Mann 1871/1971. Bestandsaufnahme und Untersuchung. Ergebnisse der Heinrich-Mann-Tagung in Lübeck,* edited by Klaus Matthias. Munich: Fink. 37–68.

Adorno, Theodor W. 1974. "Frank Wedekind und sein Sittengemälde *Musik.*" In *Gesammelte Schriften.* Vol. 2, *Noten zur Literatur,* edited by Rolf Tiedemann. Frankfurt am Main: Suhrkamp. 619–26.

Glaser, Horst Albert. 1974. "Arthur Schnitzler und Frank Wedekind. Der doppelköpfige Sexus." In *Wollüstige Phantasie. Sexualästhetik der Literatur,* edited by Glaser. Munich: Hanser. 148–84.

Seehaus, Günter. 1974. *Frank Wedekind in Selbstzeugnissen und Bilddokumenten.* Reinbek bei Hamburg: Rowohlt.

Best, Alan. 1975. *Frank Wedekind.* London: Oswald Wolf.

Burns, Robert A. 1975. "Wedekind's Concept of Morality: An Extension of the Argument." *New German Studies* 3: 155–64.

Dedner, Burghard. 1975. "Intellektuelle Illusionen. Zu Wedekinds *Marquis von Keith.*" *Zeitschrift für deutsche Philologie* 94: 498–519.

Friedmann, Jürgen. 1975. *Frank Wedekinds Dramen nach 1900.* Stuttgart: Hans-Dieter

Heinz.

Gittleman, Sol. 1976. "Sternheim, Wedekind and *Homo Economicus.*" *German Quarterly* 49.1 (January): 25–30.

Lorenz, D. C. G. 1976. "Wedekind und die emanzipierte Frau. Eine Studie über Frau und Sozialismus im Werke Frank Wedekinds." *Seminar* 12.1 (February): 38–56.

Kuttenkeuler, Wolfgang. 1977. "Der Außenseiter als Prototyp der Gesellschaft. Frank Wedekind: *Der Marquis von Keith.*" In *Fin de siècle. Zu Literatur und Kunst der Jahrhundertwende,* edited by Roger Bauer. Frankfurt am Main: Klostermann. 567–95.

Geißler, Rolf. 1978. "Kunst und Künstler in der bürgerlichen Gesellschaft. Wedekinds *Der Kammersänger.*" *Literatur für Leser* 7.2: 156–60.

Peacock, R. 1978. "The Ambiguity of Wedekind's *Lulu.*" *Oxford German Studies* 9: 105–18. This appeared in German also: "Zur Problematik der Lulugestalt." In *Bild und Gedanke. Festschrift für Gerhart Baumann zum 60. Geburtstag,* edited by Günter Schnitzler. Munich: Fink, 1980. 343–56.

Stroszeck, Hauke. 1978. "Ein Bild vor dem die Kunst verzweifeln muß." In *Literatur und Theater im Wilhelminischen Zeitalter,* edited by Hans-Peter Bayerdörfer et al. Tübingen: Max Niemeyer. 217–37

Bovenschen, Silvia. 1979. "Inszenierung des inszenierten Weiblichkeit: Wedekinds *Lulu* —paradigmatisch." In her *Die imaginierte Weiblichkeit.* Frankfurt am Main: Suhrkamp. 43–60.

Harris, Edward P. 1979. "The Liberation of Flesh from Stone: Pygmalion in Frank Wedekind's *Erdgeist.*" *Germanic Review* 52: 44–56.

Hibberd, John L. 1979. "Imaginary Numbers and 'Humor': On Wedekind's *Frühlings Erwachen.*" *Modern Language Review* 74: 633– 47.

Höger, Alfons. 1979. *Frank Wedekind. Der Konstruktivismus als schöpferische Methode.* Königstein: Scriptor.

Jelavich, Peter. 1979. "Art and Mammon in Wilhelmine Germany: The Case of Frank Wedekind." *Central European History* 12: 203–36.

Klotz, Volker. 1979. "Wedekinds Circus mundi." In *Viermal Wedekind,* edited by Karl Pestalozzi and Martin Stern. Stuttgart: Klett. 22–47.

Nef, Ernst. 1979. "Der betrogene Betrüger wider Willen." In *Viermal Wedekind,* edited by Karl Pestalozzi and Martin Stern. Stuttgart: Klett. 48–59.

Rasch, Wolfdietrich. 1979. "Das Schicksal des Propheten." In *Viermal Wedekind,* edited by Karl Pestalozzi and Martin Stern. Stuttgart: Klett. 60–73.

Schumann, Willy. 1979. "Frank Wedekind—Regimekritiker? Einige Überlegungen zur 'Majestätsbeleidigung' in den 'Simplicissimusgedichten.'" *Seminar* 15.4 (November): 235–43.

Stern, Martin. 1979. "Begleitwort." In *Viermal Wedekind,* edited by Karl Pestalozzi and Martin Stern. Stuttgart: Klett. 4–6.

Wagener, Hans. 1979. *Frank Wedekind.* Berlin: Colloquim.

———. 1979. "Frank Wedekind: politische Entgleisungen eines Unpolitischen." *Seminar* 15.4 (November): 244–50.

Kalcher, Joachim. 1980. "Frank Wedekind: *Tod und Teufel.*" In his *Perspektiven des Lebens in der Dramatik um 1900.* Cologne and Vienna: Böhlau. 292–410.

Mennemeier, Franz Norbert. 1980. "Frank Wedekind." In *Handbuch des deutschen Dramas,* edited by Walter Hinck. Düsseldorf: Bagel. 360–73, 568–69.

Muschg, Adolf. 1980. "Frank Wedekind: *Mine-Haha.*" In his *Besprechungen 1961–1979.*

Basel, Boston, and Stuttgart: Birkhäuser. 43–45.

Wagener, Hans, ed. 1980. *Erläuterungen und Dokumente. Frank Wedekind. Frühlings Erwachen.* Stuttgart: Reclam.

Willeke, Audrone B. 1980. "Frank Wedekind and the 'Frauenfrage.'" *Monatshefte* 72.1: 26–38.

Harris, Edward P. 1981. "Freedom and Degradation. Frank Wedekind's Career as a Kabarettist." In *The Turn of the Century. German Literature and Art, 1890–1915,* edited by Gerald Chapple and Hans H. Schulte. Bonn: Bouvier. 493–525.

Höger, Alfons. 1981. *Hetärismus und bürgerliche Gesellschaft im Frühwerk Frank Wedekinds.* Copenhagen and Munich: Fink.

Kuhn, Anna Katharina. 1981. *Der Dialog bei Frank Wedekind.* Heidelberg: Carl Winter.

Salvesen, Hugh. 1981. "A Piece of Snuff from Pandora's Box. New Light on Karl Kraus and Frank Wedekind." *Oxford German Studies* 12: 122–38.

Medicus, Thomas. 1982. *Die große Liebe. Ökonomie und Konstruktion der Körper im Werk von Frank Wedekind.* Marburg an der Lahn: Guttandin & Hoppe.

Nolting, Winfried. 1982. *Literatur oder Kommunikation.* Münster: Aschendorff.

Jelavich, Peter. 1983. "Wedekind's *Spring Awakening:* The Path to Expressionist Drama." In *Passion and Rebellion. The Expressionist Heritage,* edited by Stephen Erich Bronner and Douglas Kellner. South Hadley, Mass.: J.T.Bergin. 129–50.

Kuhn, Anna Katharina. 1983–84. "The Deceitful Artist in German Expressionist Drama." *University of Dayton Review* 16.3 (Winter): 9–18.

Chick, Edson M. 1984. "Frank Wedekind and his *Lulu* Tragedy." In his *Dances of Death. Wedekind, Brecht, Dürrenmatt, and the Satiric Tradition.* Columbia, South Carolina: Camden House. 11–45.

Hibberd, John L. 1984. "The Spirit of the Flesh: Wedekind's *Lulu.*" *Modern Language Review* 79: 336–55.

Pickerodt, Gerhart. 1984. *Frank Wedekind: Frühlings Erwachen.* Frankfurt am Main, Berlin, and Munich: Diesterweg.

Schuler-Will, Jeannine. 1984. "Wedekind's *Lulu:* Pandora and Pierrot, the Visual Experience of Myth." *German Studies Review* 7: 27–38.

Gerlach, U. Henry. 1985. "Wer ist der 'vermummte Herr' in Wedekinds *Frühlings Erwachen?*" *Maske und Kothurn* 31.1–4: 101–11.

Gonçalves da Silva, M. Helena. 1985. *Character, Ideology, and Symbolism in the Plays of Wedekind, Sternheim, Kaiser, Toller, and Brecht.* London: Modern Humanities Research Association.

Midgley, David. 1985. "Wedekind's *Lulu:* From 'Schauertragödie' to Social Comedy." *German Life and Letters* 38: 205–32.

Schröder-Zebralla, Josephine. 1985. *Frank Wedekinds religiöser Sensualismus. "Die Vereinigung von Kirche und Freudenhaus?"* Frankfurt am Main, Bern, and New York: Lang.

Stewart, Corbet. 1985–86. "Comedy, Morality and Energy in the Work of Wedekind." *Publications of the English Goethe Society,* n.s., 56: 56–73.

Weidl, Erhard. 1985. "Philologische Spurensicherung zur Erschließung der *Lulu*-Tragödie Frank Wedekinds." *Wirkendes Wort* 35: 99–118.

Hibberd, John L. 1986. " 'Die Wiedervereinigung von Kirche und Freudenhaus.' Wedekind's *Die Zensur* and his ideas on religion." *Colloquia Germanica* 19.1: 47–67.

Boa, Elizabeth. 1987. *The Sexual Circus. Wedekind's Theatre of Subversion.* Oxford: Blackwell.

Hibberd, John L. 1987. "The Morality of Wedekind's *Der Marquis von Keith.*" *Deutsche Vierteljahrschrift* 61.3 (September): 510–30.

Vinçon, Hartmut. 1987. *Frank Wedekind.* Stuttgart: Metzler.

Diethe, Carol. 1988. *Aspects of Distorted Sexual Attitudes in German Expressionist Drama.* New York, Bern, Frankfurt am Main, and Paris: Lang.

Pankau, Johannes G. 1989. "Exhibitionismus und Scham. Zur Problematik der Ich-Konstitution in Wedekinds *Die Zensur.*" In *Kein Funke mehr, kein Stern aus früh'rer Welt,* edited by Elke Austermühl, Alfred Kessler, and Hartmut Vinçon. Darmstadt: Georg Büchner Buchhandlung. 289–310.

Skrine, Peter. 1989. *Hauptmann, Wedekind, and Schnitzler.* New York: St. Martin's Press.

Kieser, Rolf. 1990. *Benjamin Franklin Wedekind. Biographie einer Jugend.* Zurich: Arche.

Vinçon, Hartmut, ed. 1990. *Die Büchse der Pandora. Eine Monstretragödie,* by Wedekind. Historisch-kritische Ausgabe der Urfassung von 1894. Darmstadt: Häusser (Pharus III).

Grimm, Reinhold. 1991. Introduction to *Frank Wedekind Yearbook 1991,* edited by Rolf Kieser and Grimm. Bern, Berlin, etc.: Lang. [ix]–xiii.

Kieser, Rolf. 1991. "The Opening of Pandora's Box: Frank Wedekind, Nietzsche, Freud, and Others." In *Frank Wedekind Yearbook 1991,* edited by Kieser and Reinhold Grimm. Bern, Berlin, etc.: Lang. [1]–15.

Ritter, Naomi. 1991. "The Portrait of Lulu as Pierrot." In *Frank Wedekind Yearbook 1991,* edited by Rolf Kieser and Reinhold Grimm. Bern, Berlin, etc.: Lang. 101–40.

Dowden, Steve. 1992. "Frank Wedekind" In *Twentieth Century German Dramatists, 1889–1918,* edited by Wolfgang Elfe and James Hardin. Dictionary of Literary Biography 118. Detroit and London: Gale. 252–63.

Hibberd, John L. 1992. " 'Sein frevler Mund / Tat das Bekenntnis schrecklich kund': Another Look at *Tod und Teufel.*" In *Frank Wedekind Yearbook 1991,* edited by Rolf Kieser and Reinhold Grimm. Bern, Berlin, etc.: Lang. 101–25.

Kim, Kwangsun. 1993. *Die Lieder in Frank Wedekinds Dramen.* Helicon 13. Frankfurt am Main, Berlin, etc.: Lang.

Index

DUE